BEATING ABOUT THE BUSH

David Read was born in Nairobi, Kenya on the
23rd April 1922. In his colourful and varied life,
he has been a metallurgist, soldier, vet, cattle-dealer,
hunter, safari guide, aviator, fisherman and boat
builder, living and travelling across Eastern and
Southern Africa. He currently works as an agricultural
consultant on a coffee estate on the slopes of Mount
Kilimanjaro.

David Read is the author of two other books,
"BareFoot Over The Serengeti", the true story of his
childhood with the Masai in Northern Tanzania, and
"Waters Of The Sanjan", a Masai historical novel.
He is married with one daughter and lives in the
foothills of Mount Meru, in Northern Tanzania.

ISBN: 9987-8920-3-5

ALSO BY DAVID READ

Barefoot Over The Serengti
Waters Of The Sanjan

David Read

Beating
About The Bush

Tales From Tanganyika

Published by David Read 2000

Copyright David Read 2000

A CIP catalogue record for this book is available from the Tanzanian National Archives.

ISBN: 9987-8920-3-5

Cover design by Samantha Goodwin Email: *design@habari.co.tz*

ACKNOWLEDGMENTS

I would like to thank the following for their kind words of encouragement, well-meant words of objective criticism and undying support throughout this entire project:

Patrick Fletcher, Adrianne Mills, Rennie Barnes, Felicity Tessaro, Sally Prentice, Mary Edwards and Bobby McKenna

I would like to dedicate this book to Pat, my wife, and Penny, my daughter, for tolerating me so long.

David Read, Momella, 2000

INTRODUCTION

Beating About The Bush is an autobiographical novel, charting the remarkable life of David Read between 1936 and 1952, in Tanganyika, as it was then known, in East Africa. It is intended as a direct follow-on from his earlier novel, "Barefoot Over The Serengeti", published in 1979, which covered David's childhood in the eponymous area that is now the most famous National Park in the World.

David was born in Kenya in 1922, where he spent the first seven years of his life with his mother, who was running a hotel for travellers and hunting parties in Waso Nyiro in the Rift Valley, where she remarried a genial Czech, Otto Fischer and in 1929, they moved to Loliondo in Northern Tanganyika (modern-day Tanzania) where they set up a small trading post. There were no other European families for a hundred miles in any direction and so he fell in with a group of Masai boys of his own age, developing a particular friendship with a boy named Matanda. Over the next seven years, they roamed the Serengeti plains, together, naked and free, trapping birds, hunting warthogs and accompanying the Masai stock to grazing pastures as far afield as Ngorongoro Crater and the Great Rift Valley.

"Barefoot Over The Serengeti" is about his life during this period, his friendship with the Masai people and his schooling in the customs and life-style of this highly-individual nomadic tribe of pastoral warriors. At the time, he was considered something of "an uneducated savage", but his Masai friends taught him moral values, a respect for life and bush-skills upon which he claims to still rely upon to this day, seventy years later, in "the modern world".

"Beating About The Bush" picks up David's story where "Barefoot" left off, with his parents moving to the Lupa Goldfields to try and salvage their livelihoods after a catastrophic series of events that left them almost destitute, reliant on David's hunting skills and the help of their Masai friends. As the book moves from Mission School life to veterinary training, active service in Abyssinia, Madagascar, and Burma, to the Parsee burial grounds of India, meetings with the King and Queen to privileged encounters with the Ndorobo

people, there is a sense that it is the people rather than the events that have been the most important thing in a quite fantastic life.

If your knowledge of pre-Independence Africa is coloured by Happy Valley glamour, colonial suppression and Hollywood stereotypes, then this book will provide a humane and sympathetic account of how many people lived at a time when the rest of the World had other things to care about. Rich in anecdote, wise in ethnic insight and affectionate in it's telling, Beating About The Bush pays homage to a life in which people are more important than ideas and experience is more rewarding than possessions. And there is not a pith helmet in sight.

The Editor.

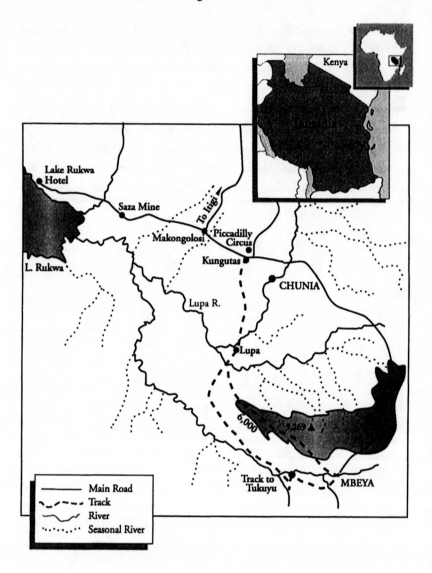

Map of South Western Tanganyika and the Lupa Goldfields, 1936

Chapter One
A Brief Education

After an idyllic childhood in the Serengeti, running wild with my Masai friends, immersed in their culture, surrounded by wildlife and free of cares, it was becoming apparent that the spectre of change was looming. Our farm in Loliondo, on the Kenya/Tanganyika border, owned by my mother and my stepfather, Otto, had suffered some serious setbacks and we had been living a very frugal life of late. Rinderpest, a killer disease in cattle had swept through our herd of trek oxen, leaving only a few survivors, a plague of locusts had decimated our maize crop and a drought had strangled the area's water supply over the previous year. These problems had been aggravated by the General Depression which had practically stopped trade between East Africa and the rest of the World and the rise of Fascism, which had demanded that the attention of the British Administration be turned to matters closer to home.

One day in early 1936, Otto called me in and told me that there was not enough money for the farm to run properly and we could not even afford to replant the crop recently decimated by the locusts and drought. In order to try and rectify our terrible financial problems, and make it easier for my mother and myself, he was going to the Lupa Goldfields, where he hoped to make enough money for us to follow him. My mother and I lived for eight months on what I could snare in the way of birds and small animals and on the occasional meagre purchases of tea, sugar and mealy meal. The local Masai people helped us with milk, and their young boys, who had been my only friends, hunted with me. I was prevented from using a .22 rifle or 12 bore shot gun as ammunition was too expensive, but I was proficient with a bow and arrow. Whilst my bush-craft was equal to that of any Masai boy of the same age, living off the land under nearly starvation conditions proved to be a great strain on both my mother and me. Eventually when the letter from Otto finally arrived with the money for us to follow him down to Lupa, but our relief and excitement at finally leaving behind what had been tough times, was tempered by my utter desolation at leaving Matanda behind. Matanda had been my closest friend and ally for most of my life, closer to me than my brother and our parting proved to be one of the most difficult of my life, despite the attempts at stoicism that boys, especially Masai ones, adopt to hide their tears.

We moved from the farm at Loliondo to the Lupa Goldfield in time for Christmas 1936 and upon arrival, my step-father took one look at the rags my mother and I wore and drove us straight to Mbeya to get us decently clad. After the deprivations of the past year it was overwhelming to be comfortable again, although the comfort was relative and of a primitive sort - we could now buy tea and sugar and have less than threadbare clothes. There were further aspects of our new life that we had not considered whilst at Loliondo. I was now fourteen years old, just over six feet tall, but had only completed less than a year's schooling in my life. Thus, it was decided that I should go to the new Christian Missionary Society (CMS) School at Arusha, in Northern Tanganyika, over 730 miles away along one of the most rudimentary roads in the country. I thought life was suddenly rather exciting, although I had strong reservations about the need for further education.

The sudden intrusion of life at boarding school proved to be a far more unkind world than I had anticipated. I was far behind in the work, at a far lower standard of ability and could barely read or write.

When I arrived I was initially put in a class suitable for my age but could not cope with the demands being made on my untrained mind and was sent down to a level more in fitting with my qualifications. That was shaming enough, but I was also bullied and called "white nigger" by many of my peers because of my less than cosmopolitan bush childhood, which made life even harder to bear. Most of the children, and especially the girls, could not be bothered with me believing my lack of knowledge to be a mark of stupidity rather than a result of an incomplete education. The majority of them had been reared in Africa but none had lived a life as isolated from European influence as I, which led to their notions that I was some sort of tribal freak. As the days passed and time softened the harsher opinions of my first arrival, some of the others began to realise that I was not quite as uncivilised as I might have first seemed and two boys of my own age took me under their wing. Jeff Hollyer and David How-Brown were to remain friends for the rest of my life, and Fate would conspire to knit together our paths frequently over the coming years. The characteristics that were to define them as adults, were already branded upon their personalities with Jeff to remain the ginger, short and stocky one with David also of the same colouring, blessed with an open outgoing character that was simultaneously honest and truthful.

Mr. Forehead, one of the masters, together with one of the female staff, took me in hand and started the slow business of educating me to the standard attained by my peers. Luckily I was not alone in being so backward as there was an Afrikaans boy, strong as an ox and a good sportsman, who had received as little education as I and with his moral support, and that of Jeff and David, the bullying eased up and I began to climb the scholastic ladder. By the end of the second term I had made reasonable progress and a natural ability for mathematics had placed me among the top ten of my class. I had spoken Swahili, Kikuyu and Masai practically all my life, and so encouraged by Mr. Forehead I took Swahili as an extra subject, proving to be the most fluent in the school, amongst both students and staff. This linguistic accolade was strictly limited to the African languages, because my written English, and particularly my spelling, fell way short of acceptable and still proves difficult for me to this day.

Eventually, the much-anticipated end of the school year hove into view and we all prepared to depart for home and the precious eight weeks of the August holiday. When the day came we piled into the school bus, filling it with the noisy bustle of luggage and students all too eager for home and freedom. The bus took us from Arusha to Dodoma, in the centre of the country, a journey of about 270 miles, from where most of the children were to catch trains going east to the coast or west to the lakes. There were five other boys and girls and I from the same area who were to carry on southwards in Mooloo Manji's Royal Mail Transport, a rather grandiose term for what was little more than two saloon cars. Donald Bousfield and his sister Lorna, as the eldest in the group, were in charge of us for this leg of the journey, but their duties entailed nothing more than comforting some of the younger children. The long rains had arrived early and the Ruaha River was in flood, sweeping over the bridge in a vicious brown torrent, forcing us to sleep overnight in the saloon cars at Chipogoro. The whole thing was initially a great adventure, which at first we entered into with a joyous spirit, but when we woke up after a damp and cramped night we were slightly subdued. By morning the waters had receded sufficiently for the cars to creep across the bridge in low gear with us walking and sliding ahead to remove debris and check that all was well on the crossing. The journey from Dodoma to the Lupa took four days but that first holiday at home provided a longed-for release for me, a great letting off of bottled up energy and frustration and if my mother had known how I spent most of that holiday, she would have been horrified.

My brother Norman was a good five years older than me and was working at the Saza gold mine where he kept company with a crowd of rowdy young men. Apart from the boat they owned between them, they borrowed others from the Bousfields and on weekends, they would drive down to Lake Rukwa, put up at the Bousfield's Hotel and from there go fishing or harpooning crocodile. I was now fifteen and my brother Norman very condescendingly allowed me to tag along on these expeditions, either as a dogs-body, punch-bag or perhaps, as bait - I never really knew. Crocodile hunting was a dangerous and somewhat hair-raising sport at the best of times but we added a few rules of our own, just to heighten the risk. The boat would be driven out under its own power to within a hundred yards or so of a place known to attract sunbathing crocodiles, where we would switch off the engine and propel the boat forwards quietly with paddles. Going inshore as close as possible, the crocodiles would then be disturbed from their sleep as they lay sunning themselves on the banks of the lake and with tremendous splashing, threshing and flashing of jaws, they would make for the open water, where the young men would be waiting for them. They carried harpoons attached to ropes or chains, which were fastened to the boat, and when the crocs dispersed, the nearest crocodiles would be speared with a spring-loaded harpoon, which opened up once inside the animal. It could be a lot more difficult than it seemed and sometimes we would approach twenty or more, secluded, sandy bays along the shoreline without success. However, once a harpoon was firmly embedded in a crocodile, events would move at such impossible speed that the only thing to do was to let the creature tow the boat along until it tired itself out or died from the effects of it. More often than not, one of us, more foolhardy than the rest, would decide that one harpoon was insufficient to hold the prey and insist on thrusting in another. This usually ended up with him being pulled into the water or losing his balance and falling in, but in either case the cable had to be cut, and quickly, and the man picked up. On some occasions the boat was turned over and everyone thrown out but this usually took place early on in proceedings, in shallow water, and so there were no serious mishaps. The Rukwa crocodile is a very large and powerful animal with a fully-grown male weighing close to a ton and reaching up to 22 feet in length. In those days they had plenty of fish to eat and so attacks on humans that might be playing, fishing or hunting close to the water were rare. If, as often happened, a crocodile had had a long battle and was tired, it would make for land and then we would play our own rules which required each man to try to be the first one to wedge the mouth open with a stick. I thought this was highly dangerous as the crocodiles would only have their mouths wide open when attacking but I think in retrospect that this was probably the attraction. Once the victor had inserted the stick, the crocodile would be swiftly killed, measurements would be taken, congratulations bandied about, and we would all retire to the Rukwa Hotel bar where the rest of the month's salary would be happily disposed of.

The fact that I was permitted to accompany these young men and that I was involved in crocodile baiting, gave me a certain prestige amongst the youths of my age group. While the young men were drinking in the bar, we youngsters - the Bousfields and other visiting boys - would play, fish and swim among the crocodiles. At this time it was not the done thing to make too much of a friend of someone considered as "backward" until they had proved themselves in other fields but through my displays of outdoor derring-do I came to be accepted for the first time by my European peers.

My journeys to and from school always seemed to be such adventures that I remember more of the travelling to school than I do of the term-time. Sometimes it was impossible to return home for Christmas as this holiday was at the height of the short rains and the fairly primitive mud roads would be impassable. After my first full year at school in 1937 the roads were thought to be acceptable and we embarked, as usual, on the school bus for Dodoma, with one of the teachers as escort, to spend Christmas with our families. Although the rains had not been heavy, the roads were a morass of mud and potholes and we got as far as Pienaar Heights, about 135 miles from Arusha, before our troubles started. The bus was too heavy, the road too steep, and the mud too slippery for an easy ascent. The bigger boys had to get out and cut brushwood to lay along the wheel tracks and then they had to push while the older girls had to walk. The mud was thick and slimy and clogged our shoes, which made walking and pushing very difficult whilst the road was too narrow for the bus to turn round. With no options to go back or to reverse down the hill, we had to persevere with this Sisyphean task until we reached the top of the hill, pushing in the dark and driving rain with our clothes soaked before we were even half-way on the first leg of our journey. To me the activities of the day had been fun and rewarding, and while most of the others, and the teachers, complained about their cold and soggy state, David How-Brown, Jeff Hollyer and I felt we had had a most worthwhile time. We hoped eagerly that calamities would continue to occur, so as to relieve the boredom of the long and uncomfortable trip with a little adventure. It was on that day, while we were covered in mud, pushing the big bus with all our strength, shouting instructions to the driver, falling flat on our faces in the wet, trying to avoid the spraying mud of the wheels that spun and failed to grip, that a lasting friendship between the three of us was, if you will excuse the pun, cemented.

It was four in the morning by the time we reached Dodoma, and everyone had missed their connecting trains. Those who were going east, like Jeff and David, were told that they could travel on the early morning goods train going to Morogoro, but would have to sit in the Guards van, which delighted them and those travelling to the Lakes would go on at ten the next morning. Only three rooms had been booked at the Railway Hotel for the teacher and those of us going south, and these were given to the girls and small boys, leaving the rest of us to sleep in the hotel lounge. Our companions for the night were a motley crew of sleeping drunkards who had been unable to get home. Our coming in had disturbed them and, waiting until the teacher had gone to bed, they started their party all over again, plying us youngsters with drink. We thought this was a great adventure until daylight came when we had to face our escort, Miss Read. She was a zealously religious Church Missionary Society lady, thin, with a bun at the back of her head, and glasses which gave the impression of a very fierce hawk, but underneath she had a very kind and soft heart. On this occasion, for some reason, which I did not understand, she frowned at me in particular, saying she had expected better of me and that all her good work of the past term had been for nothing. I felt very bad about this as she had been extremely kind to me, giving me extra lessons every evening and helping me with my work. I had been her favourite and everyone knew it but now she was very angry with me and let me know in no uncertain terms that her blue-eyed boy had let her down. Predictably, my reputation amongst my peers received quite a boost from this episode and at that age, the opinions of friends are far more important than those of the teachers.

As usual, Mooloo Manji, the transporter from Iringa, had sent two saloon cars to take the Lupa youngsters south to Sao Hill. Early in the morning, after Miss Read had finished her sermon on the evils of drink, we set off from Dodoma, suitably chastised and feeling a little queasy from our introduction to alcohol the night before. It took a long day to cover the one hundred and eighty miles to Sao hill as conditions continued to deteriorate under the relentless rain and we did not arrive until ten that night.

On this journey the first sign of my acceptance as a social equal by the girls was given when Edith Kerchona volunteered to sit in front of the car with me, a most daring thing to do and we sat in rigid silence for many miles. I have been told that I have an irreverent streak and, squeezed beside Edith that day, the desire to shock her grew stronger and stronger. This trait, to attract disapproval over trivial matters, is something I have never been able to curb and my chance came at the Ruaha Bridge when an African walked up to us with a bowl of eggs for sale. I bought five for five cents and began to break the shells on the mudguard of the car and nonchalantly swallow the eggs raw, tossing them down my throat like oysters. The boys and girls all walked away unimpressed, saying I was a disgusting pig and that they could not bring themselves to talk to me but I continued to eat my eggs, feigning enjoyment because they were not very fresh. When we started off again I was invited to the back seat with Maureen Hickson Wood, Lorna and Donald, the elite of Arusha School. Our parents met us in Chunya the next day and I was very pleased when several mothers approached mine to invite us to visit them during the holidays. I assumed this was at the instigation of their young and I was secretly delighted at being accepted as one of them at last.

My parents were now doing quite well and had moved from Kungutas to Makongolosi where Otto could work the river beds and swamps in the wet season, moving to the hillsides when the water dried up, and then operating with mechanical dry-blowers. Prospecting in the river beds and swamps was done with two-man "debe-boxes". These were small sluice boxes, six feet long, nine inches wide, with six-inch high sides. Across the bottom were one inch slats at three inch intervals and at the top end of the box was a triangular guide which sloped backwards. The box was supported on two long adjustable legs at the rear and two short fixed legs at the front. When the box was set up and regulated for the required slope, one man fed the grid with earth and checked the bigger pieces which did not fall through for gold nuggets, while the second man fed water through the grid to wash the soil down the box, the heavier metals sinking to the bottom and held by the slats. When sufficient earth had been washed through, one man removed the wet waste soil from the tailings end of the box and the other man cleaned the box into a pan and washed away the earth in the conventional manner, leaving the gold exposed at the bottom of the pan. The dry-blower was similar to a grain-grading machine, with a sieve down the front in the shape of a wide, short sluice box with a continuously moving riddle. It was powered by a small petrol or kerosene engine and operated by a team of about fifteen men under the charge of a headman. The sieves were cleaned out every hour and the headman then carried out the final sifting of the heavy metal from the earth. He did this either by washing it, if there was enough water, or by swishing the pan, allowing the lighter earth to fly out and the heavier metal to settle at the bottom. When only a small deposit lay in the pan, he blew on it and so was able to pick out the bigger pieces of gold. The remaining gold dust and other metals were put into a jar of mercury until it became saturated with gold and the mercury was then burnt off. This method was less conducive to theft than the "debe-box" but even so it was found that the larger nuggets were seldom handed to the rightful owner, no matter which method was used.

My report from school had apparently been good and my step-father had a surprise for me - a second-hand Ariel motor bike. As I was too young to hold a licence I was told not to go on the main road that ran from Mbeya to the Saza Mine but all the places I would be likely to visit could be reached by rough car tracks or footpaths, providing there had not been too much rain. One day I was on one of these rough tracks, on my way to see a girl, when I skidded on a corner. The motorbike landed on top of me, pinning me to the ground, with the heel of my right foot stuck in the frame and the rear wheel slowly working its way through my boot and foot. Fortunately a car drove up within a few minutes and a couple and their young daughter, a girl of about my age, jumped out and stopped the motorbike. I was in bad shape and bleeding heavily as they bundled me into their car but the nearest medical help was a Dr. Swanepoel at Picaddilli, near Kungutas, about 15 miles away, so I was taken directly to him. My rescuers had stopped the bleeding with firmly tied strips of shirt and the girl sat beside me holding my injured leg across her knees. I badly needed to relieve myself and asked them to stop the car. The girl's mother told her to hold me by the shoulders while I leaned out from the seat of the car. I could not bring myself to undress in front of the young girl so I struggled out and tried to move to the rear of the car but in doing so I knocked my foot and it started to bleed again. Both mother and daughter had to come then and help me get back in the car and by this time I was beyond worrying and they could have stripped me naked for all I cared.

Fortunately the doctor was at home and after one look at the damage said I would have to be stitched up immediately. There was no anaesthetic available so I was given a large tot of whiskey and when my parents arrived, I was forcibly held down, sewn up with seven stitches, the wound cleaned with Jeyes Fluid and iodine and then dressed with iodoform. It was ten days before the stitches were removed and the changing of the dressing every other day left our house reeking of iodoform.

Otto had taken under his wing a European who was down on his luck and in order to get him back on his feet, gave him the job of helping control the two thousand labourers we now employed. This man had to share my rondavel room during the holidays, which meant that, unfortunately for him, when I was home his African girlfriend had to be banished. He accepted this situation whilst he was sober, but as soon as he had had too much to drink he became abusive and very nasty to me. A few nights before I went back to school, when he had been on the bottle for three days and nights, he suddenly picked up his rifle just as I was getting into bed. He lurched over and dragged me on to the floor, gave me the rifle and ordered me to "shoot them".

-"Shoot what?", I asked him.

-"Those niggers" he said, pointing to the roof. "They will get me if you don't".

When I did nothing, he turned on me saying I was a "nigger kid" and that was why I would not shoot my own kind. He grabbed the rifle from me and fired two shots into the roof before I managed to wrestle the gun away from him, which fortunately was just as Otto walked in, and seeing what had happened, told me to spend the rest of the night in our sitting room. When he had recovered Otto gave him, and another man named Williamson, a small gang each, some tools and rations and sent them both off to prospect for themselves. I do not know what happened to the first man but Williamson became famous when he found diamonds at his Mwadui mine and the Williamson's Diamond Mines, which was later to flourish, was founded.

Due to my motorbike accident I had not seen much of the other youngsters and was a week late returning to school. I had company on the journey, a German boy by the name of Kurt Hunke, who was a few months older then me and had been to school in Europe. He was tall, fair, good looking and quite an athlete and was also very advanced scholastically, speaking excellent English. We got to know and like each other on the four-day trip to school, and my own standing at school was much improved by his friendship. The older boys were divided into the bullies and the others and, although I was still a target for the former, they did not try anything when my friends were about. In the carpentry shop one day I saw one of the day-boys removing some tools and as only a handful of us were allowed in the workshop without a master, I told him to put the tools back, otherwise the privileged few would be blamed. His reply was to let me know that he did not take orders from "white kaffirs", which inevitably led to a fight. Others came running to watch but when I began to bleed furiously from a wound behind my ear the fight was stopped. The boy ran away and was not seen for the rest of the week but when Donald and Charlie Stevens reported to the headmaster that they had seen him use a nail in the fight, the boy was sent for and given corporal punishment. The boy was Greek, and the punishment was given in the presence of his father, who waved his arms about dramatically and gave loudly his low opinion of the British. Mr. Wynne-Jones, the headmaster, understood no Greek and carried on regardless with the caning of the Hellenic backside. The boy was made to apologise to me afterwards, and in the perverse way of youth we later became quite good friends.

Charlie Stevens was my age and the top sportsman in the school, outshining us all in practical skills, but academically he was on a level with me although he had been at school since he was seven. Capable, and a born leader, he was highly thought of by both staff and pupils and made a very good prefect and so when he came to me one day and asked if I knew why paraffin from a bottle would not ignite, I felt flattered to be consulted. I told him that it needed heating first, unlike petrol, which would ignite when cold. Petrol would be no good, he said, as it would blow up and he explained that he wanted to make a stove from a Pascal sweet jar for the next Scout safari. If I was willing to try it out with him, we could borrow the blow-lamp from the workshop to heat up the jar.

The operation was carried out in the senior dormitory during the afternoon rest hour and everything went smoothly and we had got the flame at least four feet high when the jar suddenly exploded, setting fire to the mosquito nets which hung coiled above each bed. Very quick action was taken by us to save the day and no one was hurt, except for David How-Brown who sprained an ankle when he jumped out of the dormitory window. The fire was put out in record time and the damaged mosquito nets re-coiled with the burnt parts turned to the wall in an attempt to hide the evidence. We gave one of the juniors a burning bakelite bicycle pump to walk about with, so as to attract attention away from the senior dormitory, but the master Dickie Forehead had heard the bang and came to investigate. When he saw the small boy with the burning pump, he marched the child off to the washroom where the pump was put under the tap and the boy ticked off with an order to go back to his dormitory to rest. Our immediate problem, however, was to deal with the burnt nets, but as it was half-term the next day we resolved to somehow obtain new ones to bring back with us on the Monday night.

Charlie had invited me for half-term to his mother's coffee farm at Two Bridges near Moshi, which was not only a great compliment, but also a most sought-after offer because he had the use of a car and several suitable places to go shooting, on both his mother's and his aunt's farms. We had a marvellous weekend shooting green pigeons, fishing in the rivers, eating what we liked and shooting buck in the coffee plantation by torchlight at night. On the second day we had a competition to see who could kill the greatest number of creatures in half an hour sitting where we were inside the house, armed with .22 rifles and hard-nose ammunition. After many hits, Charlie spotted a gecko lizard on the wall and fired at it, but the bullet ricocheted and hit him on the arm. Luckily it was a clean hole through the fleshy part and we raced to his aunt's house where she dressed the wound and promised not to tell anyone. I cannot remember what Charlie's mother had to say about her bullet-scarred walls, but no doubt she drove us back to school with some relief.

We found our elaborate arrangements to cover up the fire damaged nets had been in vain as Miss Vance, the senior matron, had sniffed out the burnt nets when checking the linen in the dormitory. She then extracted the whole story from some of the junior boys who had not gone home for the half-term weekend and the next morning at Assembly, Mr. Wynn-Jones lectured us before ordering all senior boys to report to his office. Charlie and I received two strokes of the cane each morning for three days and we had to replace the damaged nets from our pocket money.

For some time tunnelling in the school grounds from the river bank had been carried out by a group of five senior boys. When several of these left the school, interest waned and the tunnels were neglected, but during my second year the Tunnelling Committee decided to revive the work. They invited three new members to join them and to my surprise I was amongst them. I was given a long lecture on secrecy and hard work but when I asked what the tunnels were for, no one seemed to know. They just thought it was good idea and would be first class for midnight feasts, although it is worth considering that at the time any explanation would have satisfied me such was my pride to have been included in the secret mission. When I was younger I had experienced acute claustrophobia when I first wriggled down a porcupine hole and I must admit I did not look forward to digging in a confined space but after a few days I grew accustomed to it. At the end of the first week we had cleared all the fallen debris and boxed in the soft sides. We were ready to start on new ground and very soon came across hard, impacted soil, which was tough-going. Sweating as we worked we realised there was a shortage of fresh air, so a small chimney was opened which also let in some light but this part of the tunnel then collapsed and had to be cleared, leaving us with a large space, which we named our feasting room. At about this time we discovered there was another party tunnelling away a little above and across our front. Jeff and I had just finished our stint at the face and were in the wash-house when Charlie ran in to say we must go back to the tunnel as there had been an earth fall and two fellows were trapped inside. It alarmed us to realise that the ventilating hole was on the wrong side of the collapse and we fought down our fear as we ran for the river. The quickest way to rescue the trapped pair would be through the rival tunnel but we could not waste time searching for the other team to seek their permission, so we clambered straight into their tunnel, Charlie leading the way with a torch. The narrow entrance led into a large cave and, in the light of our torch, eight very surprised faces caught in the middle of a feast turned to glare at us. There were two girls and six boys in the party and had there been room for manoeuvre they would have certainly have roughed us up, but as soon as they heard the reason for our invasion, their hostility was forgotten and they set about helping us. Fortunately the collapse had been from the surface, allowing some air to reach the trapped boys, but the tunnel was too narrow to turn round in and all they could hope to do was to move backwards. When they found they could go no further, they panicked and it was with great relief that we were able to clear away the small amount of earth which separated the two tunnels and get them to safety.

Shocked by this near-tragic experience, we gathered outside in the bright sunlight with ashen faces and agreed a temporary halt to our excavations. Inevitably the story leaked out and we were thoroughly cross-examined by the headmaster and the parents of the two girls, although it should be mentioned that it was established that the girls were there only for the feast and not for any scandalous reason. We were told to attend the headmaster's study the next morning before assembly and that we should be prepared to be sent home for good. However, in the event, the morning brought us three strokes of the cane from Mr. Wynne-Jones' practised hand and the girls were sent home for the rest of the term.

A few days later four of the older boys including myself were invited to the headmaster's house for tea, where we rattled our tea cups nervously, laughed too loudly at all his jokes and were eventually taken off to his study for a very interesting lecture about sex. We were told all about masturbation and how bad it was, in all its forms, for our health before moving on, to our astonishment, to include "mental masturbation" and why boys had wet dreams. He told us the new swimming pool at the school would soon be ready, and we would be well advised not to pay too much attention to the bigger girls when they appeared in their swimming costumes. After all, he said, we would only be seeing a little more of them than we did when they played tennis or hockey. All this seemed to us somewhat unnecessary as on certain days we had swum at the Arusha Hotel pool and had been frequenting the peepholes in the partition between the boys' and girls' changing rooms for some time. We were further advised that if and when we felt randy we should take a cold shower. After this first lecture, all the bigger boys in turn were called to Mr. Wynne-Jones' study, at regular intervals, and given further pieces of fascinating information. The girls were having similar talks with the female staff and we exchanged information to everyone's great delight.

Interestingly enough, later events proved that either the girls and boys were cleverer than the staff or were a great deal more moral than they were given credit for. One day just after the pool had been completed, Charlie and I were on our way to supervise the junior swimming when we were called over by an older girl called Dorothy, who had been a pupil herself until that year and now taught in the kindergarten. She told us she was in a quandary as to what to do as a new master, an Australian, had been making passes at her. Dorothy looked a very attractive and mature twenty, yet she was only eighteen and the master concerned was about thirty and that day, she breathlessly told us, the master had put forward an improper but flattering proposition. Now, blushing, horrified and excited, she appealed to us for advice. Privately thinking we would have done exactly the same thing had we had the opportunity, we listened gravely and told her to keep well away from the man and to say nothing to anyone until we had thought out what to do. This was now our little secret and Charlie and I planned to make the most of it. In truth, we were far more conservative than we liked to think and in the end sought an audience with the headmaster that evening. He was not very sympathetic at first and warned us not to make up stories but he eventually decided to consult Dorothy herself. We were sent out into the corridor to wait while she told her story, then two further confidantes were summoned before we were all stood before Mr. Wynne-Jones and lectured on secrecy and the good name of the school. The master in question left for Australia a week later - there was a rumour that he was to become a priest - and no more was heard about the incident but the result was that the headmaster did not call us for any more talks on sex.

It was rapidly becoming clear to me that life at school was capable of providing incident which whilst it might not compare to Masai life in the Serengeti, was at least capable of distracting me from my loss of it. This education lark was proving to be less scholastic, and more enjoyable, than I had initially feared and I was discovering that wisdom is what is learnt when you are not being taught.

Chapter Two
The Last Days At School

When Easter came around, we were uncertain as to what to do. Two weeks holiday at Easter was far too short a time for the long journey home, so most children from distant parts of the country remained in the area of the school, staying with friends or relatives. Dickie Forehead, my favourite among the masters, invited Jeff Hollyer, David How-Brown and me to go on a camping trip with him. Dickie was one of the most academically gifted, and one of the nicest men I have ever known but unfortunately found it very difficult to discipline a class of unruly children, because he was far too kind. On his own, away from the school or out in the bush one could not find a more interesting person or a better friend. I owe most of my small amount of education to him, and the greater part of that was absorbed outside the classroom. He was a very religious man and later joined the Church Missionary Society but he never forced his beliefs on others nor lost that sensible worldly outlook that differentiates the spiritual from the zealouts.

Dickie had a shotgun and a bird licence for certain game birds in season, which he did not use himself but he did allow certain of the older boys to use it and this was one of my privileges. When we had gathered a small tent, cooking utensils, sleeping bags, fishing tackle, digging and car tools, basic foodstuffs and all the other odds and ends necessary for a ten-day safari, there was not much room left in the old B Model Chevrolet Box Body. Dickie and two others sat in front and the third squeezed himself into the back with all the kit. On the way we shot some yellow-necked spurfowl for our supper and reached Babati, just over a hundred miles away just as it was getting dark. We had been given permission to use an old rest camp on Lord Lovelace's farm for the first three nights and when we arrived, we were relieved to find a large stack of firewood cut and ready, but there was no water. The river was some way distant and so, when we had unloaded the car, Jeff and I set off to fetch water in a couple of clean debes. A debe is one of the greatest inventions of our time and very useful in everyday East African life. It was made of tin and designed to hold four gallons of petrol or paraffin, but had a hundred different uses, including grilling steaks over four sheets of the East African Standard newspaper, baking bread, or as the Africans most often did, cutting and flattening out the tins to make efficient roofing tiles. We approached the river through an area teeming with game, some of it dangerous, and were entirely dependent on the car headlights. The crossing was too shallow to fill the debes and so we walked a short distance further along a footpath through thick elephant grass. Jeff went a little way and then would go no further from the security of the car lights and turned back, but I was so used to mixing with game both in daylight and at night that it did not worry me at all, so naturally I started to show off. After bringing back the first debe I went far further than I needed to fill the second can when suddenly, to my horror, a rhino charged, presumably having caught my scent or heard the clang of the debe against a stone. Of course anything like this always seems much more frightening when it occurs in the dark; one cannot see the cause of the commotion or where to run. I just stood petrified until I heard the animal breaking through bush on the far side of the river. Jeff shouted to me in panic from the car but I did not answer until I got near enough to be seen but he thought I had been killed by the rhino, and so lost his temper with me for not replying earlier. He had realised he could not start the car alone as it required two people, one to swing the starting handle and the other to press the accelerator and had worried for his own safety too. Although rather shaken myself, I managed to calm him down and we drove back to the camp in silence.

Neither Dickie Forehead nor David How-Brown believed our story, as Jeff, the youngest in the party embellished the incident with such vivid detail that it sounded far more dramatic than it had really been. Although most of the boys in the school lived in areas populated by game and had a fair knowledge of it, few if any had been as closely connected with wild animals as I had. At first I was presumed to be showing off, then thought to be fanciful, but, towards the end of the trip, their attitude changed and I found I was being consulted about matters concerning the bush. When it came to discussions on other subjects however, such as world affairs or the infinity of space, it was either explained to me in slow simple English or I was just left out of the conversation altogether.

At our first camp we spent most of the time walking in the Ufiomi mountains while Dickie took samples of rock and studied the formation of the different layers of the ground, indulging his interest in geology, which he was fond of explaining in detail. This did not appeal to me but David and Jeff absorbed it all and were fascinated whereas I was more excited by the lively doings of the numerous rhino in the area. We were charged as many as five times a day, and none of the attacks were serious but they kept us alert, however, and I found the sensation invigorating. The others talked of adrenaline and how fast the body reacted to danger, but I did not know what adrenaline was and kept quiet, content to enjoy the sense of impending danger and the effect it had on my heartbeat.

On the next part of the trip we moved to the western side of Lake Babati, as far as we could get with the car, and camped about two hundred yards from the water. This camp, although very pleasant in the day-time and shaded with trees, had to be abandoned after the first night as we were plagued by mosquitoes and were forced to move further away from the lake. Dickie and Jeff spent hours looking for stones, but David and I busied ourselves fishing for barbel, which were easy at the time because the rains had just finished and the water was clear. The African tribes prefer barbel (a type of catfish) to most other fresh water fish, but the average European will not eat them, considering their taste too muddy. In my opinion, a good barbel, at the right time of year, takes a lot of beating and is certainly no more muddy than some of the bream and bass I have eaten, with the added benefit of fewer bones. Dickie who would eat anything that was put in front of him and as long as there was enough, was not sufficiently interested to comment on it, which was fortunate as we boys knew nothing about preparing fish dishes. We knew how to cook meat suspended over an open fire, but game meat is usually too dry to be roasted on coals as it has little fat and so we bought eggs from the local natives. First we tested them in a bowl of water; they were bad if they floated and they were fresh if they sank to the bottom. For our evening meal I shot game birds or small buck, accompanied by boiled rice, which came out of the pot in one solid chunk and our memorable safari bread, which was as solid and heavy as mahogany.

Babati was known in those days for its one and only shop, owned by Shere Mohammed, which sold everything one could possibly need, including rare luxuries such as tinned food and whiskey, and was a regular stopping place between Arusha and Dodoma. It has also become well known through the fame of its beautiful women, the Wafiomi, who are an offshoot of the Hamitic Wambulu tribe. These women carry a reputation throughout East Africa for their grace and beauty and have the added bonus of retaining their looks and figures to a ripe old age. Several wealthy and, in some cases, titled European men, out in Africa on hunting safaris, saw, tried and liked the area and its people and bought farms in the vicinity. They built good houses, laid out colourful gardens and spent the winter months there, sometimes bringing with them their girlfriends from Europe and sometimes befriending the local Ufiomi girls. The shop had been opened initially to serve these people and it traded well for many years, slowly building on its reputation as hunting safaris and travellers began to pass through the area. It was a godsend to other travellers such as ourselves and we were able to stock up with a few choice items to relieve our dreary cooking. At the end of ten days we had walked many miles, seen a great deal of game and enjoyed ourselves immensely - with the exception of the food. Dickie when asked, said he thought it had been all right, but the rest of us hungered for a decent, well-cooked school meal.

We arrived back at school from this trip a few days before term was to begin, just in time for preparations for the annual attempt on Mount Meru. Mount Meru is a spectacular fifteen thousand foot mountain that would be famous were it anywhere else, but is overshadowed both in height and in reputation by its more famous cousin, Kilimanjaro, across the steppe. It looms over the town of Arusha, nestled in its foothills, and is such an important part of town life, providing the water and climactic conditions that make the town so habitable, that few people who live there have not considered climbing it. This was an annual event and boys over the age of fifteen were, with their parents' consent, allowed to make the attempt. I had taken part in the previous year's climb from the west, but at 13,500 feet many of the boys had dropped back, unable to make it, and the exercise was aborted. This year there was to be no repetition of that and the mountain would be attempted from the south. It would be heavy going through the bamboo forest, but after that there was a solid rock ridge without the volcanic ash surface which was so tiring and frustrating when approached from the west. The western flank rises in great steps, one step up and then a flat open glade, followed by another climb through thick well-watered forest, then another open glade, with more forest, up to the edge of the volcanic ash at about 12,000 feet. From that height to the top the surface consists entirely of loose ash, making the climb a slippery and exhausting business. On the northern and eastern sides is the huge crater, encircled by 2000 ft high sheer cliff walls and a primeval floor of cedar forest. Strangely-shaped, wizened trees are festooned with Old Man's Beard and the core of the volcano itself rises from the floor of the crater in a grey, grim cone. It makes for an almost primeval atmosphere that is a far cry from the arid steppe to the south. We found the climb up the steep southern face hard going, with the first part through cedar and loliondo forest. We reached the bamboo belt at about 8,000 feet and it was so thick that the only way to walk through it was to follow the winding game tracks, which were difficult to negotiate and required constant attention to avoid meeting the rhino, elephant and buffalo that also used them. We slept that night at a point just above the bamboo in a well-protected gully near a beautiful spring of clear mountain water, where it became clear that some of the boys had found the climb very demanding and Jeff and I were quite sure that before long the expedition would be turned back. We thought the party far too large, convinced that someone would feel the altitude and become mountain sick, which would necessitate bringing the whole party back. We decided that on the following day, we would make our way to the front of the party and just keep going until we reached the top, even if the rest of them went back. We knew we would get into serious trouble when we arrived back at school, but we were determined to see our names on the "Conquered Meru" Board in the school hall.

On the second morning we left at first light and in about three hours we were well out of sight of the others, so we had a short rest before continuing, until after a breathless two hours, we reached the summit, with sweeping views across to Kilimanjaro and Kenya. We signed the book, had a quick look at this privileged perspective on Africa, before sliding and stumbling back down, catching the rest of the party, already on a return journey, an hour and a half later. Several of the boys were nursing sore stomachs as they had been eating ice for reasons best known to themselves. We thought this state of affairs completely justified our dash to the top, and when Dickie, the master in charge, asked us where we had been, we were quite honest and told him we had reached the summit. He told us he would speak to us when we got back to school, but said that as no one had witnessed our achievement, we could not be listed on the Board until one of the masters had been up and verified the book. We heard no more about it until a week later when our names were called out at Assembly and in a few days the Board shone with its new additions. We felt very pleased and proud of ourselves.

It was a Sunday evening when we got back to school after the climb up Meru. Everyone else had returned after the holidays and there were also some new boys and girls to whom we were introduced. Sadly, my friends Donald and Lorna Bousfield had left and David How-Brown was leaving soon also, but I was moved up a form, even though it was not the beginning of the academic year, which meant I was now in a class with my own age group. I was also put in the lst XI hockey team and selected for the school rugger XV, signs to me that I was finally an accepted part of the school. I was never really an outsider but at that age and after the dramatic upheaval of leaving behind what amounted to a Masai childhood, I clung to these emblems of acceptance as a form of security. There was further pride when I was moved to a junior dormitory as dormitory leader, which I knew was the first step towards being made a prefect. When this happened to me, I felt I did not want to be a prefect if it meant leaving my friends and I found my new duties involved more than just controlling the junior boys. I had also to protect them from the bigger bullies, especially on the days when they went shopping and they would bring their sweets and tuck to me for safekeeping, before anyone could remove their purchases by force. I had more fights looking after the juniors than I had had before which, if it was a free-for-all, I invariably came off best, but one particular bully challenged me in the boxing ring. I had not the faintest idea how to box and consequently suffered a good thrashing in front of the whole school, not only once but for four Saturdays running. The boy in question was gaining so much prestige that I knew I would have to resolve the matter one way or another. Things came to a head one Friday when a girl called Jessie Dare reported that her little brother had had his tuck taken by one of the bullies, who chose that moment to walk by. When I asked him about the boy's sweets, he told me to mind my own bloody business otherwise his friend - my enemy - would sort me out on Saturday. I took hold of the boy and gave him a couple of slaps, the sweets were returned and the boy went off to report me to his friend. Owen was with me when the two bullies returned and demanded the sweets back. Feeling courageous with his friend in attendance, the boy I had cuffed took a swipe at me and, as I grabbed him, my enemy came for me. This time there were no rules or referees and Owen was there to hold the other chap back and in a very short time I had the bigger boy on the ground in the middle of a quickly growing crowd. I was just about to release him when one of the prefects shouted, "Now's your chance to sort him out for Saturday night!" By the time I had finished with him I had extracted an apology, a promise that there would be no more bullying and that I would never again be challenged in the ring. The promises were kept and certainly no bullying took place again in my presence. The story went round the school like wildfire and before going home for the holidays, Mr. Wynne-Jones called me into his study and referred to the incident, informing me that next term I was to be a prefect and that I should continue to protect the younger boys.

Once term finished in 1938, I immediately left for the Lupa full of plans for further adventure and I had only arrived, when my brother Norman turned up from Saza Mine, where he was still working and invited me to go to Mbeya for the weekend. My mother thought it would be a good idea for us to have some time together, now that I was away as much as he was and so off we went. Norman was courting a girl there at the time and we went straight to her parents' house where, despite our late arrival, both the girl and her mother were waiting up for us. We were given something to eat and a bed was made up for me on the sitting-room sofa and once everyone had disappeared, I drifted off into the sleep that comes so naturally at that age.

Early next morning, a girl about a year younger than me appeared with a cup of tea. I would not see Norman until later as he and his girl had gone to play tennis and the parents had left for work and so the young girl asked me if I would like to go for a walk up to the reservoir which supplied Mbeya. On our way up we saw some African women washing their clothes, and themselves, in a stream. They were quite naked and made no attempt to cover themselves, even though we had to pass close by. To me it was the most natural sight in the world and I scarcely glanced at them, but after a little while the girl turned to me and said,

- "Did you notice that all those women were shaved except one? Why wasn't she shaved?"

- "Where?" I asked, pretending innocence.

- "Here". The girl pointed to between her legs. "Stupid! Where do you think?"

I told her I did not know the customs of the local tribe but if they had been Masai, it would have meant the woman was sick in some way, and that it would have been a warning to the men to leave her alone.

By the Sunday evening I was bored by the entire weekend and only too glad to set off home with Norman. Driving along in silence to Makongolosi, the road lit by our headlights, we watched bemused as a wheel passed us by, appearing so suddenly that for a moment neither of us realised its significance. Norman suddenly swore one of the finest of his collection of Anglo-Saxon oaths as it dawned on him what had happened. He stopped the car and I climbed out to go in search of our rear wheel. When I returned pushing the errant wheel, he had jacked up the car from where we could see that the nuts had worked loose and the bolts had sheered off. This required the type of action that comes so naturally when one lives in the Bush for a while and we simply took a nut and bolt from each of the other three wheels and got back safely by midnight.

Norman had invited me to join his crowd on Lake Rukwa the following weekend for a crocodile hunt, but it meant my having to make the journey as far as Saza on my old bicycle. After my accident, I was thought to be unsafe on my motor-bike, apart from which all the local policemen knew I had no licence. On the Friday morning I pedalled the twenty-five miles to the Saza Mine, with my trusty Mannlicher .256 slung across my back in case of lion. Saza was the largest and most developed of the mines, extracting reef gold from deep below the surface, and belonged to East African Goldfields. I knew from Norman's talk that there were shafts, lifts, buckets and underground rails and my greatest dread was to be taken along on a tour underground. I carefully arranged my arrival to coincide with the time Norman would be working in the power house and there would be no chance of his seeing me until he finished work in the evening.

I arrived just after lunch but instead found Hutchinson, the labour officer with whom Norman shared a house, still eating. In true East African style, he insisted that I share his meal and afterwards invited me to go around the mine with him. I had no choice if I was not to suffer my brother's teasing and was fine until we got to the head of a shaft, where I was handed a helmet and ordered into a large bucket, together with Hutch and one of the other European miners. I was not asked if I wanted to go, but simply told to sit down and keep my hands on the inside rail. Very quickly the bucket swayed its way to three hundred feet below the surface, where we climbed out into a gallery, lit only by the carbide lamps carried on the helmets of the miners. The carbide, a mineral powdered fuel, gave a very bright light and also a very strong smell of turpentine. The walls dripped with water and the heat, smell and noise were extreme. We made our way along the gallery for about a hundred and fifty yards and then the tunnel narrowed and decreased in height until we could only just stand. At the working face, two men were preparing holes for dynamite charges but they stopped to talk for a few minutes with Hutch, who was on an inspection of the working conditions, following complaints from the miners. When he was satisfied with what he had seen and heard, we returned to the surface where I was relieved to see daylight once more. Strangely, although I had hated being underground and was very apprehensive, in some way it had a fascination for me which I could not explain then or since, and I wanted to go down again.

A group of eight of us, including my brother, left for Lake Rukwa by car before dawn the next morning. The boat was ready on the lakeside and we clambered aboard and were soon chugging our way into deeper water. The lake was a little choppy and the large barbel, some of them weighing a hundred pounds or more, were having trouble getting below the surface, so we had some fun shooting these with the smaller harpoons. Just as we approached one of our favourite crocodile bays we ran into rain, which became a cloudburst. We were quickly drenched and sat uncomfortably for the next two hours, dangerously awash, with water coming in at us from all directions. Visibility was down to a few feet and it was all we could do to keep afloat, frantically baling at the same rate as the water was entering. When the sun appeared at last, we abandoned all thoughts of shooting crocodiles and went back to Bousfield's Hotel on the shores of the lake, where Norman and his friends consoled themselves at the bar.

I had a happy time fishing with the Bousfield boys, with whom I had been at school the year before, until a lunch of fresh Tilapia such as I have never tasted before or since, and quite as delicious as trout. After lunch, some of the people who had been in the bar, among them some women, joined the boys and girls for a swim. Lorna Bousfield was with us and, for the first time, I saw her as a woman in a swimming costume and I remember thinking to myself how wonderful it would be to see her with nothing on, proof, if it were needed, that I was growing up. She had the most beautiful figure, standing there on the edge of the water, and most of the men eyed this beautiful seventeen year old girl with approval.

Later on, Donald Bousfield suggested that we try fishing lower down the shore, where the native fishermen came in with their netted catches of Tilapia, which were then gutted along a lengthy stretch of beach and attracted large shoals of Barbel and Tiger Fish. Tiger fish are scaly and have long sharp teeth and, on Lake Rukwa, they used to run from a couple of pounds up to twenty pounds in weight, with the average around the four-pound mark. Great care has to be taken when extracting a fish-hook from the mouth of a Tiger Fish, if one does not want to lose a finger and it has the reputation of being one of the most active fresh water sporting fish in Africa. I have caught tiger fish on Lake Rudolph (now Lake Turkana) in Kenya and also on the Zambezi, both in the river and on Lake Kariba, but nowhere have I seen them as big or lively as on Lake Rukwa. When going after these fish today, one should reckon on having a strong rod with a modern spinning reel and a six-pound line, with a strong steel trace. Even so, one can still count on less than fifty per cent of those caught being boated, because as soon as the tiger feels the hook, it leaps well out of the water, trying to shake itself off. Fishing from a boat, I have seen Tiger Fish fly right over the boat and land on the other side, and sometimes land in the boat itself, whereupon all wise people remove themselves to the furthermost point or even take to the water, so vicious are the teeth. As youngsters, we had nothing more than cotton twine, a hook which had no eye, no trace and baited with something shiny or a piece of meat, yet we caught Tiger Fish by the dozen. Lake Rukwa in those days was a fisherman's paradise.

Unfortunately for us, it rained for the rest of the weekend and we were unable to go out fishing as much as we would have hoped. The adults spent their time in the bar and when it closed at four in the afternoon, I was the only one in our party capable of driving. Staying at the hotel were two other groups, with a couple of women who remained sober, but the owner of one of their cars refused to allow his wife to drive, insisting that despite his condition he would still make a better driver. As a consequence, they came to grief turning the vehicle over in the muddy road and all five occupants ended up in Saza hospital. We were travelling just behind the fated car and managed to get it back on its wheels and moved to the side of the road. Three of the most seriously injured people were put into the car I was driving and, with one of the women to look after them on the journey, we set off for Saza. It was quite an ordeal as, besides my being unlicensed to drive, it was a very slippery road and I had to do my best to go carefully so as to jolt the accident victims as little as possible. It was almost dark when I turned back again to fetch the remainder of the injured but thankfully, the men had sobered up enough to follow in my tracks to the hospital and I met them on the way.

The next morning I left to return home and, on the way, called to see Moira. Her parents, like most people on the Lupa, lived in a temporary house made of poles thatched with grass for both walls and roof, rather like living in a haystack. Modern history prefers to portray colonial life as one of mansions, servants and huge gardens but in some regions, people worked very hard, in very primitive conditions. An area like the Lupa Goldfields was scattered with digs, prospectors, machinery and basic shelters intended only to keep out the sun and preserve a modicum of privacy. As I leaned against one of the supporting poles, I suddenly felt an excruciating pain in my right arm and jerked it away and as I did so, a pink scorpion fell to the floor. The last thing I remembered was being caught by Moira's father, Mr. Shearer, before I collapsed onto the earth floor. It was some time before I came round, to find myself in my own bed at home and whilst I have felt various forms of pain in my life, nothing has been so severe as that sting. I am told it is only a particular type of scorpion that inflicts such agonising pain, normally those small ones with a sting larger than the pincers. Indeed some years later, I was stung on the foot by the large brown scorpion, hero of many an apocryphal bush tale, and there was no comparison in the degree of pain.

A great friend of my mother's, Mago, our nearest neighbour, was married to an older man Mcque who was infirmed with bad gout but had a very healthy bank balance. Mago had a boyfriend John, who, on the pretext of visiting us, called on her at weekends. He would come to our house, put his things in my room and after dinner, when we all went to bed, change into his pyjamas and disappear into the night. Being a naturally inquisitive boy, I followed him one night as he headed straight to the lady's house, as I had suspected, where she had been waiting to let him in. They fell into each other's arms and I sat, fascinated, watching through the gaps in the grass wall. They did not believe in dimming the light or in covering themselves and when at last they fell asleep exhausted under the mosquito net, I felt I had seen enough to stand me in good stead in the future. The episode amply filled the gaps in the basic sex education attempted by an embarrassed Mr. Wynne-Jones at school, and I was tired. In any case, I was being bitten so badly by mosquitoes that I decided to leave but as I did so, I made a noise among the flower pots and awoke the lovers, startling not only them but myself as well and I ran off as fast as I could. I ran in the opposite direction to our house, as I thought that tactic would prevent suspicion falling on my head, and then, by a roundabout route, returned home and slipped into bed, pretending to be asleep. It was not a moment too soon for the man came tiptoeing in, breathing very hard, and bent over my bed for a long, long time. Satisfied at last that I was asleep and had never moved from my bed, he climbed into his own, but only for a very short time because, to my great surprise, he went outside for the second time that night and did not return until early next morning. The neighbour called on my mother during the course of the day with a story of burglars and how she had had to "call poor John because she was frightened". My stepfather snorted somewhat and said he supposed that was as good an excuse as any and we all laughed but I could see then that Otto was a trifle bored with the pair of them. John did not say anything, but the girl had made a fool of herself by trying to explain away an incident which none of us could have known about anyway, and it was obvious she was covering up for something. They left shortly afterwards and Otto turned suddenly to me and asked me what I knew about the events of the night. My stepfather was always very sharp but I told him and my mother what had happened, and Otto thought it a great joke, but my mother gave me a dressing down, presumably out of loyalty to her friend.

The following weekend, John appeared again, but the ending was to be tragic for the lovers, as the old husband returned unexpectedly, caught the couple *in flagrante delicto* and gave an albeit doomed chase to John, waving his crutch in a violent manner. Both houses were in an uproar and John, who was a big man, scuttled into his car like a frightened rabbit and was not seen in the district again. Our neighbours vacated their house and about a year later the old man died, leaving his young, adulterous wife the car he had given her and precisely one shilling. She contested the will and, quite some time later, my parents were called to give evidence. I was called too, but by that time I was fortunately in the army and when my C.O. asked me if I wanted leave to attend the case, I declined. In the end, the lady lost both her boyfriend and her rights to her husband's estate.

There was more incident before my return to school that was to provide light relief from the rigours of gold-prospecting in the area. When the new road from Mbeya was constructed, it had, through necessity, to cross the Lupa River, and the point chosen had been through an alluvial claim, worked by "Snakejuice" Wilson. This digger was an old misery, curbing any activities which his pleasant wife, and equally pleasant quartet of daughters, might have enjoyed in the community with his moods and despondency. The girls were about my age, but seldom had an opportunity to mix with other youngsters and I do not think they ever attended school. The family had to eat, however, and Mrs. Wilson was grudgingly allowed to go to Kungutas, once a week, to shop, accompanied by one or two of the girls. She became friendly with my mother, which led to me getting to know the daughters and to hearing the story of the bridge.

When the bridge was built, "Snakejuice" 'turned his back' and allowed the workers to use rock picked up on his claim; rock which could only have contained small quantities of gold, but gold nevertheless. Once the construction was complete, he raised a hullabaloo, saying he would break the bridge down unless the Government compensated him for the gold contained in its building, which everyone thought was a great joke, egging "Snakejuice" on. A case did eventually come up, only to be promptly thrown out of Court but this was the only topic of conversation up and down the Lupa for quite some time and the cause of many a round of drinks. The bridge became known as the Gold Bridge and, I believe, it is still known by that name to this day.

Eventually I had to return to school, but things were a little different than before. During my third (and last) year at school in 1938, when I was in the senior form, tension between the Germans and other European nationals in Tanganyika was running high. These feelings filtered down to the schools too, particularly between the German school at Oldeani and ours, which was English, at Arusha. As the inter-school sports were due at the end of the term, it was decided to organise a half-term camping safari for the twelve oldest boys in each school, in the hopes of paving the way towards a friendlier entente on Sports Day. Mr. Wynne-Jones had instigated the safari and had gone to considerable pains to make it a success but unfortunately, he did not take into account the affects of European politics and group rivalries on the minds of boys. On our arrival at Ngorongoro, it was found that the so-called "boys" from Oldeani were mostly between seventeen and nineteen years old and appeared to be fully trained soldiers. The only games they would play were military ones, which were all they knew, and they spent a great deal of their time attending politicised lectures in German, doing military exercises and parading. We were told to try and co-operate with them, but when they taunted us by saying that soon Germany would take back Tanganyika and kick us all out, we inevitably resorted to fisticuffs. It was a miserable weekend, with our having to listen to insults and pretending to fraternise with them, in the name of international harmony.

The only thing the trip did was to increase our determination to beat the Oldeani School when Sports Day came around, a victory we were to achieve very well. The Greek school also took part and, in fact, the German school earned the lowest marks, with Arusha a contented second, behind the Olympian efforts of the Greeks. A special song had been composed, honouring all three countries, and this was supposed to be sung at the end of the three-day event and initially, the

Germans refused to join in, only reluctantly doing so after a lot of persuasion and a few threats. The whole affair opened the eyes of the authorities to the covert politicisation that was going on at Oldeani under the guise of education.

Shortly after the infamous Sports Day, I was called to the headmaster's study for a talk about my future. I was told there were two alternatives open to me. I could go to Plumtree School in Rhodesia, where I had been accepted to complete my matriculation, or I could be apprenticed to the Geological Survey Department as a metallurgist. My standard of education was not up to it, Mr. Wynne-Jones said, but I could remedy that by taking a correspondence course in three subjects. He told me I could have an interview with Mr. Oates, the Chief Metallurgist, when he visited Arusha in three weeks' time and suggested I write to my parents for advice. My mother replied promptly that it was my decision but, if I could not make it myself, then I should consult Mr. Wynne-Jones. He pointed out to me that if I went to Plumtree it might mean two, or even three, more years at school, as I was still far behind for my age, and this would take me up to the age of twenty. In practical matters I seemed to be well advanced, and, for that reason, he thought the best thing to do was to go for the apprenticeship. He told me it was by no means certain that I would be successful, but he thought I would stand a good chance of getting one of the three apprenticeships being offered. I would have to study two additional subjects by correspondence and he offered to arrange for me to be coached at the Mission School at Dodoma. This talk with the headmaster left me startled and aware for the first time that life was a serious business and that I was on the cusp of adulthood. I was also frightened because I had enjoyed my last year of school and did not look forward to leaving it all behind. It was all too reminiscent of when I had been forced to leave behind Matanda and my Masai friends in the Serengeti and come to school in the first place. The sense of dislocation, the loss of hard-won friendships and the fear and frustration of trying to prove myself again, were things I had vowed to avoid at all costs.

Later on, I was called to the headmaster's study to be introduced to Mr. John Harris, Chief Assayer for the Geological Department in Tanganyika. He told me he had come to interview me for the post of apprentice assayer and that, if successful, I should be working under him. He then outlined my numerous drawbacks, the methods by which I could overcome them, and what would be expected of me in my duties. He ended the interview by saying I would hear from him in due course, but it was so obvious to me that I had failed to make an impression on him, that I felt relieved that I did not have to try to make a go of such a complicated sounding job. I wrote to my mother that night, telling her about the interview and suggesting that I might wait until I was of age before joining the Forces, or perhaps go to work on a farm. She replied immediately, saying she had heard that I had been successful with my interview and she recommended I take the apprenticeship, whether I liked it or not. Thus, when school closed, I did not go home for the holidays but travelled straight to Dodoma to start my new career, and a new life.

Chapter Three
Apprenticeship In Dodoma

It was a Friday, and long after dark, when I reached Dodoma from Arusha. I went straight to the one and only hotel in town, the Railway Hotel, where I was to live for the next few months until the Department found a small house for me. Waiting at the desk was a note from Mr. Harris asking me to report to him first thing in the morning and also a note from my mother, saying she would arrive over the weekend to stay with me for a week while I settled in. She had also realised that I probably had no clothes apart from what I had been wearing at school so a shopping expedition would be necessary.

The hotelier, a Greek, regarded me with suspicion and wanted to know how long I was going to stay, what meals I would require, and, most importantly, how I intended to pay. There was no question of my moving an inch further into the hotel until I had satisfied him with a reasonable reply. After a lot of grumbling, coupled with threats such as handing me over to the police should I fail to produce a deposit by noon the next day, I was finally, grudgingly, shown to my room. Later, while I was eating my first meal of the day, and feeling rather alone and abandoned, the Greek approached my table with a broad grin and a slap on the back.

-"Why didn't you tell me you were Mrs. Fischer's son?" he said loudly.

I was more than welcome at his hotel, he said, even without paying. This about face was a great surprise to me and when he offered me a drink on the house I accepted eagerly. He gave me Ouzo with soda, which went down rather too fast, only to return again shortly afterwards when I left the dining room.

It was not uncommon to see Greek hoteliers in those days, the success of their hotels founded on their position at the hub of local Greek social life. The Greeks had been farming in Tanganyika for some time but after the First World War, when the existing farms and estates were taken off the Germans, many Greeks and Cypriots bought them at an extremely good price. Once settled, their families came over and a substantial Greek community grew up, with their own churches and schools. In modern Tanzania, most large towns have an Orthodox Greek Church and Hellenic schools and there is one town in Central Tanzania, Kinamba, that has such a Greek influence that it is known as "Ulaya Ugiriki" (Greek Europe) by the Tanzanians.

That night I felt completely lost and alone, worrying about what would happen the next day and wishing my mother could arrive in time to be with me when I met Mr. Harris and the almighty Mr. Oates in the morning. I am ashamed to say I shed quite a few tears that night and had little sleep as the feelings of loneliness overwhelmed me. I had left school with something of a basic education and was now on the verge of adult life in a strange town, without friends, family or any idea as to what the future held for me. In body, I was a man, but emotionally and scholastically, I was still a boy and I was not certain which was the more dominant character. Nine o'clock the next morning saw me in Mr. Harris's office, where for over an hour he explained to me my duties in the immediate future and what would be expected of me. He seemed a quiet-spoken kind man of about 40 years old, clean shaven and dark-haired with large thick glasses. He was very well qualified for his work, which, with his friendly manner, earned him the respect of the local community. He could obviously see how uncertain I was of myself and was very gentle, but without letting me forget that he was my superior and very senior to me in every respect. He said, however, that should I find myself in any difficulty, or have any doubts about anything, I had only to approach him for help or advice. He then invited my mother and me to dinner at his house and, later in the evening, to the Club to meet the local residents. I was taken round the laboratories, offices and workshops and was introduced to all the people in the Department as we went along. The second in command was a man called Eades, who knew my parents quite well. He and Mr. Harris had accompanied me when I met Mr. Oates for the first time. They had warned me that he was a very moody man, clever, but not given to enjoying a sense of humour and advised me to answer any questions he asked me but otherwise, to remain silent.

The man I saw was very thin and over six feet tall with a completely bald head, an animated Adam's apple and very thick glasses. I had been told he was an intelligent man and a Doctor of Geology but he somehow reminded me of an unhappy vulture that had eaten something indigestible. Not once during my interview did he look at me, or even lift his eyes from the papers on his desk nor did he shake hands, or offer any other form of greeting. The only thing he asked me was

- "Why were you late in getting to Dodoma?"

Before I could reply, he said to Mr. Harris,

-"You know what to do with him. Put him to work and report back to me at the end of next week".

I was ushered out of the office and Mr. Harris explained to me that I should have very little to do with Mr. Oates and not let his peculiarities concern me. When I returned to the hotel I was pleasantly surprised to find my mother sitting on the veranda waiting for me. She looked very smart, in a grey coat and skirt, and wore sheer silk stockings and she had even had her hair permed. I was rather taken aback and took a little time to get used to her changed appearance, since normally she wore her hair cut short and straight and always wore trousers for comfort and convenience. She told me she had been to Dar-es-Salaam where she had had her hair done, having grown tired of dressing in trousers and working like a man and from now on things would be different. She never did wear trousers again but her work pattern continued as before and she was always busy.

The Greek manager came to talk to us and it was agreed that he would let me have a small room, with full board, for Shs.120/- (£6) a month. Laundry would cost an extra Shs.15/- a month, which meant that out of my salary of Shs.150/- a month, I should have Shs. 15/- left over for other things. I was quite sure this would be plenty, but my mother said I could not possibly manage and promised me a further Shs. 50/-.

Later that day the tailor in the Dodoma Silk Store measured me for a suit and work clothes, undertaking to have everything ready by the following Saturday before my mother left for home. I also put my old bicycle up for sale and was offered Shs. 37/50 for it as long as I took a new one, which would cost Shs.120/-, which I could pay for in instalments over the following year. I was a changed man, albeit under my mother's guidance, in less than a week.

The total European population at that time was about thirty, including women and children, and Dodoma Club was the only place for Europeans to meet, greet, entertain and socialise in the immediate vicinity. It was said that wherever there were two Englishmen, there was a club, and in Dodoma, it had a bar, sports field, tennis court and dance floor for social occasions. We had all been brought up to believe sports to be an important part of an active life and so we would play cricket against local Indian teams, rugger against other Clubs in the colony and were occasionally soundly beaten in football by the local teams. As drink plays a major part in social life in the Tropics, the Club was also where we would socialise, swap stories and meet new people and it was a great way for someone new to the area to immediately feel settled.

At the Club that night, I met Chrystal, John Harris's German wife who openly showed her dislike of me from the start, so much so that even my mother noticed. Chrystal was quite pretty with blond hair and blue eyes but always seemed inclined to draw attention to herself, a result, I suspected at the time, of an inferiority complex.

Whether it was because I was so very junior, the only young man in town and therefore an easy target or whether it was because I was British, I never quite knew. My mother immediately advised me to keep away from her, wherever possible but this open distaste for me tended to help rather than hinder my relationship with her husband. John Harris, a quiet and ineffectual man in his wife's presence, always tried to be particularly pleasant to me when she was not about. He also went out of his way to keep us apart and would give me work to do in the evenings if he knew there was tennis on at the Club and his wife was playing. If there was a camping-out shoot, he would make some excuse for them not to go if he knew I had been invited to take part but it was not always possible to arrange things so easily. Nevertheless, I got the impression that a number of people seemed to be sympathetic.

Some times, however, there was no way of avoiding confrontation. On one occasion, I partnered Dr. Shelley's daughter, a charming girl of about my own age, in a tennis tournament and we were doing quite well until our turn came to play against Chrystal Harris and her partner. Chrystal immediately started on me and eventually reached such a peak of rudeness to me that Yvonne Shelley eventually burst into tears and walked off the court, which may have been the intention. Chrystal however had not reckoned on Yvonne's mother, Mrs. Shelley, who was very French and very tough, marched straight onto the court to slap Chrystal's face, calling her a Nazi gold-digger as she did so. There was a shocked silence before the club members began to clap and shout for more. Embarrassed at the trouble caused, I climbed on to my bicycle and started to ride back to the hotel, only to be called back to the Club, where Yvonne and I were given a prize, despite not having finished the tournament. The tennis captain said a few pleasant things about my play and Chrystal did not come to the Club again for quite some time.

At this time I was taking an International Correspondence School course, so as to fill the gaps in my scanty education and John Harris had kindly offered to help with the mathematics and chemistry and so on Sundays he would come and see me at my house. After the debacle at the Club, I was sitting on the verandah when he walked in. My immediate reaction was to apologise and try to explain to him what had happened at the Club, but he put me immediately at my ease by apologising for Crystal's behaviour, saying that she had not been very well and if it happened again I should not take any notice. He assured me that what happened after work and outside the classroom had nothing to do with him and would in no way reflect on my work. I thanked him for being so kind and told him I would try and keep away from the Club, but he would not hear of this. He insisted that we both go to the Club at once and be seen together and that day I had my first beer at the Club.

My first working week was a matter of obeying instructions and getting to know the routine. My mother had assured me that she would come back and settle me in my new house when I was allocated one, and I saw her off on the Royal Mail lorry for the Lupa, early one Saturday morning. I then set about immersing myself into my new life. My duties called for me to be at the laboratories every morning at 6.30 in order to let in the cleaner, before work started at 7.00am. The day would then be spent preparing soil samples and carrying out tests until the end of the day, when I had to check that all the electrical switches, fuel and gas taps had been properly switched off. Every other Saturday someone else would open up the offices, which would give me an extra half-hour in bed, once a fortnight. If anyone planned to work on Sundays, I had to be prepared to open up the offices as usual and if the vulturine Mr. Oates was working on Sundays he would expect me to be about. Thus, over the next three months, I had to work two or three nights a week up to nine o'clock, losing at least one complete weekend in three and becoming something of a recluse. I was made a member of the Club at half rates, because I could ill afford the full rates and anyway, the times of my work duties made it difficult to go there as much as I would have liked.

It was the last week in August 1939, when I was told I could go home for three weeks because of building extensions to the Geological Department that would require the offices to be closed. Mr. Harris told me to complete a section of my correspondence course and then I would be free to go, mentioning that on my return I could move into house No.62, which had been allocated to me. Yvonne and her mother had undertaken to move my kit to the new house, as soon as the occupants left at the end of August, and so the next day I left for the Lupa.

War was on everyone's lips. I filled in forms to join up, eager to do my bit like everyone else, but was told I could not do so until I was eighteen, in April 1940. John McFee, who owned the bottle store in Chunya and had been an Army Reserve Capt, in the last war told me that if war was declared, I would be on call and that, as the most likely prospective commander in the event of war, I should keep him informed of my whereabouts.

On Saturday 2nd September, we went to watch a rugger match at Chunya. It was between the Goldfields XV made up of half British and half Afrikaans men - a very strong team – playing a team of mixed German and Afrikaans players. It was a very passionate, very rough game with more at stake than the usual bar bills. It eventually degenerated into a fight, and feelings were running so high that most of the Germans and a large number of the Afrikaans finally left but not before abusing their fellow countrymen who played for the British. I got the impression that a lot of the Germans who had left had done so more to avoid trouble than to show sympathy to the Nazi German faction.

At this time, my parents and I were living on the lower Lupa River. Our nearest neighbours were two bachelors, Richard Turnbull and Charlie Goss, who had been elephant poachers in the Congo and now mined on the Lupa. Like everyone else, they were waiting for news of the outbreak of war and had been on the bottle for the last three weeks. We had been unable to get a battery for our wireless and we were over at the bachelors' house to hear the news. Their house, like other houses in this part of the world at the time, consisted of a thatch roof borne aloft on poles. An open veranda spanned the width of the house, with bedrooms at the rear, with open pole walls - cooling breezes were important in temperatures which ranged from 50 in June to 100 degrees Fahrenheit in January and February. At about 2.30 in the afternoon we heard the British Prime Minister announce that we were at war with Germany.

Generally speaking there had always been a good camaraderie amongst the various nationalities mining in the Lupa. Everyone was struggling to make a living and the general feeling was that there was enough to go round and so it was easier to get on than to make a hard life harder through quarrelling. When someone struck gold, for instance, and a party developed, a sum would be left at the Goldfields Hotel for everyone to drink on the house. It was never stipulated who could and who could not drink, nor was anyone ever refused. Once it became inescapable that there was going to be a war, things began to change and certain sympathies amongst a few of the groups, both British and German, made themselves felt. The majority of the settlers felt that it was not their concern and for the sake of maintaining a peaceful status quo, it would be easier to stay well away. The agitators, however, would not allow this and once war was declared, rivalries moved out of the bar and into everyday life. It is regrettable that things happened like this, and had there been a little more warning and a little more organisation, then things might have been different, but at the time, we did what we thought best. Perhaps in the case of Tanganyika, there was a certain justification in our actions because the colony had originally been German but was handed over to the British by the League Of Nations after World War One. Now that it was under British administration, and they were organising us into units, it seemed apparent that the Germans should be kept from trying to regain their colony, which was, after all, our home.

When war was declared, the general feeling was of relief that everything was out in the open and something was to be done to curb the Nazi menace in Europe. Everyone set about reorganising themselves according to their new Allied or Axis status. My stepfather was Czech by birth but a British naturalised subject and was told to keep a low profile until such time as he was called upon to take an active part. That day I was given a box-body car and, with my Mannlicher .256, reported to Captain McFee, who formed us into groups who were despatched to round up all the Germans, together with their arms and ammunition. The Goldfields Hotel was set up as a temporary prisoner of war reception and interrogation camp and I was sent with another European and two native *askaris* (policemen) under the charge of a "Lands and Mines Inspector" to round up two Germans who were believed to be hoarding arms about fifteen miles out of Chunya. Before leaving, we were warned that they might have rounded up a gang of supporters, and that we should exercise care in approaching them and if we should find that there were too many of them for us to handle satisfactorily, we were to take up positions that would stop them escaping and one of our party would return to Chunya for reinforcements. We had three vehicles between us but decided to only take mine and another. The leading vehicle was to have the Mines man and the two askaris, with Hans, a Scandinavian of about thirty years old, and myself in the following car. Neither Hans nor I knew where we were heading, but he knew the people we were to arrest and did not think there would be any shooting. If there was, he said, he hoped I could shoot well as he hadn't fired more than twenty rounds in all his life and had never used a rifle, despite having already been issued with the standard army .303

By the time we neared the house it was getting dark and we stopped some way off so as not to alert them. Hans was to stay with the vehicles whilst the man in charge, with one askari, was to lead, and when they got near the house and compound, were to go round and cut off the track on the far side. The other askari and myself were to get as close to the house as possible and take up our positions. No shooting was to take place, except in self-defence and if nothing happened within an hour, Hans was to go back and get assistance.

Apart from the askaris, no-one had much idea of what we were doing. We were playing at soldiers - with live ammunition, weapons and a cause - and I doubt whether even the askaris had much idea of how to handle things, if they went wrong. It was getting darker all the time and our excitement was mounting to breaking point. Shortly after the other two had left us, an African, with a woman carrying a load on her back, came walking down the road. We spotted them and hid behind some trees on either side of the road. The man stopped when he got to my particular tree and said "Jambo Bwana" (hello) immediately picking me out from my carefully-sought hiding place. I did not quite know what to do next and stepped towards him with my rifle half-pointing at him until the askari stepped out of the shadows causing the man to explain his presence until he was curtly told to shut up and simply answer questions. We learned that there were three German men and a woman and child at the camp. The house servants and labour had been told they could go, as there was no more work for them and that they could take whatever they liked, but nothing from the two cars which were loaded and waiting outside. The Germans were apparently drinking lots of beer - they did not have any guns near them and they were waiting for the Government to come and take them away. The man was a house servant and said he would take us up to the Germans if we so wished, adding that their names were Mr. and Mrs. Kaufmann.

As we advanced towards the house with the man and askari, we could see the Germans sitting round a table in the light of a single pressure lamp. A dog started barking at us and, before I could say anything, a torch was flashed in my face and a voice said,

-"Good evening. If you have come to collect us, we are ready to go". Mr. Kaufmann turned around and seeing me, asked "Aren't you Otto Fischer's step-son?"

I said that I was, and then recognised the couple as having been neighbours of ours at Makongolosi. We stood wordlessly and rather embarassedly looking at each other until the Mines man, who was in charge, turned up. A body search was carried out for weapons and when all the arms and ammunition had been handed over, we had a drink together and waited for Hans to arrive with the car.

Chunya was a hive of activity, with Germans coming in to hand themselves over and men and women with their families coming in from all over the Lupa, volunteering to help. The town was in chaos, with the necessary administrative organisation seemingly non-existent. When the groups of volunteers found there was nothing for them to do, they all congregated in the Goldfields Bar instead of going home, and the longer they remained the drunker they became and the more disruption they caused. Some were abusive to the Germans and others spent their time taking drinks out to their German friends, who were not allowed in the bar. By the early hours of the morning, the situation became intolerable and orders were issued to clear the hotel and send them home. I was one of those chosen to guard the Germans and prevent others approaching them. Every time I tried to stop someone from doing so, I got a mouthful of abuse. No drunk, old-time, tough miner was going to be ordered about by a boy of seventeen! Fortunately, after about three hours of this, we were sent off to rest, before going out again to bring in those Germans who were known to be still at large.

Just before midday, I awoke in the front seat of my car where I had fallen asleep and went over to the hotel in the hope of getting a meal. Everything was closed but as I was walking away disappointed, I heard my name called. Sydney Mayer approached, waving at me,

-"Have you got a car, man?" he enquired in his strong Afrikaans accent.

I said that I had, and so he then asked me if I had any particular job on at the time, which was not the case, although I mentioned that I needed something to eat.

-"Come, jong, we have a job to do at Piccadilly which will take us out of this f....... place, eh."

Sydney, Piet Udendaal and I, with three askaris, then went in search of two Germans who were reported to be beyond Kungutas, on the Itigi road, about forty-five miles away. We bought some bread and tinned food to take with us, as we had no idea how long we would be away. By the time it became dark we had still not located the German camp, so we made an overnight stop at the side of the track. We had shot an impala on the way and this was roasted on the fire. We sat round the camp fire, eating a meal of bread, tinned butter, roasted venison and lukewarm beer. As we had left in such a hurry, no-one had thought of bringing mosquito nets and so we suffered acutely, particularly just before dawn. I had found that by stoking the fire and remaining within the range of the smoke, the problem was a little easier, but the other members of the party thought the mosquitoes were the lesser of the two evils. When dawn broke, the cause of our troubles became apparent when we stumbled across a number of prospecting trenches in the black-cotton soil nearby, in which the mosquitoes were breeding.

We searched diligently for the Germans. Every African we saw had either just seen them a few days previously or had never even heard of them and after three days of fruitless searching, we gave up. We returned to Chunya only to find that they had in fact handed themselves in before we had left to search for them. At this news, Sydney and Piet decided that they could not stand the chaos in Chunya a moment longer and, leaving all their possessions behind them, went to join the army.

I stayed on for a few days, by which time things had settled down and there was some semblance of order. I took the opportunity of seeing John McFee and, unknown to my parents, asked him to put in a good word for me to join the army. He thought it best if I went back to my job and, meanwhile, promised to see what he could do on my behalf.

Apart from the odd German who shouted about the situation being temporary, predicting that in six months the Germans would be back in control of the Government and that any of us who did not treat them with consideration and respect would suffer, there was very little antipathy or bad behaviour on either side of the Lupa. Stories came through to us later about a few who were awkward. One was a Dr. Ekhart at Mbeya, who was sent back to Germany in one of the first exchanges of prisoners. There was also a Mr. Dam, who was known to be a fiery character and had left his wife and children on a farm on the southern side of Lake Rukwa and gone off into hiding. He was missing for some time but was eventually caught on the border, trying to enter Portuguese East Africa (Mozambique), and was interned. This man caused quite a lot of trouble whilst a prisoner of war, but when the war was over, he was allowed to remain in Tanganyika because of his wife and children. His wife, with two small sons, remained at Sumbawanga, running their farm alone and when lions worried their cattle, she was reputed to go out hunting them alone, with a pack of Ridgeback dogs. She survived the war very well, when one considers she was the only European, with her two little boys, in a vast and unfriendly area. It was said that she and her husband did not live together again. He later married an Englishwoman and they had another family and farmed at Esimingore on the eastern shores of Lake Manyara. Sad to relate, after Tanganyika's Independence in 1961, he and a girl-friend were murdered - chopped up badly by persons unknown and left for dead, and the farm has reverted to bush.

I cabled my office in Dodoma asking for a week's extension of my leave but it was refused. "There is a war on and you are needed here". As it happened, I returned one day late because the buses were so erratic, due to the upheaval of the war, and moved into my new house. Yvonne and her mother had been very kind and had not only made the place ready for me, but had also employed a servant, a man of the Ugogo tribe whose name was Sewegi. The tradition in East Africa is that it is usually the men who take employment while the wives grow crops and rear the children, usually seeing each other only during their annual leave.

When I reported to the office next morning, I was taken to see Mr. Oates, having already been warned by John Harris that I would in all probability be in trouble for being late. He advised me that I should not make any excuses unless asked to do so, adding that he had some good news for me when it was over. In the event, Mr. Oates never gave me a chance to say a word. Looking at his blotter pad, without raising his eyes, he told me that I was useless and a disgrace to the Europeans of Tanganyika, that he was going to put me under special surveillance and the next time I stepped out of line, I would be severely punished. He then called John Harris to take me out and see that I was given something useful to do. At that moment, I thought John was going to interrogate me and that I would have to endure the whole business all over again. I had decided that if this was the case, then I would resign immediately from the Department and join the Forces. I don't know if John sensed my hardened attitude or whether he was showing his usual remarkable kindness, but all he said was, "You can now forget what Mr. Oates said, as he did not mean it", and handed me an official letter confirming my appointment, with an increase in salary. I now earned a total of Shs.200/- (£10) a month. He told me that Chrystal had invited me over to their house for supper that night to celebrate my official appointment and with Yvonne also at the dinner, a very enjoyable evening ensued. It appeared to me that Chrystal's change of attitude was rather forced, but nonetheless she told me I was always welcome to come to their house and that if I needed anything in my new home I should let her know. After dinner, when the time came for us to leave, John offered to drive both Yvonne and me home, but Chrystal said she thought him a spoilsport, suggesting that we might like to walk home and have time to ourselves. After we had left, Yvonne ventured the opinion that I should not trust Chrystal, likening her to a snake that would strike at the first opportunity, a comparison with which I entirely agreed, based on my experiences with her.

The situation slowly ordered itself for a while, and we continued with our lives. One of the first visitors to my new house was a tall thin man, rather serious, called Mike Hooper, who lived next door and was the Officer in Charge of the prisons. On this occasion, he appeared ill-at-ease with something haunting his mind. When I asked what it was, he told me that he had applied to join the Army because he could not endure his job any longer. He explained that he had never minded the just hanging of murderers in the past but he could not bear hanging women, but that he had just found an exception. After sending his servant for some beer from his house, as I had none, he started to relate a most gruesome and horrifying story.

He told me that in a certain part of the Singida District of Tanganyika there were a number of hereditary chiefs, who were always vying for position. Over the years they had built up banks of blood feuds and this had been going on for years, long before the Germans occupied Tanganyika in 1884. The witchdoctors, who were invariably women, were always consulted before a murder was committed and had seen their chance of benefiting from this prior information by hatching a deplorable plot. They would buy young boys shortly after birth, then break their arms and legs, resetting them so that when the child learned to walk, it would do so on all fours. They then removed their tongues and kept them in cages, feeding them to a large extent on raw meat, denying them any human contact. Some witchdoctors kept three or four of these boys, and when a wealthy man died and there was to be a sharing out of his property, the dead man's relations would call the witchwoman in to murder closer relatives, so that they would be entitled to a larger share of the property. Provided the relative paid the price, the witchwomen would send out their cripples to do the deed. Should the cripple be seen by anyone, it was considered fair game and would be speared or clubbed to death, but these were the luckier ones. In most cases the trained cripple killer would be successful, and would even feed on its victim, leading to stories of werewolves, cannibalism and juju spirits. It was extremely difficult for the European administrators of the area to determine whether death had been caused by genuine lion or one of these "lion-men", since there were many man-eating lions in the area. Although, of course, the local natives knew the details they were far too afraid of the witchwomen's power to talk. The Germans had tried to put a stop to these activities before the 1914 war but had not completely succeeded and the practice had begun again on a fairly large scale. The British administration had been worried about these rumours for some time and sent some of the best Game Department men to destroy the lion in the area. One of these men heard that the Germans had hanged a great many people in the region in the past and suspected that there was a good deal more to the matter. Later, he saved one of the cripples from being killed and managed to arrest some of the would-be assassins, who eventually spoke up and the story came out into the open. By the time Hooper had finished his grisly story, he had consumed about a dozen bottles of beer and I, who hardly ever took even a glass, was through my second bottle. Just then, Frances, the Provincial Commissioner's nanny, appeared and tried to persuade Hooper and me to go to the Club. The next day a woman was due to be hanged and, although Hooper would not be doing the actual hanging himself, he was nevertheless responsible for seeing that everything was carried out according to the law. This would be his last execution before his resignation and return to England. Frances had, I suspect, been sent over to make sure he did not make himself ill, and they left, while I went gratefully to bed. Years later, when I was in Singida with the Veterinary Department, I heard the story of the lion-men confirmed.

The next day, I had been invited out on a baboon shoot, which required us to leave immediately after work, find the troop and keep in contact with them, so we could see where they would roost for the night. Once they had settled down, we would take up our positions round them, and two reliable marksmen would be sent nearer to pick them off but if the animals tried to escape and, provided they were still up the trees, the rest of us could take a shot. These shoots were very well organised and only good and experienced hunters would be invited by the Game Department to take part in them. The whole exercise was only carried out in response to a number of complaints from the native inhabitants of the area, about damage to their crops from baboons, and was seen to be a necessary procedure. They took place on clear, moonlight nights and afterwards we would all go back to the Club, where the ladies would have a good meal for us and a party would usually develop, dancing until daybreak. On this occasion I had to be at the office the next morning early as Oates had given our Italian mechanic permission to do some of his own private work in the laboratory on the Sunday. I had to be there early to show the man where he could work and what he could use before going back to the laboratory at midday to close it. The mechanic had finished his work and departed, leaving everything seemingly in order, and so I locked up and returned home.

Next morning I had some work to do with platinum crucibles, which I placed on the asbestos pads to cool down while I did further work. When I went back to check them, I found that one had a hole through the bottom and another had been badly damaged. I was mystified and could not understand what had caused the damage but I knew I was in for trouble. I had only recently been allowed to use the crucibles and I had been given a careful lecture on how highly prized and expensive they were. John Harris was in his office adjoining, behind glass panels, and noticing my agitation, came over to see what was causing it. I was overcome and speechless and could only point at the crucible with the hole in it. John could not contain himself and spoke very strongly, telling me I was nothing more than a headache to everyone that had the misfortune to work with me when suddenly he stopped and got the magnifying glass from his table. He looked at the asbestos pads and handed the magnifying glass to me, saying,

- "There's your trouble - have a look".

Through the looking glass I could see two small drops of solder stuck to the asbestos and when the hot crucibles were put on the pad, these had melted, merged and caused the damage. John then asked me if the Italian mechanic had been given permission to work on those pads. I told him he had been specifically told by me not to do so and fortunately John knew the Italian disliked me and seldom listened to what I said. He was summoned and John apologised for reprimanding me but said that Mr. Oates would, nevertheless, hold me responsible since I was expected to be in the laboratory whenever anyone was working in it.

When questioned, the Italian denied having used the pads, saying that he knew they were not to be used and so I was asked to leave the room while John questioned the man again. After a while, the Italian emerged smiling and John told me that he would not admit to being in the wrong and although he would tell Mr. Oates that he knew the Italian was to blame, I should brace myself to shoulder the entire responsibility for what had happened,

-"I will see Mr. Oates now", he said, "Wait here until I call you". After five minutes or so, John came out of the office.

-"Mr. Oates will see you tomorrow", he said, "Be prepared for the worst".

In the afternoon, Mr. Eades, who was the overall number two in the Department's hierarchy, sent for me, but by this time I had made up my mind to tell them that I had decided to join the Army. Mr. Eades was very pleasant and explained that I was held responsible even though I had not personally left the solder on the pads. He went on to say that Mr. Oates was very annoyed and would probably expect me to pay for them but I was not to worry, he went on, because the senior staff would raise the money behind the scenes and they would also see that the Italian mechanic was given a severe reprimand. I thanked him and told him that it would not be necessary to raise the money, since my parents would pay, and that I had decided to join the Army, since I was obviously not cut out for a future with the Department. Eades told me he expected better of me. I was growing up, he said, and I should learn that I could not always run away from my problems - I should rather learn to face up to them.

Something obviously went on behind the scenes, because when I went to Mr. Oates' office the next morning, he did not have very much to say, other than that I would have to pull myself together and pay for the crucibles, once new ones has been costed. I never did hear what the cost was, and I was spared having to pay for them. This incident did me a great deal of good, and I suddenly gained confidence in myself, realising that even after an occurrence such as this, Mr. Oates was prepared to overlook matters rather than losing me to the Army.

About a month later, my new-found confidence was put to the test. I was told that the Italian mechanic would be working in the laboratory again, this time making something for one of the bosses. I said I would happily remain in the laboratory all Sunday but that I could not accept any responsibility for what the Italian did. John then reminded me that these were Mr. Oates' instructions and if I felt like that, I should go and tell him so. I boldly knocked on his door, entered without permission and told him how I felt. To my surprise, Mr. Oates told me to leave the keys with him on Saturday, adding that I need not turn up on Sunday and that I should have a break for a change. When I related all this to John, he congratulated me, but suggested that I should not repeat the exercise too often.

I had been invited to the Shelley's for lunch on Sunday and, whilst I was there, a policeman came to report that some Indian Boy Scouts had been attacked by bees. They had been camping in the hills to the north of Dodoma and some of the worst cases had been taken to hospital but some boys were still missing. As bee stings had never had any effect on me, I was keen to find out how fierce these particular bees were and so I asked Mr. McLeod, the police officer in charge, if I could help in the search.. African killer bees are actually not much different from the common bee, except that they are smaller and generally more numerous in a group. They are certainly more aggressive, a result perhaps of having more predators and disturbances than their European counterparts. Their reputation for killing comes from the sheer numbers that attack the victim and the stronger allergic reactions produced by their larger stings. Most of those who die generally do so as a result of this allergic reaction.

We finally reached the spot below the hill in question and, no sooner had the askaris and others got out of their vehicles than they were attacked by the bees. Instead of standing still, which is the sensible response, they took to their heels, waving their arms and running in all directions, which made the bees angrier still. Whilst McLeod was trying to organise his force into some order, he too was set upon and resorted to hitting at them with his hands. It was now well after mid-day, the sun was very hot and the bees at their most active, and in a very aggressive mood. I was stung a few times but, other than removing the sting when I could see it, I did not take any notice of them. McLeod ordered the askaris to move away to a quieter place. By now there was only one small boy still missing so one of the askaris and I went up the hill to search for him and the higher we climbed, the less active the bees became. We came to a rocky outcrop near the summit, close to where the boys had been camping, and split up to search round it. We found nothing and were just about to quit, when the askari said,

-"Did you hear that?"

We heard a sound about thirty yards away. We found the boy, hidden by a rock on one side and a bush on the other, where he was lying down, sobbing softly. He did not have many bees around him but he had a nasty bump on the side of his head. He stopped crying as soon as he saw us but refused to get up as he was petrified of being stung. I removed my shirt and covered his head with it and we carried him away from the rocks whereupon he began to walk with the shirt over his head and each of us holding a hand. When the others saw us approaching, they came towards us but I waved them away, as they were still surrounded by bees and went a little further on, where McLeod picked us up in his police car. His face and hands had begun to swell and, together, we were all driven to the hospital.

On the way there, the boy, who appeared to have recovered but for the bump on his head, told us that when the bees attacked, everyone ran in different directions and he had slipped and fallen over and that was the last thing he could remember, until we appeared on the scene. He did not have a single sting, probably because he had been lying perfectly still. At the hospital there were a great many people, mostly Indian, who had come to meet their sons. One group was very quiet and sad but suddenly one of them recognised the boy with us and, within seconds, we were surrounded by his excited and relieved relatives. Doctor Shelley insisted that McLeod and I have an antihistamine injection, but I demurred. I did, however, allow the nurse to remove about fifty stings from my head, and after taking my temperature, she told me the stings did not appear to have had any ill effect on me. The doctor insisted that I be taken home and told me to go straight to bed, adding that he would come along later to see me. By the time I had been taken home and had a bath, I could not even feel the stings, and only had a tingling sensation.

Later on, when I was having a cup of tea, Frances came in to tell me that she had been sent over by the Provincial Commissioner to see if I was all right and to tell me that he was very pleased with me for what I had done and would have come to tell me himself, had he not had to visit the hospital. One of the Indian boys had died and another was in a critical condition. Soon other people began to turn up to see how I was and to congratulate me for something I did not consider worthy of praise, since the bee stings had no adverse effect on me. John Harris asked me to give him the office keys, as I would not be expected to come to the office the next day, which was splendid news, about which I would not argue. The next day I heard that the askari with me had been presented with a gift of money by the Indian community and had been congratulated also by the Provincial Commissioner.

Unbelievably, more was to follow. In the evening a car arrived at my house with the little boy's father, the Scout Master and the leader of the Indian community, all to thank me in person. Then a few days later, at the next Club Night, the District Commissioner, John Griffiths, stood up and apologising for the absence of the Provincial Commissioner, who had asked him to speak on his behalf, made a very congratulatory speech to me. I ended up being shaken by the hand by most of the men, kissed by the ladies, including even Chrystal and, by the end of it all, there was barely room in the Club for my enlarged head. My new-found confidence, however, was to be short-lived.

After the back-slapping at the Club, I went home to bed, only to be suddenly awoken in the early hours of the morning, by a man scrambling around my room. I was scared stiff and my dog Shenzi, who was lying on my bed, was uncharacteristically silent, which led me to think that he must have been killed. I began to shout and the intruder leapt for the door, which was half open, tore it off its hinges in his enthusiasm, tripped over it and the door fell on top of him. I was so frightened that, instead of following him and grappling with him, I stood rooted to the spot and watched in the semi-darkness as the man picked himself up and managed to make his getaway. My neighbour, who had heard the commotion, rushed in to investigate and found me still standing by my bed. In the end, the intruder turned out to be none other than my servant who had borrowed my suit without permission and was sufficiently drunk to forget to see if I was in the room before he surreptitiously returned it. This episode had a rather bad effect on me and I kept away from the Club out of embarrassment.

A weekend or two later, I was on guard duty with some askaris, looking after a passenger train loaded with German civilian prisoners of war. I had the misfortune to be responsible for the section of the train from the Lupa, and on one of these cars was one of my old school friends, Kurt Hunke. While his sympathies were with the British, he had nevertheless been interned and this had made him very bitter causing him to switch his allegiance to the Nazi cause. He asked me if he could walk to the shops, knowing that I would have to refuse and then started to bait me before finally challenging me to put my gun down and come into the train, where he would teach me a lesson. I was no match for him at the best of times, but I would not, in normal circumstances, let a challenge like that pass, without making a good attempt. I told him not to be such a bloody fool, to which he replied that I was "just a yellow English Sweinhund, like all the rest". Some of the other young Germans took up the cue until, finally, the District

Officer in charge turned up and wanted to know what the hell was going on. The Germans said I had called them bloody fools because Kurt had asked to go to the lavatory. Without being given the chance to put my side of the story, I was promptly moved to another portion of the train. After the train left, I was given a serious talking to by the senior police commander, Mr. McLeod, and when I tried to put my side of the story, he simply said that was not what he had heard.

One result of this was that I seemed to have lost my former prestige and I took to licking my wounds of pride at the Military Staging Camp outside Dodoma instead of going to the Club. Most members of the community did not approve of the camp because its patrons were known to be rather wild in their after-hours habits, a reputation not altogether undeserved. One evening when I was there, Hamish, the Army Service Corps Warrant officer, brought a mixed party of men and women from one of the convoys travelling from Nyasaland now (Malawi), to join the forces in Nairobi. The rain chose that evening to put an end to the seasonal drought, quickly making the earth roads treacherous and so Hamish asked me to put the girls up at my house for the night. On the way to the hotel to collect their luggage, the road beneath the street lights was crawling with large black scorpions which crunch under the wheels as we drove over them. When we reached the hotel the girls refused to get out and there was nothing for it but for us to carry the girls in. There was a large crowd at the bar so we stayed on to wait for the scorpions to thin out and passing the time with drink, until Hamish dropped the girls and a drunken me off at my house..

The next morning I awoke with a bad hang-over and sent a message to the office to say that I was unwell and could not attend, but inevitably the whole story soon leaked out and when I went along the next day, I was immediately called to Mr. Eades' office. I was made to feel that I had really overstepped the boundaries of decency and responsibility - a decent chap getting drunk and then taking two young girls back to my house, brazenly, for all the world to see, went beyond the pale. What would the parents of the girls think when they got to hear about it, as surely they must? Did I have no sense of responsibility and more interminable moral preaching.

After the incidents of the previous weeks, I felt that my every action seemed to cause offence to some punctilious member of the community or other, and so I decided that I could wait no longer and the next day, I sent a cable to Manpower, Dar-es-Salaam. Manpower was an organisation formed to regulate the flow of eligible people into the forces. Their task was to ensure that those qualified to fulfil important roles and tasks within the existing system or those important to the wartime infrastructure did not join up. My cable was simple, stating that as I was nearly eighteen years old, I would like to be released from my job and join the forces. Whilst waiting for a reply, I became depressed and lay in bed at night condemning myself and trying to justify my recent behaviour to those who seemed so keen to condemn me. For about two weeks I could not bring myself to go to the Club or to the Army Camp and even hated going to the office, where I would meet the people who had castigated me. Yvonne tried to persuade me to play tennis a couple of times, but I refused, making the excuse that I had too much study to do, but even that was difficult with my mind haunted by my misdemeanours over the past three months.

The final crunch was yet to come. Mr. Oates told me that he would be working late in the laboratory on some experiments and asked me to clear a couple of gas chambers for him and leave him the keys. He said I was not to turn the gas off but should call in on Sunday morning to see that all was in order for the following Monday. On the Sunday mid-morning I went into the laboratory but Mr. Oates was still working, so I collected the keys from his home that evening and early the following morning I went in to let the cleaners in. Whilst I was working in the sample room there was an almighty explosion, from one of the chambers and I rushed over to find Mr. Oates on the glass-strewn floor, suffering from what seemed to be fairly extensively burns. John Harris and Mr. Eades immediately dashed Mr. Oates to hospital, whilst I turned off the gas in the affected chamber, had the place cleaned up, and returning to my sampling a little shocked at the incident. When John Harris returned, he called me to his office to tell me that Mr. Oates was holding me responsible and John wanted to get the facts straight before Mr. Eades returned. What had apparently happened was that Mr. Oates continued to work after I had left on the Sunday and the Italian mechanic, seeing the laboratory open, had gone in to speak to Mr Oates who asked him to turn the main gas supply off. Concentrating on his experiment, he did not remember to turn the chamber switch off and so when I came in that morning, I only checked the empty chambers, before turning on the gas main. By the time Mr. Oates came to light up the stove in the chamber he had been working in, it was full of gas, which ignited.

When Mr. Eades returned, a staff meeting was called and I was called in to tell my story. Mr. Eades asked me if I had checked the gas switch in the chamber in question to which I said "no". I explained that I would never touch anything that Mr. Oates was working on, as I would get into trouble and did not consider Mr. Oates, of all people, capable of leaving a gas switch on in an empty chamber. He then told me that Mr. Oates would have to be taken to hospital in Dar-es-Salaam and that an official investigation would be held to apportion blame. Whilst he did not personally blame me, he said I had been careless in my duties, this very unpleasant accident could have been avoided and I should try and be more responsible in future.

The worry and depression were probably instrumental in bringing on a very nasty attack of malaria and I was kept in bed for a week, with additional time off work. During this time, most people in Dodoma were very good to me and I was reassured that the accident was not my fault and even the District Commissioner, Jock Griffiths, took the trouble to come and see me also, suggesting that I forget all about it. Gradually, life became worth living again.

After a hockey match against the local Indian team, when we had been soundly thrashed, John Harris came and told me that they had received a cable from the Manpower Office for my release after 1st

April, which was only eleven days away. He was glad, for my sake, but considered I was doing the wrong thing. I had a chance of bettering myself within the department and did not need to rush off to fight the war when there were so many other people in less responsible positions keen to do so. I was, however, steadfast in my resolve and made the preparations for my departure. Finally, the day came and all that remained was attend a *baraza* (meeting) arranged by Jock Griffiths so as to parade two Africans and myself before all the Chiefs of the district and all the Government officials, before we left for the War.

Chapter Four
Joining The Forces

I spent two days at the 2/6th Battalion The King's African Rifles Headquarters at Moshi, northern Tanganyika, where I was joined by two other volunteers, who were to accompany me to Nairobi. The Kings African Rifles were a little known infantry unit consisting entirely of volunteers from tribes across the British East African colonies. The original KAR were formed by Lord Lugard in Uganda and consisted of Sudanese and Somali soldiers but slowly the Regiment grew to include most tribes, with the notable exception of the Kikuyu of Kenya, who were considered to not be of martial standard. All the officers were British, but warrant officers, non-commissioned officers etc, right down to the rank of sergeant, were mixed European and African. The traditional uniform had been a khaki drill tunic, khaki shorts, a *tarbosh* with black tassel derived from the Sudanese origins, blue puttees and no foot gear; the askaris never wore boots. Now however, with the KAR about to fight outside of East Africa for the first time, they wore the more conventional uniform of the Allied Forces. After reporting at Moshi, we were given railway warrants and told to make our own way to Nairobi in Kenya. We embarked on the train at Moshi in the late afternoon and it was dark by the time we left Taveta, the border post between Kenya and Tanganyika. I knew the driver of the train, Joe Hannen, and he invited me to accompany him in the engine, which I was happy to do, even though I was dressed in a clean white shirt and my only pair of grey flannel trousers.

The railway network in Kenya and Tanganyika was served by steam locomotives and, as there was an abundance of wood but no coal, large quantities of logs were stored at most stations, and these, together with an overhead water supply, met the refuelling requirements of the engines' steam boilers. Each engine had a driver and two stokers, whose job it was to keep the wood fire going, but as time went on, the consumption of wood, together with the supply of wooden sleepers for the track, made the system inefficient and the system was converted to diesel power in the 1950s throughout East Africa. As we chuffed along in the gathering darkness, we noticed eyes shining in the beam of the engine light and recognised large herds of Impala, Grant's and Thompson's Gazelle, Kongoni, Eland, Zebra and sometimes a Rhino and smaller herds of Giraffe and Oryx. On two occasions the train had to slow down to allow giraffe to cross the line and once we stopped altogether to give a herd of elephants the right of way, hazards that do not normally interfere with trains elsewhere in the world.

After the train had stopped at Maktau, midway between Taveta and Voi, the Asian station master and a colleague emerged from his office with double barrel shot guns informing us that there was a pride of lion about fifty yards from the station water tank. There was little protection in the cab of the engine, so we all made a dash for the station building, although before leaving, Joe managed to give a really good string of blasts on the whistle and this seemed to have the desired effect, so far as the lions were concerned. As I reached the light of the pressure lamp in the station, I noticed my white shirt and face were now black and my hair full of particles of wood ash and my shirt and trousers were never to recapture their original colour again.

Joe asked the stationmaster why they were making such a fuss about the lions, which were, after all, always roaming the area. Mr. Singh told us that this was a new pride that had already killed a number of cattle and given chase to some tribesmen in the area. He said the Game Department people had been informed and it was expected that the pride would soon be dealt with. When we asked why the station staff did not do something about the lions, Mr. Singh explained that they only possessed shotguns, which would be unsuitable for lion as they were too weak. It was all very exciting and reminded me of the tales of Colonel Patterson who had travelled through the same area dealing with lions when the nearby railway was constructed. In the event, we were delayed at Maktau for a considerable time before the train could be refuelled, because of the proximity of the pride and so Mr. Singh produced curry titbits and bottles of whisky and many tales were recounted and a good deal of liquor consumed.

One of the stories was about the time when the Governor of Tanganyika visited Manyoni station and whilst he was being entertained by the station master, after having completed the inspection of the station, the station master's three sets of twin daughters were ushered in to be presented. After they had left, the Governor asked Mr. Singh if he and his wife always had twins? Mr. Singh replied,

-"Oh no, Sir. Thousands and thousands of times nothing at all!"

We arrived at Voi Station, which was the junction of the Tanganyika and Kenya railway systems, in the early hours of the morning and were shunted into a siding. Voi station was a boisterous place in the early hours of the morning with shouting and whistles and sudden chuffing and squealing of brakes, the shuddering crash of linking carriages and vendors crying their wares of eggs, bananas, chickens and chapatis. The train was split, with our part hitched to the Mombasa - Nairobi train, which had come up from the coast and so, in due course, we proceeded on our way to Nairobi. After a childhood running free in the bush, I had developed a profound interest in game and vegetation, and on this journey from Voi to Nairobi, my interest was also assailed by Patterson's story of the "Man-Eating Lions of Tsavo", which I had read at school. So it was that most of the way to Nairobi was passed with my head out of the window, hoping to catch sight of the famous man-eaters or something equally as noteworthy. The country was blanketed with thick bush, punctuated by the occasional bigger tree and waterhole left over from the rains. The rains had also meant that the country was well covered with tall, rippling grass, making it difficult, especially at speed, to spot anything under a certain size. Away from the tracks, I saw some elephant and a few giraffe, the only animals large enough to be visible above the low scrub, but nothing of importance. Later, however, the occasional clearing began to appear, increasing in both size and number the further we travelled from Voi until, after Machakos, the country became more open and heavily packed with game.

After arriving in Nairobi, I reported to the Railway Transport Officer, and after signing on as a Volunteer for an unspecified period to serve in His Majesty's Forces, I was sent up-country to Eldoret for training in the Kenya Regiment and given the number LF 1148. The journey from Nairobi (5000ft) to Eldoret (7500ft.) was a nightmare. We were transported in open lorries in heavy rain that seemed to accompany us most of the way and so we were all soaking wet and very cold when we arrived after midnight. The sergeant who escorted us however was unsympathetic, believing that we were too lowly to speak to in a civil manner, referring to us as a shower of rabble, although this did not worry me particularly as we were all being treated the same. One of the older men however objected to it, and the response he got went along these lines:

- "What do you want me to refer to you as? Gentlemen? None of you will ever be that, or bloody refugees, which would be better suited. I would like to remind you that you are in the Army now - poor bloody Army - and when you talk to me, you stand to attention, and address me as "Sergeant".

This little homily was to have repercussions later. At Eldoret we were taken to the mess at the camp which was sited on the Eldoret Race Course and was still in the process of being turned into the army barracks. The mess, as such, consisted of a very large roof, supported on timbers, with no walls and there was a large fire lit outside. We were given a very thin soup and then taken to the barrack rooms, where there were rows of ground sheets laid on the concrete floor. We were told that two blankets would not be enough as it would be very cold and if we had any of our own, we should use them, or failing that, we should double up. We were told not to get in the habit of doubling up, as we were not in an Indian Regiment at which point some of the uniformed soldiers began to laugh, but we were too wet, cold and miserable to appreciate the subtleties of barrack-room humour. The Sergeant then announced that we would be on parade early the next morning, under a Corporal Gillett, and breezed out of the room without so much as a 'goodnight'. The racecourse stables had been turned into sleeping accommodation for the non-commissioned officers, and large sectional wooden quarters were still being constructed for the recruits. We were all being trained as N.C.O.s and Officers for the King's African Rifles and for specialised units such as Reconnaissance, Engineers, Artillery and the Service Corps. All the senior instructors were from British Regiments and a large proportion of them were from the Brigade of Guards.

On our first morning, we were given a short talk about general behaviour and discipline by the Regimental Sergeant-Major, Charlie Broomfield. Documentation was followed by the issue of uniforms, for which we were split into three groups. I went first to collect my boots and tried to explain that I took two different sizes, soon learning that the Army has no time for such finesse and that they would fit well enough after half a dozen route marches. I was then given some socks, which felt as if they were made from sisal or camel hair, a tunic that fitted like a blanket, a complete set of buttons and some brass badges. My appearance was a far cry from the dashing brave warrior that I had once envisaged.

By the end of the morning we had all collected some items of our uniform but most things were out of stock. I was busy polishing up my buttons, when I heard a shout from the other end of the Barrack Room.

-"Orderly Officers' inspection - stand by your beds".

I heard a lot of shuffling but was far too interested in my buttons to take any notice until the next thing I knew, the Sergeant was standing by my bed-boards bawling at me.

I struggled to my feet muttering, "Sorry, Sir",

At which he bellowed again, "You do not call me 'Sir', you address me as Sergeant and stand to attention when you speak to me".

My humiliation was not yet at an end. When the Officer reached me, he asked me how long I had been in the Army. I replied "One day, Sergeant" and at this the other recruits started to laugh. The Corporal was detailed to deal with me and, at our first break, gave us a lecture on Army ranks, how to address them and when and whom to salute. This was chiefly for my benefit, as I seemed to be the most ignorant on these matters.

My next mistake was to salute our Company Sergeant-Major, Allan Bobbitt, a couple of days later for which I was made to walk round the camp for half-an-hour, saluting and addressing officers and N.C.O's in the correct manner. C.S.M. Bobbitt did not let me forget this incident, knowing that it embarrassed me and he made great capital out of it. Another misfortune that attended me in the early days, before the instructors learned our individual names, was that I was generally picked out because I was one of the tallest and so was always chosen to answer questions:

-"That tall fair-haired man - would you come and show us how to sight this rifle?" "Would you like to tell us the answer to so and so?"

Needless to say, most of the time I did not know the answers.

After we had been in the Army for about a fortnight, we were given our first Swahili lesson, conducted by a Kenya-born officer whose knowledge of Swahili was limited to the up-country version, which paid little attention to grammar. He was also one of the people who referred to me as "the tall fair-haired man" but on this occasion, I was able to get my own back, because my knowledge was actually far wider than his. I am not an expert on KiSwahili but can speak a grammatically sound dialect well, and can hold my own even in a country like Tanganyika where the purest Swahili in Africa is spoken. Kiswahili is a relatively new language derived from a mixture of Arabic and the Bantu languages originating from West Africa and developed along side the slave trade as a language of business. The origins lie along the coast (swahele means "coastal person" in Arabic) from where it was brought by Arab traders, but is now the *lingua franca* of East Africa and the official language of Tanzania. So it was that I was able to flex my linguistic muscles until, during the lesson, a disagreement arose and I was taken to a Captain who spoke good Swahili. After a few questions he told me I would be needed to help him with extra lessons for some of the men destined for the K.A.R. units whose language skills were lacking and I was to report to him when the time came. At last, it seemed, things were improving.

Or so I thought. It was my custom, when shooting from a prone position, to steady myself by placing my right foot over my left, which was not the done thing. We were on the practice range before moving on to the Rifle Range proper when my unconventional stance was noticed. I was naïve enough to protest thinking that my logic would win through, but instead was told by Sergeant Davidson that things must be done the regulation Army way. As a punishment, I was made to splay my feet outwards, flat on the ground and to remain in this position under the burning sun for an extra hour after the Range. We wore khaki shorts, so I became badly sunburned behind the knees with continuous movement leading to the burned skin cracking, and becoming infected, so that for three days I could not walk. I had not recovered completely when we went to the Rifle Range proper. It so happened that one of the men who had been good at most things shot very badly that day and the Sergeant remarked that he expected that sort of performance from someone like me, but expected better things from him. When my turn came, the Sergeant decided to demonstrate how to shoot, so being out of his direct sight, I was able to cross my legs, as I preferred. He managed to score three bulls and two inners - I scored five bulls but he glanced down the line and noticed my legs were crossed. My shooting was disqualified and I was put on a charge but this did not stop the Sergeant from entering me for the rifle competition at the end of training. However, in the event I did not take part as I was transferred to the Officer Cadet Training Unit before the competition took place.

At about this time, volunteers to train as pilots in the Royal Air Force were called for. I put my name down, was medically examined, took an examination with the other applicants and promptly forgot all about it. One day, whilst on the Adjutant's parade, a number of names were called out, including mine and the R.S.M., Charlie Broomfield, told us the Army must be in a very bad way, as we had been chosen to go to the Officer Cadet Training Unit. He added that, should any of us be sent back to the Regiment as failures, he would deal with us personally, which would be very unpleasant. We were sent to Nakuru where my brother Norman had been in charge of the Demonstration Platoon, a special platoon consisting of 35 men that have been expertly trained and are then used to train other units by example. When I arrived there, he had already left, but his car was there with a note to the effect for me to use it. However, a Mrs. Spears, who worked in the office, had seen my name on the list of new cadets and had decided not to pass the note on to me, since she found the car very useful herself, only later allowing me to use it occasionally.

Ever since my resignation, an argument had been burning between myself and my old Department in Tanganyika, who were supposed to make up my pay, but had claimed that I had not been released by them when I volunteered to join up. It was a rather unseemly disagreement, especially as I had tried to be as amicable as possible on my departure but in the end they relented and a sizeable cheque arrived for me. The use of a car and some extra money caused my popularity to soar overnight, especially with the less fortunate cadets who were surviving on the negligible army pay. One Saturday afternoon when I had the use of my brother's car, I took two of my friends and a couple of girls to Lake Nakuru, a beautiful Rift Valley soda lake that is home to thousands of flamingos. The water level was very low at the time and so we drove across the soda crust to get sufficiently close to the pink swathe to see them, when I drove a little too close to the shore. Suddenly the car broke through the crust and sank down to its axles in the thick black mud that lies beneath it. There was no way of getting it out, so we had to walk back - to Nakuru, a distance of some four miles. It cost me Shs.500/- to have it recovered and the incident caused a great deal of hilarity back at the Unit and provided me with the first of many unheeded lessons on the difference between impressing people and making a fool of yourself.

Shortly after this I received a salutary lesson, while on parade, this time on keeping in step. I was proudly marching my way across the parade ground, congratulating myself on having stayed out of recent trouble when R.S.M. Bobbitt, who had moved to O.C.T.U. with us, gave the order,

- "Cadet Read, as you are - remainder change step".

We had been at O.C.T.U. for six weeks, when five of us were told we had been accepted for pilot training in the R.A.F. We would be leaving for the Eastleigh airbase just outside Nairobi, and then we would be posted to a training school in Canada or Rhodesia (now Zimbabwe). We were joined by two other men at Eastleigh, only to find the place was seriously overcrowded, without even sufficent beds or eating utensils to go around the crowd of cadets looking for them. Eventually we were each given a mattress and blankets and told to find room on the floor, between beds and I was unfortunate enough to choose an area between a drunken aircraft engineer and a religious fanatic. After much discomfort and frustration wedged between these two social extremes, I awoke on the third night, to find a man urinating all over me. I grabbed a pillow and, pushing it into his groin, pushed him away from me, causing him to fall over his bed, which was an iron one on rollers, shooting it across the floor to collide with the neighbouring bed and thereby making a great deal of noise. The whole barrack room woke up and my abuser was on the floor, with blood streaming from a cut on his head, which prompted a full-scale battle between the ground staff men and the pupil pilots, making the most of the opportunity to enjoy the traditional rivalry. The next day we pupil pilots were given a good dressing down by the Station Commander and moved to another barrack room.

It happened that my brother Norman was to be married the following week-end and I was supposed to be his best man. My leave was refused because of the barrack room altercation, but Norman, who was an officer, intervened, wielding his authority sufficiently for me to eventually be granted my pass. The marriage was to take place at Nairobi's Cathedral of the Highlands with all the pomp and splendour of an officer's wedding in the Colonies but the wedding unfortunately got off to a bad start when the parson responsible for the vestry key did not turn up on time. Norman and I had only just returned from an all-night stag party at the Long Bar in the New Stanley Hotel and needed to be dragged from our hangovers by the bridesmaid's husband, who then ordered us to get dressed for the occasion. Frantically late and decidedly half-dressed we ran to the Cathedral dodging rickshaws and cars until we got there, straightened our ties and, looking suitably composed, assumed our positions. Casually, I carried on my search for the ring, which I was sure I had put it in my breast pocket, despite the numerous searches that said I hadn't, when Norman suddenly stumbled into the middle of the aisle. Everyone stood up, thinking the ceremony had begun, when in fact he was looking for the parson with the vestry key and avoiding the gaze of the bride, who was in a state of rage. Fifteen minutes later, the man with the key appeared and the service began its time-honoured ceremony slowly heading towards the time when I should produce the ring. Search as I might, through all my pockets, I could not find it and it was only when I was asked to produce it that a blushing bridesmaid reached into my inside pocket and, with a flourish, handed it to the Groom.

That wedding weekend had been my first experience of what I considered real luxury encountering facilities that my life in the services and childhood in Tanganyika had not bestowed such as electricity, a flush lavatory in a tiled bathroom, an eiderdown, sprung mattress and soft carpets. It was the first time I had seen built-in cupboards. I had been used to a long-drop lavatory, anything up to fifty yards from the house, rammed soil for floors, grass mats and paraffin lamps. Baths were free-standing, made of galvanised iron, with water brought in by hand in four-gallon "debes". Luxury is a seductive concept to a man in the Forces,

My new sister-in-law and I got on very well. She was a great girl in my opinion, with a good sense of humour and whenever the opportunity presented itself we would conspire to play some practical joke on Norman. In his turn, Norman would pretend to protect me and disapprove of my companion when he was with his brother officers. Then I, as a mere LAC (Leading Aircraftman), would bring up something that would embarrass him, such as my exploits with certain girls of whom he did not approve and so forth, but despite the banter, we all got on very well and these were happy days.

Shortly after my brother's marriage, the R.A.F. contingent, proud in our new blue uniforms, was despatched by sea to Rhodesia for training. One of the men, who became a great friend of mine, was an Irish Canadian from the Lupa Goldfields with whom I differed in just about every respect. He was six years my senior, short and stocky, tough and courageous, whilst I, on the other hand, was a thin, wiry six foot two inches and still growing, and far from tough.

When we reached Durban, we were delayed there to await the arrival of an Australian contingent going to Rhodesia with us, which provided us with an idyllic twelve days of freedom. We were all supposed to wear shoulder flashes showing the country we were from, and as Kenya was at this time considered to be an operational zone, we were treated like heroes home from the front, a misconception that we were more than willing to endure. We had plenty of invitations from girls to go to their homes or join them on the beach, where we all swam naked. The Warrant Officer who took us for physical training got wise to this pastime, however, and made us strip to have a dip in the ice-cold sea first thing in the morning. He would then accompany our ablutions and exertions with very loud remarks about our anatomy within earshot of the girls waiting to collect us in their cars nearby. We could hear their roars of laughter but fortunately he did not link names to his descriptions. By the time we were to leave Durban, most of the others and I were madly in love and, in the passion of youth, were all determined to go back and marry our respective girl-friends, come what may. Thus our time in Durban passed all too quickly, which was probably just as well as we were all becoming emotionally involved and running short of cash. All too soon we were on the train travelling from Durban to Salisbury in Rhodesia.

We were such a small group from Kenya that we amalgamated with the Australian contingent, as opposed to the South African, Rhodesian and British cadets that made up the other groups. Once again, the training camp in Salisbury was not ready for us, so we went temporarily to Belvedere for about two weeks, and had very little to do. It was during this period that a friend Jimmy and I went up to a hot dog stand in town, proudly wearing our new R.A.F. uniforms. The girl who was serving said,

-"Sorry, we are out of everything and about to close", adding in an urgent whisper "Get going out of here before you get into trouble".

She had hardly spoken the last word, when a group of about twenty men, all speaking Afrikaans, surrounded us and the next thing I knew I was on the ground with a boot in my face, being kicked and beaten all over and I could hear similar treatment being inflicted on my companion. Then a man armed with an iron bar approached us menacingly, I got another boot in the face, heard the girl scream and then passed out. When I came round, I was surrounded by three members of the British South African Police, one of whom had his hand round my head. Jimmy was being propped up by a couple of policemen, his face and clothes covered in blood, unrecognisable except for his R.A.F. uniform. The only other person present was the girl from the hot dog stall, who insisted that she hadn't seen anything.

We were taken to hospital by ambulance and stayed there a week. The police tried to play down the incident for political reasons, but our Australian compatriots, who had more or less adopted us, had better ideas and were bent on revenge. The girl of course knew very well who the culprits were and where they lived and had already told the police that she thought they were members of the Ossewa Brandwag, a pro-Nazi movement that had been causing trouble throughout Southern Africa, harassing and attacking Allied Forces. After threatening to take her into the middle of Salisbury, strip her naked and shave her, the Australians extracted the names of some of the men and where they lived and the entire Australian contingent decided to pay them a visit. The Afrikaners refused to come out of their houses and account for themselves, so their cars were smashed, doors and windows broken and their houses ransacked until finally, the Australians withdrew, content with their handiwork. The incident prompted the authorities to take strong measures against the pro-Nazi movement, which was very strong in South Africa at that time, perhaps united against the common English foe.

At Gwelo, we started our flying training. Jimmy and I were posted to different flights as we were under different instructors and my instructor, a man called Harvey, always referred to his students as "fellows", a habit I have carried to this day. He was a Sergeant Pilot Instructor and a first class tutor and had it not been for the fact that he was a heavy drinker and indulged in uncensored language, I am sure he would have become a commissioned officer long before I met him.

In light of how I was to spend much of my later life in a plane, it seems strange now that I had never been in an aeroplane before. I was to be taken up, in the first instance, to get acquainted with the air and so climbed into the back seat of a Tiger Moth, shown the speaking tube and told how to strap myself in and subsequent conversation thereafter was minimal. A garbled explanation about "switches on" and "switches off" came over the speaking tube, which I failed to grasp or hear properly, before the plane roared into life and we were on the move. Everything seemed perfect from up there and I enjoyed the sensation of being in the air. A voice came over the air,

-"How does it feel, fellow?"

-"Wonderful", I replied.

-"Good, keep it that way" was the last thing said before the plane tipped upside down, and a couple of inches looseness in the harness convinced me I was going to fall out. I did not dare let go of the sides of the cockpit, which I had clutched in alarm until suddenly we were the right way up again for a few seconds, only to lurch threateningly over to the other side. This time I complained that I was going to be sick.

-"Make sure you do it over the f...ing side" was the wisdom imparted by my instructor.

Having been put through loops, turns and dives, I was so scared and disorientated that I was almost beyond caring, or so I thought until the engine suddenly stopped and there in front of me was the propeller, hardly turning. The pilot pointed the nose to the ground saying,

-"The bitch has packed up on us".

I could see the ground looming up rapidly and I was quite convinced that this would be the end of us but when we were within what seemed only a hundred feet of the ground, the engine roared into life and we went on to make a perfect landing. I had to be helped out of the plane by the ground crew.

Harvey came up to me and said,

-"Well, how did you like that?"

-"I didn't", I said.

He then put his hand on my shoulder and said, "That was the way to find out your reaction. You'll be all right, and won't have to do anything half as bad again."

To his credit, Harvey later came round to the quarters and invited his three new pupils to have a drink with him. He had the enviable gift of making us feel important and after an hour of his stories and his camaraderie, my rather shattered confidence was restored.

Harvey had a girlfriend, Moira, who lived not far from the camp and she happened to be a friend of my Bulawayo girlfriend, Janet. A party had been arranged at Moira's house and Harvey asked me if I could come along. When I accepted Harvey told me he was going to show me a novel way of doing the RSVP and handed me a weighted envelope in a sock, which was to be delivered by air as close as possible to the target. The house was surrounded by tall trees, except for a small gap, which was usually downwind from the house and so we flew over in a Tiger Moth and came in just below the trees. As we reached the gap, the plane rolled, I dropped the sock and we pulled out upside down. I was warned by Harvey that I was never to try this particular flying exercise myself.

Jimmy and I shared a room, and on this particular week-end we were being punished for some misdemeanour or other, and had been refused week-end passes. Our girls had come all the way to Gwelo from Bulawayo and we were not going to see them and so we went to the Mess to drown our sorrows, returning to our room somewhat drunk. We found that if one gave the ceiling boarding which lined the dividing partitions a good thump one could get through and so after some drunken discussion, we decided to take a run at the walls with our heads. At the crucial moment an Orderly Sergeant walked in with the intention of telling us that our girls were at the gate and we were free to go and see them, only to find us headbutting partitions, which earned us a charge. We were given a severe reprimand and made to pay for the damage, which meant we would not be seeing the girls for a considerable time. Shortly afterwards we were moving for the next stage of our training to Cranborne in Salisbury but before that the first member of our East African contingent had an accident. His plane went into a spin and he could not get out of it, or out of the plane, before it crashed. He spent the night on the ground, having suffered several broken bones, covered only in his parachute and was found the next day, in a very bad state. Surprisingly, however, he survived this mishap and was flying again in a very short time.

Both Jimmy and myself had fared poorly in our theoretical work tests, and we were worried that if we did not do better on the next course, we would be removed from training. So during the next three months at Cranborne we hardly ever went out and we got down to some serious study until the course was finally over in April and we found ourselves waiting about for our postings. While at a party at the Highlands Hotel in Gwelo we met up with a crowd of girls who were leaving the next day on the train from Bulawayo to Salisbury. We were also going on this route by air on a cross-country exercise and a plan was hatched by six of us to "shoot up" the train the girls were on. Thus, whilst on exercise, the six planes did a couple of swoops each over it in mock attack but unfortunately, unknown to us, our Chief Ground Instructor was also on board the train and recognised the planes. Diving at trains was, of course, strictly forbidden and the six of us were caught and grounded for two months. As we were due for some leave, Jimmy and I were sent back to East Africa and told that after our leave we would be grounded for a further four months. We were both from Tanganyika, where there was no conscription, and we had been signed on as pilots only and so had effectively been discharged from the service. Jimmy remained in Kenya and later joined the Pioneer Corps as an officer; I went back to the Lupa to see my parents and lick my wounds.

After three weeks on the Lupa I was impatient to get back into the Army. At Mbeya I heard that a convoy from Nyasaland was on its way to Nairobi and I was introduced to the Convoy Commander, who seemed only too pleased to have someone join them who was familiar with the route. The convoy consisted of two small vehicles and eighteen troop carriers, driven by "Cape Coloureds" (men of mixed race from South Africa), and a party of 180 troop reinforcements for the 1st and 2nd Nyasaland Battalion. In charge of the convoy was Eric Whitehead, a young English officer going to join the Service Corps, and three young women Pat, Rosemary and Dorothy, on their way to join the First Aid Nursing Yeomanry known by their quite innocent acronyms as FANY's.

The night before our departure we had a party at the Mbeya Hotel, paid for by my step-father, who was doing quite well on the Lupa at the time. Another officer on the convoy, Mike, had already come to an understanding with Pat, which left Dorothy, Rosemary, Eric and me unattached. Dorothy was a good-looking, vivacious blond with a beautiful figure and a liking for getting her own way whilst Rosemary was dark, of Maltese extraction, placid and kind-natured. I was spoilt for choice. One of the lorries was set aside for our group and it was agreed that Eric and I would take it in turns to lead the convoy, while the others rested in what we called the "passion den".

Unknown to the Convoy Commander, the Cape drivers had become well stocked up with Nubian gin at Mbeya so by the time we reached Chimala, where we spent the night, they were in very good form, staying in the convoy yard, about three hundred yards from the Chimala River Hotel, where we were staying. We were having a drink at the bar when the owner-manager of the hotel asked Eric if there would be any objection to some of the guests going to the yard to listen to the music. The coloured men had three guitars and an accordion and as soon as they saw us they clearly felt encouraged. A couple sang to the accompaniment of the guitar and another man was a comedian who told jokes in the typical Cape-coloured style and accent, acting the parts as he spoke. They were better than a great many professionals I have seen and the huge wood fire and the dark bush all round added greatly to the atmosphere. The event was a great novelty to us, starved as we were of entertainment out in the vast distances of Africa. At midnight the Cape Sergeant announced the last song before fire out, which was "Sarie Marais" and then we retired. I received a goodnight peck from Pat and Rosemary, but a proper kiss and hug from Dorothy, which kept me awake most of the night, analysing the possible meanings. By the time we reached Dodoma two days later, Mike let us know that he and Pat planned to get married.

At Dodoma I decided to show off my new friends and took them to the Club, where I knew most of the people would be on a Saturday night. Mike said he could not come as he was running short of cash but when I told him the night was on me thanks to a £100 given to me by my step-father, he changed his mind. This was the first time I had been back to the Club since leaving to join the Forces and, although some of the people I knew had also left, many friends were still there so we had a good party. John Harris was on safari but Chrystal was there and surprisingly made a great fuss of me, perhaps as a show of allegiance towards the Allied cause. Our uniforms prompted invitations to spend the night in many different homes but we chose to return to our lorry, where all six of us slept. We were all invited to a curry lunch at the Club the next day and some people offered us the great luxury of a bath at their homes before we were to set off. Unfortunately Sunday turned out to be rather a fiasco, as we were suffering from the effects of the night before and, added to this, the rain started early in the morning and did not stop all day. When we reached the Kilema river, it had been in flood. This is a sand river about a thousand yards across and, although it is impossible to cross when the water is running high or when it has been dry for a long time and the wheels dig in, it is possible to cross when the sand is wet and compacted after a flood. Knowing this from past experience I was able to persuade Eric to let me take over one of the small trucks and attempt the crossing when the time was right. Luckily I crossed without any difficulty, then walked back and positioned troops where the sand was softest. I put the best drivers in the remaining five trucks and then led them across with me driving the "passion den". The drivers were told not to change speed and, in this way, we managed to get the convoy successfully across just before dark. As if to prove the point, a Somali lorry attempted to cross shortly after us, but became bogged down in the sand. We decided to camp that night on the bank, since it was too late to reach Kondoa Irangi, still about twenty miles away. We were able to pull out the Somali lorry with our troops, which was just as well, because shortly afterwards the river came down in full spate. My luck in having this local knowledge was greatly appreciated by the members of the convoy, especially as Eric had wanted to return to Dodoma to "await instructions".

The next stretch of our journey to Babati, which would normally be one day, took us three days because of the wet, muddy roads. We were, by this time, running short of food and drink and everyone was getting irritable. Drink was no longer available in the shops because of the war, except on ration to civilians and so when we reached Babati, I stopped outside my old friend Shere Mohammed's shop and luckily he was there. After a hearty greeting, I asked if I could have a word with him privately. I explained our predicament and he said he would see what he could do in the drink line. He told me he could provide fresh supplies of bread, butter, meat and vegetables. The convoy was established in the camping site, a mile or so further on, and I returned later with Pat to collect the supplies, among them a small cardboard box, for which I had to pay cash. I had been used to buying at the NAAFI and was astounded at the price I had to pay for a bottle of gin, one of a lowly brand, and six bottles of Tusker beer, all at highly inflated prices because of the war.

Morale rose as soon as we produced the drinks box and thankfully the men insisted on splitting the cost between us. We had been in the same clothes, without a real wash, since we left Kilema, so when I took my towel and a set of clean clothes and announced that I was off for a bath in the river, Dorothy and Rosemary asked if they could join me. Pat and Mike declined, saying that they would keep an eye on the camp until we got back. We walked downstream until we found a quiet secluded spot and, no sooner had I put my things on the ground, than Dorothy and Rosemary began to strip. Dorothy made the remark that one of us had to start and added that they would have had to wait until dark if they had let "the shy boy" lead the way, which I took as a challenge and within seconds the three of us were standing naked. I found it very difficult to look straight at the girls at first, and to stop the nature of my response being too obvious, I dashed straight into the cold water.

When we got back to the camp, we heard that the Sergeant had reported to Eric that two of the vehicles needed some attention before we could go on and, secondly, that the drivers had found a good supply of Nubian gin and wanted to know what action he should take. After some discussion it was decided to rest up the next day, on condition that they abstained from drink until we left. That night, to the delight of the girls, the drivers put on a good show for us, every bit as good as the one at Chimala and after the necessary repairs, which took two days and allowed us a good rest, we moved on to Arusha.

On the morning we left Arusha, I was not feeling too well and, by the evening when we arrived at Namanga, I was running a high temperature that was obviously a result of malaria. I was given a room at the hotel to sweat it out and the two girls took it in turns to apply cold compresses to my head to keep my temperature, which causes malaria microbes to become active, down. I took my own quinine and aspirin, refusing to take any of the new drugs, which, in my opinion, were not as effective. After the bout of ague that always accompanies malaria, my temperature eased and, since I refused to be left behind, I was laid in the back of a truck and taken to hospital in Nairobi, where I remained for the next five days. A couple of days after my admission, Dorothy came to see me in her new uniform, carrying a large bunch of pansies. Although very sick, the other inmates of the ward saw the humour of this and burst out laughing. She told me that Eric had gone further north with the convoy and that Mike was leaving that evening to join a unit in the Northern Frontier Province at Garissa. Rosemary and Pat, who were both qualified secretaries, had been posted to Command Headquarters in Nairobi and she was to be sent to the driving pool, until she received her posting. This effectively meant that our little gang had come to an end and whilst I was very disheartened at my new predicament and isolation, I was certain something would turn up.

It did so whilst I was in the Military Hospital, when a curious situation arose. I was in fact at that time a civilian; I had been transferred from the Army to the R.A.F. and then discharged from the Air Force, prior to re-joining the Army. When my particulars were being taken down on admission to hospital, I had to do some quick thinking. I gave my Kenya Regiment number LF 1148 and my rank as "Officer Cadet" in the Kenya Regiment. I was then asked how I happened to have an R.A.F. uniform, to which I replied that I was not in a position to explain. What happened behind the scenes, if anything, I never knew but I was not questioned any further and I found that I had become a soldier again.

Chapter Five
Active Service:
Abyssinia and Madagascar

It is not my intention to write about the War, a subject that I feel other people, more qualified than myself, have already covered in some detail. I do, however, think that some of my own experiences, which differ slightly from the more conventional war accounts, might be of interest here.

At this time, the Kenya Regiment hardly existed, even as a training unit, as a result of the previous course cadets having finished their training and been posted elsewhere. The instructors themselves were either on leave or in the process of being posted elsewhere and there were only about twelve new recruits, one of whom was my old friend from school, Jeff Hollyer. The only training these recruits seemed to be getting was drill, which was being carried out by N.C.Os from the neighbouring Details Camp, where those soldiers who had yet to receive a posting were stationed. I was put in charge of the recruits, but without any rank. A week later I was posted to the 2/3rd Battalion Kings African Rifles at Nyeri, which had been formed from part of the old regular 3rd Battalion of the Kings African Rifles.

The majority of troops in the new Battalion were recruits from the Kalenjin and Kamba tribes, but there were also some Samburu and a smattering of other Kenyan tribes. Most of them were recruited direct from the native reserves and were only able to converse in the local dialects of their tribes. Kiswahili was the forces' *lingua franca* in this region, and most of the Kenya upcountry people, Africans and

Europeans alike, spoke (and still do) a poor imitation of it. As I spoke good Swahili and Masai, and a little Kikuyu and Kalenjin, I was able to make myself understood better than most, which eventually became known to my Company Commander, Charles Corbett and, in due course to the Acting C.O. Major Bombo Trimmer. He attended a lecture I was giving the Company on Kiswahili, and after that I was detailed to give Kiswahili lessons to all the officers and N.C.O.s and to do some oral translating at the bigger parades. The Samburu warriors, who speak Masai, were finding it particularly difficult to adjust to Army routine having come to the army from their tribal life miles away from modern "civilisation", with completely different disciplines, customs and culture. They were used to their tribal food, consisting of fresh killed meat charred over open fires and a junket made of blood and milk and were very proud people, naturally wary of commanders who did not understand their customs and background. Understandably they requested *en masse* to be transferred to D Company in order to be under the command of someone who spoke their language and understood their customs and beliefs but this, however, was not Army policy so their request was rejected. When these men had been recruited, they had been told that in six months time, after their training, they would be given leave but when the Battalion was brought up to full strength and the troops were to be moved up North, they had yet to be given it. When they asked about their leave, they were told that as soon as the last Italian stronghold in Abyssinia (now Ethiopia) had fallen, they would all go on leave as promised.

In April 1941, the 21st Infantry Brigade, consisting of 2/3rd, 2/4th and 3/4th Battalions K.A.R. and Brigade Headquarters embarked at Mombasa for Gondar in Abyssinia, via Asmara in Eritrea on two very old ships of about 10,000 tons. It was something of a relief after many months of training in various countries with various companies to finally embark for active service. I must admit to feeling rather excited at the prospect of visiting a new place and seeing some action against the Italian enemy, which, we suspected, would involve little actual resistance.

After leaving Aden, one ship, the "Norde Munde", which I was in, broke down in the Red Sea and the already grim conditions on board steadily worsened as we wallowed about in temperatures of 110 degrees F for a few days. It was hopelessly overcrowded, the ship was without electricity, had no power to move and the troops below deck were getting very little fresh air. We had already had an outbreak of cerebral spinal meningitis in the cramped quarters and the troops could not be left down below in these conditions, so the top decks were taken over. British Officers and N.C.O.s were paired for group administration purposes, and I went with a young officer of about my own age named David Sheldrick from one of the other two battalions. We were allocated a section of the lower and upper deck and it was our responsibility to see that every man on our deck had a fair share of fresh air at about four hourly intervals. This went on for three whole days but even so, during this time, there were some nineteen regrettable deaths from the meningitis. All our fresh supplies of frozen meat and other perishables had to be thrown overboard because the refrigerator was out of action and we began to believe it was only a matter of time before scurvy started to appear. Finally, on the third morning, we were taken in tow to Massawa on the western side of the Red Sea, where we disembarked.

We did not remain in Massawa for very long. A very narrow gauge train was at the station waiting to take us up the escarpment to Asmara, but the train was so narrow that it was only capable of taking two companies at a time and I, fortunately, was in the first contingent. At Asmara we were loaded onto troop carriers and taken off to Adowa, where we remained in training for about six weeks. Adowa had a certain infamy at the time, for the fact that during the Abyssinian/Italian War in 1935/6, a large number of Italians were surrounded, captured and systematically castrated by the local tribesmen. Once we were mobilised, we climbed further up the Walshavit Escarpment road, built by the Italians in 1936/40, and one of the most impressive pieces of road engineering I had ever seen, climbing 3,000 feet up what appears to be a sheer wall, to the highlands surrounding Gondar. We were now in the enemy patrol zone and moved forward on foot but at Amba Georgis, a section of our South African-piloted Tomahawk Fighter Aircraft concluded that we were too far forward and took us for the enemy, strafing our own troops. We tried everything to persuade them that we were Allies, but without success, so we had to resort to returning the fire, which stopped them but not before they had killed about sixteen of our troops. The Italians had a couple of bi-plane fighters which they hid on the shores of Lake Tana and, every now and again, these two would also appear, loose off their ammunition at us and then disappear again. One day while we were on the high ground overlooking Amba Alagi, one of them appeared in the sky searching for a target, at the same time as one of our Gloucester Gladiators appeared. There ensued a very impressive dogfight, far better than the modern re-constructions, until the Italian plane caught fire and came spinning to earth and the Gladiator, after a loop and a roll, waggled its wings and disappeared home.

Whilst stationed there, we had a lot of fun with target practice on the enemy position, which was about two thousand yards away. When we had nothing better to do, we would set up the Boys .55 anti-tank rifles, and wait for an enemy to appear before strafing whatever we could see. Every now and again we managed to get one, whereupon we would quickly move from our positions and wait for their shells, many of which never went off, and those that did were seldom anywhere near us.

One day Sgt.Major Kruger, a much-respected bush soldier in D Company, was ordered to set fire to the granaries in Gondar. He and four men were to carry out the operation and I was to take two sections and give him covering fire for their withdrawal to the river, about a hundred yards away. Kruger's party quietly disposed of the first guard before the unfortunate man had a chance to wake up. The next man dropped his rifle and put his arms up before anyone could do anything to him and then Kruger poured a mixture of oil and petrol, leading from one granary to the next one, and set fire to the last. He brought back the prisoner and we were all safely up the river to the second line of cover before the first shot was fired. After the first shot was heard, half of Gondar must have followed suit but, again, very few bullets came in our direction. When we were all safe, with good cover in front of us and the light from the fires showing up the enemy effectively, we opened up on them just for good measure with our artillery following suit to make sure that they were all awake. It was a splendid sight to see the enemy getting the worst of the encounter and knowing that they could not fire at us. If this was war, then I was rather enjoying it.

A few days later, at Kulkubar, I got a backside full of shrapnel from a grenade that landed next to me and while I was on the operating table in a tented Field Aid post, wearing only my battle-dress top, the one and only remaining Italian plane arrived to let us know he was still about. No-one was prepared for him as we all thought he was grounded and this unannounced appearance had us running in all directions. I was left to fend for myself on the operating table, so I too joined the others scampering for cover, the only difference between us was that I had a raw backside - it could be said that I was inadequately dressed. I found a latrine hole and dived into it, getting my whole body filthy, fortunately only with earth, because the latrine had only recently been dug.

On 21st November 1941, we finally marched into Gondar, liberating the town, and occupied the Italian houses in different parts of the town. One thing we learned about the Italian troops was that they were either monumental show-offs, desperate optimists, or they spent more time making love than they did working. Every home we went into had drawers full of "Hatu Hatu" Italian condoms. Our Officers' Mess was above the Bank in the main street in Gondar, directly opposite the Battalion Headquarters Mess, in another building. On Christmas Day we blew up a good quantity of these condoms as balloons to add a little colour to festivities, and had some filled with coloured water. The Company British N.C.O.s were sharing the Mess with their officers, and a fair amount of booze had been consumed with fairly ribald remarks being thrown back and forth across the street. Bombo Trimmer produced his pistol and challenged Charles Corbett to some target practice. Charles then produced his pistol and soon water, lead and pieces of shattered condoms showered all over the normally orderly officers' messes. Everyone who thought he could use a pistol joined in, on both sides, until Charles Corbett's bottle of gin was hit, when a halt was immediately called. Amazingly, no-one was hurt.

After Christmas, the whole brigade was moved to Decamere, just outside Asmara, from where we were to be transported back to Kenya, where the troops would get their promised leave, after which the brigade would be brought up to strength and reorganised. We were in Decamere for about six weeks, during which time Frank Wheeler and I were making some progress with two young Italian girls whose husbands were in Prisoner-of-War camps. The girls were related by marriage and were working in a restaurant and they had finally agreed to let us take them to Asmara for the following long weekend, when a Despatch Rider appeared with an order that we were to report back to camp immediately. Lieut. Phil Leonard, the Orderly Officer, told us that orders had come through that we would have to move to the coast, where we were to be equipped and trained for sea landings and from there we would not be going back to Kenya but would be posted overseas. The 2nd/4th K.A.R. had already been told of these plans but the troops had refused, saying that they would go nowhere until they had been given their promised leave and whilst our position did not look too serious at the time, it might become out-of-hand once all the troops heard of the new development. The new orders were to be given to our battalion by the Commanding Officer at the early morning P.T. parade on the main parade ground.

The Acting Commanding Officer, Major Trimmer, first gave the whole Battalion a lecture on discipline and the duty of a soldier, followed by the new orders. The African R.S.M. got up and addressed the C.O.

in private, informing him that they had already heard the rumour, and that they realised that this order came from the Army Command and the C.O. had no choice but to enforce it, although this would result in bloodshed. The new recruits and most of the others had no quarrel with their officers or N.C.O.s. and they were prepared to hand in their arms and carry out their training as usual until they could discuss the orders with the man responsible for formulating them, General Platt, the Commander in Chief of East Africa Command. They then made it clear that they disliked doing this, but would not discuss this particular order with anyone except the General himself and furthermore, they were not interested in what the other two Battalions did.

We were all then sent off for breakfast and told to be back in full marching order thereafter. At 9 o'clock, all arms were stacked, and we went off on a route march, the Askaris (native troops) singing marching songs all the way. We did not return until the evening and the Askaris had behaved very well, cheerfully maintaining discipline throughout. Brigadier Channer then visited us and was given the same answer by the men about their wanting to see the General himself. The men were warned that the punishment for mutiny, which was what was brewing, was severe, to which they replied that they only wanted to see the General who had lied to them. I took it upon myself to speak to some of the Samburu, who said that they had always trusted the European, only to find that he was also a liar, just like the Indian and having lured them with promises to join the Army, he was now breaking those promises.

A couple of days later, we were told that General Platt had arrived and would address the Askaris. He started off by telling them that the only way they could get back to Kenya was on foot, which was immediately taken up as an offer and accepted. It was inevitable that the African troops, who might walk 50-60kms in a day at home (albeit with nothing to carry), would not feel worried at the prospect of an extended walk back. Similar parades were held with the rest of the Brigade, and as a result we started our march two days later, the Saturday that Frank and I had hoped to go on our weekend with the girls. So it was that we set out from Decamere, down the Great North Road which runs from Cairo to Cape Town; a group of 3500 men and 250 British officers and N.C.O.s in companies of 140 men.

That first day, we marched fifteen miles and rested on the Sunday but the following week we were covering about twenty-five miles a day, and after that we went up to thirty miles a day, except on Saturdays when we did less, and rested up on Sundays. We started off before light, each morning after a cup of tea, and were in the next camp by early afternoon each day, thereby avoiding the worst of the infernal heat. The Company transport, consisting of one lorry called the ration lorry, with cooks and a fatigue party, would clear up camp after we had left, overtake us, set up the new camp and prepare a meal with new food, water and petrol supplies relayed from the British Military bases along the route. Sometimes the pre-arranged supply points, supplied by other convoys going through, did not materialise and we went on short rations for a day or so, when lack of water became the greatest hardship. Each person carried a groundsheet as a sleeping mat when the weather was dry, and a bivouac when it was wet as well as a full pack of 60 pounds weight of equipment, rifle and ammunition. Initially, the country was dry, open grassland, bereft of trees and any other defining feature, that seemed to unfurl into the distance on all sides. The local people lived in small groups of huts surrounded by thorn enclosures, cooking in the open on dried cow dung, which could be smelt from at least a mile distant. Their settlements were usually an indication of nearby water or similar resource.

For the first couple of weeks, we suffered the tortures of blisters on our feet and exhaustion at the end of each day but one lesson that was very quickly learnt was not to take a drink until we had had a good rest and the sharp thirst had worn off, otherwise you could not stop drinking and take far too much. At first, the popular thing was to try and be one of the fatigue party so that you could ride to the next day's stop but after a very short time, the novelty wore off and troops had to be detailed for fatigue duty. Most of us found the march boring rather than tiring and when we got into camp and had eaten our meal, we had to find something to occupy our time. Sometimes we went out shooting birds or small mammals, which proved very difficult to find even in the open grassland or fishing in the scattered waterholes for anything that the villagers had not taken. Some men would play cards on Saturday nights and we would treat ourselves to a major "piss-up" on any drink we could lay our hands on with a different company responsible for providing the booze each week, and the cost shared by all who participated. Some did not drink, but nevertheless joined in the sing-songs and joke-telling that followed. We had a Sergeant Bradley, one of the Welsh Fusiliers, who was outstanding at telling unrepeatable jokes and singing lewd songs, and two priests who behaved in every respect like everyone else. Each night, just after dark, the local native girls *en route* would start a wailing noise to notify any interested persons that they were waiting in the bush. The Askaris were warned about the dangers of associating with these women, some were caught and punished accordingly but it had little effect and so after a while we turned a blind eye and accepted the problem. Some of the camp followers would trail along after the column for an entire week before turning round and returning home and whilst most of the girls were professionals, who made a few cents, some apparently did it for the sheer fun of it.

Certain areas along the route were known to be very bad Shifta areas and here we would be deployed in battle formation, with scouts out in front and on our flanks. The Shifta (Irregulars) were people who had served with the Abyssinian Army against the Italians and were, in some cases, commanded by British officers and had formed into units that were supposed to help retake their own country back from the Italians. Their practice was to go to war on horseback, sometimes with their wives and girlfriends seated behind, and riding bareback they would ambush, seemingly from nowhere, their unsuspecting prey. At the time of our march, we met with small groups of disbanded Irregulars who never attacked us or did us any injury of any sort but whose wild appearance and behaviour led us to believe they could do so at any time. As the march was becoming more and more tedious, such an engagement would have been a welcome diversion.

Whilst going through one such area, one of the ration lorries was ambushed by them and a shocking incident took place. A European Sergeant and three Africans were disembowelled, their genitals forced into their mouths and their bodies spread on the road for all to see and the lorry was then looted and set on fire. This behaviour on the part of the Shifta, after our having gained their country back for them, was not taken lightly. When we heard that the trouble had come from three villages in a valley nearby, we took time off the march, surrounded the village during the night and ordered the local headman to produce those responsible. Instead of bringing forward the culprits, they opened fire on us and tried to break away. They were pushed back, and after letting the women, children and aged out of the cordon, we once again warned them to hand over those responsible for the ambush. They replied once again with gunfire, trying to rush the line, by which stage, we could not restrain the Askaris any longer and in any case had little inclination to do so and after giving them a blast of mortar and machine gun fire, we set about them and arrested them. We were later thanked by the Abyssinian authorities for apprehending those responsible.

The whole exercise took two days off our march and the wailing women disappeared for a short time, only to return in even greater numbers later on but the diversion was soon forgotten and the routine march resumed. The scenery was changing fast the further south we went and we moved into highland country, still with no trees except a few along the river banks, but breaking the monotony of the previous weeks marching, even if it meant more climbing. The highland country was green and damp and cold at night with spasmodic showers of rain forcing us to make bivouacs out of our groundsheets and sometimes sleeping on wet sodden ground. Even when we started dropping back down into drier country, with rivers and bush and some sizeable trees, it was still cold at night, requiring huge bonfires at night which were kept going until the early hours of the morning, when we would set off on our way once again. This was an enjoyable stretch of the march during which we discovered that there is nothing more refreshing than a dip in a stream or river after a long march. Hordes of women would appear from the nearby villages and stare, which unnerved us at first but after a while we hardly even noticed them.

Just south of Addis Ababa, the capital of modern Ethiopia, we camped by some small lakes for the weekend and had some wonderful bathing and fishing. After we had left Addis, we began to come into some very pleasant country, well watered, and forested in places, sparsely populated and with a quantity of wild game that provided us with plentiful fresh meat, and nearly every day an antelope or two were shot for this purpose. From time to time, convoys passed us going south occasionally giving lifts to units from Brigade & Battalion headquarters, allowing them two or three days off the march. Officers and senior N.C.O.s were sometimes pulled off the march when we passed unit headquarters and sent on leave or organised for their inclusion on courses elsewhere.

We had been marching for over two months when we started dropping down to the Chalbi Desert. Water was becoming scarce and the heat that soared over 100 degrees F., was unbearable. We slowed down to marching only twenty miles a day, and later, when we started night marching because of the heat, to fifteen miles with water rationed for drinking and cooking purposes only because it was being carted by lorry from very long distances. At this point there was no game but there was a quantity of Guineafowl, Lesser Bustard and African Hare in the area. However, we had no shotguns and were not allowed to waste rifle ammunition, making our hunting practices a little more neanderthal and a lot more difficult. One day, however, I did managed to get a hare by stalking right up to it and knocking it out with a stick and Frank Wheeler managed to get a bustard in much the same way. Kamau, our Company cook, made one of the tastiest curries I have ever eaten out of these prizes, mixed with the usual tinned "bully beef" to make it go further.

About halfway through the desert, we came to a watering point served by a borehole, but to our disappointment the water was brackish. However some of us were able to collect enough for a good wash, after the local natives had watered their camels. It was at this watering point that we had rather an interesting interlude from the long tedium of the march - two camels mating. Imagine a battalion of a thousand men deep in the desert, with nothing to do but encourage and advise two camels how to go about their love activities. The camels met, discussed the matter by rubbing necks, before proceeding with more foreplay, and moving on to the matter in hand. The first time they missed and so had to start the whole fornicating process again, this time aided by the Askaris, determined to see consummation, yelling helpful advice such as "A little to the right", "Too high", "Too low" and so on. Bets were placed, and after about an hour, when a bullseye was scored, there came a roar of approval from the troops, which nearly resulted in all the good work being undone.

After this light diversion, we moved on again and although we were extremely fit, and had taken the earlier marching in our stride, the march through the desert tested our endurance and stamina to its limit. From the waterhole, we could see the hills of Marsabit and Kenya, in the far distance and we knew that from there we would all, in turn, go on leave, boosting our morale and lengthening our stride with a renewed vigour. At Marsabit we arrived to find notice boards directing each unit to its allotted place, diverting us to our Company headquarters, where we were re-joined by our officers and men who had gone on leave previously. Tents were on hand, ready for erection, and having shown my Platoon where to make camp, I was taken to the sergeants' mess.

The second night at Marsabit was a Saturday, and we had received a considerable ration of alcohol. Frank Wheeler and I were both promoted - he was to remain as Company Sergeant Major to 'D'

Company and I as Sergeant Major of 'C' Company - but I was first to proceed on leave and then undergo a tactical course at Gilgil, all very edifying news, and so that night Frank and I celebrated in grand style. We got very drunk and ended up having to fight to establish the superiority of our respective Companies and after making it up, and having one last drink, we staggered back through the forest to our shared tent for the last time. Halfway there, we came across a very large object, which decided to move and come towards us in what was a less than friendly manner. Frank bravely ran for it, reaching the mess tent in about twenty-five strides, whereupon the elephant (which I suspect was probably the famous Mohamed) turned slightly and continued on his way. I waited until he had passed and then proceeded to the tent rather more soberly than before until, about ten minutes later, Frank re-appeared with escort and hurricane lanterns, by which time I was already in bed. However I managed to get my dig in about the future pattern of behaviour to be expected from 'D' Company now that I had left its ranks, whereupon we all went back to the mess and continued the party. No-one believed our elephant story until the next morning when they saw the huge footprints, clearly visible, in the earth around the camp. Mohamed was the first large elephant in the Marsabit area, and a very well known animal, because of his habit of appearing at Army barracks to scrounge food. He was thought to carry ivory of between 150 and 200 pounds a side, at a time when a tusk weighing 100 pounds was considered to be very good. Mohamed later turned out to be one of the ten largest tuskers ever to be recorded in Kenya.

Back in Nairobi, I found that the Details Camp had moved to Langata, which was frustrating because it was six miles further out of the town. I called my sister-in-law, Irene, and learned that my brother was in Nairobi guarding the Duke of Aosta, who was out on a safari, and that they would all be going to India or Australia very soon. She also told me that Dorothy was in town and had been asking after me and so I asked her to fix up a date for me. At the Camp I was told that

I would be going on a Hygiene Course for eight days before proceeding on leave. I only had two weeks leave, most of which would be taken up in travelling if I went back to see my parents, so it suited me having a little extra time in Nairobi whilst deciding what to do. As a Warrant Officer, I did not need a pass to leave camp, all I had to do was sign the book, so off I went to the "big city" only to find that everyone was otherwise engaged. Irene did at least come and have a drink with me at the Long Bar to tell me that Dorothy was free on Saturday night and my brother Norman had invited us to the Officers' Club. She also told me that he did not approve of my going out with Dorothy, perhaps exercising the duty of moral control that an elder brother must wield over his siblings. Whilst Irene and I were chatting, my friend David Sheldrick wandered into the Long Bar, a little the worse for wear. Nairobi had a reasonable array of entertainment on offer, like any big town but many of the bars were only open to Commissioned officers and all closed at 10pm, meaning that one took one's entertainment where one could and did so quickly. After two months on route march and the little else to do at Details Camp, I felt duty-bound to stay on at the Long Bar after Irene had left. David had already had a few when we met, and was in his good Sheldrick frame of mind, when four R.A.F. Junior Officers walked in. They greeted us politely enough and, when ordering drinks, asked if we would have one. When David refused in an unnecessarily belligerent manner, a fight started and with us considerably outnumbered and our opponents comparatively sober, we came off second-best. The end result was that David and I were told to get out of the bar and stay out, so I stumbled off in search of a taxi back to Langata. I think the driver must have noticed that I was drunk because he coaxed another man to come in the taxi with us. Halfway between the Aeroclub (now Wilson Airport) and the Camp, the other passenger turned to me and asked how much I was going to pay. I told him six shillings, which was the going rate, whereupon he announced that I should pay a hundred shillings or be beaten up. I initially agreed to this thinking I would get out of it easily but when they got to within one hundred yards of our gate, the taxi halted and I was told that I should get out now and pay up. The passenger then opened my door, armed with a large truncheon, and ordered me to get out and pay immediately. As he stood there, I pretended to search my pockets and then suddenly kneed him in the crotch, sending him sprawling onto the ground, picked up his truncheon and shouted for assistance. The driver had also got out of the car but, when he saw his friend prostrate on the ground, changed his mind and drove off. I stood over the man, brandishing the truncheon until two Askaris, who had heard me shout for help, appeared. They would have killed the man had I not intervened. He was taken off to the Guard room and the next day I had to make a statement to the Police, who had apparently already arrested the driver of the taxi. I heard no more of the affair.

The Hygiene Course turned out to be a shambles and, in my opinion, a waste of time. However, one of the highlights of the course was a new field loo, which consisted of a slit trench with a pole down the middle at seat level and another pole parallel to this, but at about six feet above, with ropes strung from it to hang onto. This one item took a whole day to build with twenty-five students and three instructors, all ranging in rank from Sergeant up to Major mucking in. On the last but one day of the course, we were taken out to where the town of Nairobi's sewerage was dumped (in what is the present National Park). It was made of square holes in the ground (fifteen foot across), with three-foot wide paths going along and across dividing them. Some of these were full of liquid excreta and some appeared to have dry earth floating on top of them which, in fact, was only a thin crust. We were all warned not to step off the paths but one keen young Subaltern, complete with notebook, forgot the warning, or was not listening, and sank in up to his waist. A regular Regimental Sergeant Major went up to him, saluted him with due deference, and said, "Sir, I have never saluted an Officer in the shit!" before helping him out. Subsequently the Officer was sent back to Command H.Q., where he came from, and we never saw him again.

At this time, towards the end of 1942, I noticed many changes in Nairobi, despite visiting it only rarely. There was no fighting here, except the occasional altercation between members of the Forces on a rowdy leave and development had been taking place for some time but on this visit the changes were far more evident. The rickshaws, in which we travelled from place to place and which had been occasionally used for the purposes of well-spirited races had all disappeared to be replaced by the far more evident motor cars. What seemed most noticeable then was that the troops no longer carried their rifles with them in the town, whereas previously they had had to dance with them. I remember hearing of a shot going off in Torr's Hotel whilst a dance was in progress, which perhaps contributed to this new rule. Many of the better hotels were out of bounds to 'other ranks' but the New Stanley Hotel was still twelve shillings a night for bed and breakfast and another fifty cents if you took someone up to your room and needed an extra towel for them to have a bath.

Eventually I rejoined my unit, which had been re-formed after everyone had taken their leave and was stationed at Mombasa, where we spent the next four months training and digging trench fortifications around Kilindini Harbour. We occupied the Tudor Road Barracks and although the humid, tropical climate was not conducive to work and we found the going very hard because of the heat, we settled down to a very pleasant interlude. There were good sports facilities and the chance of meeting new people from the other services. One day I was told to get the names of three N.C.O.s, one from each of the other Companies, who had not been on Naval exercises, and tell them to report to H.M.S. "Foxhound". We spent the next six days at sea near Madagascar, where we met up with three other ships and proceeded to carry out Naval Exercises. One ship towed a mock periscope, which we then, in turn, tried to sink with depth charges. A large balloon representing a surfacing conning tower was attacked by the destroyers, which raced towards it at speed, firing broadsides on the turn. All the while the "landlubbers" such as myself were thrown about, bruised, battered and considerably frightened.

H.M.S. "Foxhound" was a Fleet Destroyer with an admirable ship's company that knew their job backwards and the food was some of the best I had had in the services. However, so far as the accommodation was concerned, there was absolutely no head room, and all the Mess Decks were grossly overcrowded, so that beds and hammocks, to which I never managed to accustom myself to, were used in relays. The ship was operating in company with two others on manoeuvres and we spent most of the time being flung from bulkhead to bulkhead, which was detrimental to the excellent food remaining in the proper place. It was worse for the "landlubbers" but fortunately I was not one of those that suffered from sea¬sickness.

In December 1942 a small cargo ship called the "Colombo" had lost its propeller and was lying at anchor in the Mombasa Kindalini Harbour awaiting a new one. We became quite friendly with the British crew, inviting them to join us in the Mess for Christmas and so to return the favour, they invited us back onboard the ship to celebrate New Year. By midnight, we had all consumed more South African brandy than was good for us and, attired in my best and only dress uniform, I was talked into seeing the New Year in up in the Crow's Nest. This necessitated crawling up a wire ladder, which had been greased to protect it against salt water, making progress in my state very difficult. Somehow, I got to the top and then promptly went to sleep but everyone else was obviously in a similar state and so I was not missed until the next morning. A search was instituted, but no one bothered to have a look up at the mast head, I was reported "missing" and a more widespread search ensued. A look-out was detailed to go up to the Crow's Nest to observe the proceedings and there I was discovered, very much the worse for wear. The search was called off and I was sent ashore, looking like a coal-carrying stevedore who had slept in an old Army uniform. I was in this state when I was let into the camp through the guard gate and went before the Orderly Officer, which resulted in my being demoted to Sergeant and sent off on a Carrier Course, again at Gilgil.

A Carrier was an armour-plated vehicle on tracks with an open top, fitted to carry three or four Bren guns, and had come into operation in Kenya in 1942. By this stage of the war, every batallion had a Carrier platoon and so when I got back to my Unit, I was given the beginnings of the Carrier Platoon so as to start training askaris, using four old Carriers. The intention was these carriers would be replaced and a new Platoon Officer assigned, at a later date, once the Platoon had been trained and I had only just got the Platoon up to strength when the Battalion embarked on a troopship for an "unknown destination". Two nights later we landed at Cape Diego in Madagascar following the Allied invasion of the island. Madagascar was a French colony, which after the invasion of France by the Germans, had been taken over by the pro-Nazi Vichy Government. In 1943, the island was invaded by an Allied Force and handed back over to the Free French administration, led by General De Gaulle.

After a bit of patrolling in the area with my four worn Carriers, I was finally given three new machines and began serious training with the rest of the Battalion. As a result of its novelty and mobility, the Carrier team became the Battalion's toy and had far too much attention directed towards it from headquarters. 'C' Company was commanded by a Major Colin Grey, who was very interested in orchids and on one of my excursions, I happened on some flowers which I thought might brighten up the Sergeants' Mess so I took them back with me in the Carrier. Major Grey happened to notice them and asked me where I had found them requesting that I take him to the spot. It was the practice for each Company Commander to organise an exercise in turn so, when Colin's turn came, we contrived a reconnaissance of the orchid area up in the hills above Diego Suarez, where we collected a number of plants. I was told how to remove them correctly from the tree and, in the following weeks, I collected several specimens for him, some of which were packed and sent back to Kenya by air.

We occupied the old French Barracks at Cape Diego but they

were not large enough to hold a full Battalion, so some of us had to sleep under canvas. We hadn't been there much more than a week when all the lavatories had to be fumigated and we were ordered to shave our pubic and underarm areas, and swab them with paraffin, which was to be put in our hair as well. The place was rife with crab lice, and we all had to be inspected by the doctor. A few days later, we were struck by a cyclone and lost everything from our tents, including all our Army records. This was followed by an incident when three of our Askaris were ambushed and scalped by Malagasy ex-French soldiers. Shortly afterwards, Hollyer's Platoon was on fatigue duty moving Spigot Mortar shells when a trap previously set by the French sympathisers went off and Jeff lost eighteen men out of his Platoon. Had it happened one minute earlier, or later, he himself would have been with them. As can be imagined, by this time we were beginning to dislike Cape Diego and our so-called allies. The only way we could get out of the place was by motor boat to Diego Suarez on the other side but the boat's engine ran on cane spirit, the fumes of which made everyone feel sick. The feeling of dislike was fully reciprocated between our Battalion and the few French residents in Diego Suarez but this animosity evaporated later when we moved over to the other side permanently and got to know one another better.

Shortly after our Spigot Mortar episode, General de Gaulle came to visit us and we had to provide a Guard of Honour. He kept us standing in the sun for two and a half hours and then did not say a word to our troops - not even so much as a thank you for giving Madagascar back to France, nor a word of regret over the Spigot Mortar casualties. To make matters worse, a two-man Japanese submarine had been washed ashore very close to the Harbour, so we were put on permanent alert, and had to patrol the beaches day and night until the General departed two days later. Meanwhile the Free French, who had now changed their attitude towards us, spent their time celebrating de Gaulle's visit with our rations, further fanning the animosity that burned between us. After de Gaulle had left, we moved from Cape Diego to a new camp site, twelve miles south of Diego Suarez, and found ourselves again under canvas. This was a very pleasant camp site, but full of snakes of all kinds, which insisted on coming into the tents and getting on our beds, or else settling themselves down in our boots. None were poisonous, and some people did not mind them, but most of the Africans and I could not get the idea out of our heads that the only safe snake is a dead one! Apart from the snakes, life was very good with food particularly plentiful and as much fresh duck or goose as we could eat. They were semi-wild and all it took was a couple of francs and a couple of fast movers with a stick when no one was looking and in no time at all we had a Carrier load full. If we were in need of a little more meat, there was a good eating place twenty miles south of our camp in the hills whose owner had two pretty daughters to serve the food, making it the most popular restaurant in the Indian Ocean. There were also large herds of cattle running wild so we were never short of volunteers for the "meat fatigue". Apart from the snakes, there was just one other unpleasant aspect of that part of Madagascar, a plant commonly known as the Buffalo Bean. The bean itself grew to just over twelve inches long, and just over one inch thick and was covered in very fine, needle-like hairs which, at certain times of the year, when they got into our clothes, nearly sent us all insane with the constant irritation. In fact the prostitutes in Diego would advertise themselves by saying "Me like Diego bean - never stop!".

Soon after this, it was arranged that we would go on a large exercise covering the whole of Madagascar. The old Carriers were to be taken away from us and we were to get a full complement of new ones with a new Carrier Officer. I was given the option of waiting for the new arrivals and continuing as Sergeant to the Carrier Platoon, or moving directly to my old Company on promotion. I chose the latter and was working on the lost records, whilst the Company was out on exercises, when General Platt turned up unannounced on one of his visits. He asked me a few questions, then he spotted one of our Platoons on their way back to camp, who looked a disreputable bunch, to be sure.

"Who are they?" he asked.

Our Adjutant very quickly replied, "They must be the enemy, Sir", and turned to me to tell me to find out, with a conspiratorial wink.

The Officer in Charge was well out of sight with the other Officers, so I despatched a message telling them to keep well hidden until sent for. I then told Jairo, the African Sergeant Major, to tell them to pretend that they were escaped prisoners, to direct them to the Parade Ground and get them into some sort of order. Platt walked over and instructed them to "stand at ease" and I was ordered to interpret for the General. There were a few questions and answers, which I twisted slightly to suit the occasion and when the delegation left, a message was sent to those in hiding giving them the all clear.

My Platoon Commander at Gondar had been Lt. Tony Woodcock, formerly of the Standard Bank, Thomson's Falls. (He was known as Timber Prick by his friends and straight Timber by his wife). He had got a bullet in his chest when we fought at Kulkubar near Gonda and had to be evacuated, but he had since recovered and was now our Adjutant. He approached me and asked me to visit a Samburu askari, Lopeyan, who was very ill for reasons that no-one in the medical team could fathom. When the Battalion was reforming at Marsabit after the march from Abyssinia, Lopeyen, had gone on leave to find that his girl, in his absence, had acquired a new boyfriend. Lopeyan was challenged to a duel, during the course of which somehow or other he managed to get the other man's spear, killing him with it, whereupon Lopeyan took fright and fled, leaving the spear embedded in the dead man's chest. After a period of time, Lopeyan gave himself up, as he believed that unless he could retrieve the spear, it would be used to put a curse on him. A Court Case was held and Lopeyan was set free but, as he was a deserter by this time, he was promptly re-arrested to be sent back to his unit on charges. He begged to be given time off to get the spear but this was refused. As soon as he had rejoined his unit, before completing his sentence for desertion, he fell ill and requested permission to speak to me but I was no longer in his Platoon and he was still serving his sentence. He was not free to look for me and stayed incarcerated until after a time, his condition worsened and he was moved to the main hospital. It was then that I received the message begging me to go and see him, which I did at Woodcock's behest, although I could only vaguely remember him from my Company. It appeared that the medical people could find nothing wrong with him and thought his complaint was psychological but that it was just a matter of time before he died. I was asked if I had any suggestions to make and so the Doctor and I went to see him .He was in a very bad way but was just able to relate his story and so I told Lopeyan that there might be a chance that he would be allowed to go home. By the end of the week, there was a marked improvement in his health, and he was sent back to Kenya as an experiment and retrieved his spear. Shortly after General de Gaulle's visit to Battalion Headquarters, I was able to ask a few questions concerning Lopeyan's case and Woodcock told me that Lopeyan had completely recovered and had reported back to his District Officer for duty again.

I was also told that I was to fly back to Kenya on the first available plane to attend the next O.C.T.U. (Officer Cadet Training Unit) course and was given no choice in the matter. This was Colin Grey's doing, I think, as he had broached the subject some time before I got my second promotion, and I had told him that I was not keen to become an Officer, primarily because I would lose so much pay changing from the Colonial rates to Imperial. Colonial rates of pay were three times higher than Imperial rates at this time. Anyone joining after a certain date joined at Imperial rates, but this was also the case if another rank became an officer, which in my case meant that my pay fell from £s.40 a month to £s.21 for the privilege.

The O.C.T.U. was a two-year course crammed into six months, leaving little spare time for the students. We only had one long weekend off, halfway through the course, when most of the Kenya men went home and the remainder of us went to Nairobi. John Bradley, one or two others and I made no arrangements, so found ourselves without anywhere to stay and so I borrowed Irene's car and we went up to the camp at Langata. The Mess had a wonderful fire going but was otherwise deserted and we drank till it was getting late and the firewood had run out, causing the bar to close. The Mess was made of cedar poles set in a concrete floor, the sides filled with split sisal poles covered on the outside with hessian sprayed with cement, and roofed with roofing felt. A new Mess was almost complete, so the old one we were in was just about to be demolished anyway, and so we began to pull bits off the wall to fuel the dying fire. It was not until one of our party went outside and saw the flames billowing out of the chimney that we realised that the booze had affected our prudence. After that we all sobered up sufficiently to realise just how stupid we were being and we succeeded in putting the fire out with water.

The next morning, the Regimental Sergeant Major gave us a good dressing down and a warning, and so we decided to leave the camp and try and behave ourselves. I took a room at the Avenue Hotel and later that day, with two other Cadets, went along to the new A.T.S. Mess and met three blind dates, one being a rather good looking, small, dark-haired girl called Daisy. She and I became friends, and after going out together a few more times, we decided to get engaged. That night we went to Hoppie Marshall's pub, where we met up with two other girls from the A.T.S. who joined our party. Ever the gentlemen, I offered them a drink, but they declined, and then promptly ordered their own. I offered gallantly to foot the bill, but one girl rebuffed me with the remark

- "We do not accept hospitality from men", adding "We do not go to bed with men, but we will sit with you and drink and stand our own rounds, if you don't mind".

It turned out that they were lesbians, and they were quite open and very amusing about their activities. When Daisy and I were alone, I asked her if she was a lesbian and she assured me that she was not. She could not come out the next day, which was a Sunday, but would like to see me when I had finished O.C.T.U. We three men then went back into town, where we met up with two of the cadets who had been on our Course, who told us that they had been failed and would not be returning. One of the two was a large Scandinavian, who whilst attempting the obstacle course at Elementaita, had given up halfway up a cliff leaving me to carry him up the last twenty feet, to avoid forcing the two of us and those below us, to slip back down to the bottom. He must have weighed a good two hundred pounds, and when I hauled him to the top, I collapsed for a few minutes from the exhaustion of the feat. When I got up eventually and was on the move again, he was still out for the count, but I went on to finish the course in time and this is probably what saved me from being sent back to my Unit, as I had not done well in the written exams. A week before the end of the term two others were failed, one of whom we had expected to be awarded the Belt of Honour. He was told that he would not be considered officer material until he stopped trying to curry favour with his superiors.

Halfway through our Course, we were given a talk by Colonel Francis Scott called "Blood on the Bayonet", all about prostitution in India, ending up with the strange epilogue, "after the forty-eighth man that night, the young girl had to be carried off", whereupon the Colonel broke down. Quite why we were never sure, although at the time we believed it was an expression of either heartfelt disgust or one of admiration for the girl in question. Then we were given a lecture on the duties of an Officer and a Gentleman by our Colonel, who wished us luck. The next morning we were sent on a week's leave, after which we would receive our new posting and so it was that I acquired a pip but lost a considerable amount in pay and authority.

I was given one of the new Platoons and posted to the 4th (Uganda) Battalion of the King's African Rifles who were in Burma. There were a number of Samburu soldiers being formed into this new 4th Platoon, some ex- 2/3rd K.A.R., who had requested that they come to my Platoon since I spoke their language. This was allowed, even though I was going to a Uganda Battalion and most of my Platoon would be Ugandans.

Daisy and I, now engaged, saw a lot of one another and arranged to go to Brackenhurst Hotel at Limuru for the weekend, but this was not to be. On the Thursday after Parade, all leave was cancelled and Officers were ordered to remain in camp. We were to leave for an unknown destination the next morning.

Chapter Six
India, Burma
and Demobilisation

On Saturday morning, we got off the train at Mombasa, having travelled throughout the night, and, as soon as it was dark, embarked on the troopship "Empress of Australia", headed for Colombo in Ceylon. We slipped out to sea under cover of darkness, in convoy with several other ships, before peeling off to follow our own course for the Indian sub-continent. The voyage was as pleasant as could be, considering the war-time situation, which required us to spend the nights in blackout and always under strict military discipline. The journey took twice as long as usual because of diversionary routings to avoid the enemy and the ship was overcrowded, as most troop ships invariably were. Spirits remained high however, especially amongst the African troops, the majority of whom had never left their home countries before and so were looking forward to visiting a new country. Those of us who had been abroad before were not quite as excited and so we worked hard to find our own amusement.

The ship had on board a number of "Wrens" (Women's Royal Naval Service) on their way out to Mountbatten's headquarters at Kandi in Ceylon, so most of us spent a large portion of our time, especially in the blackout, searching for Wren's nests. I was a free man by this time. I had always known that Daisy had another boyfriend of whom she was very fond and I was quite certain that I would be forgotten, despite the engagement, as soon as I was out of reach. This proved to be the case, for within a short time of arriving in Ceylon, I received a letter from Daisy calling off our engagement and so it was that Iris became the focal point of my attention for the duration of the journey. When we arrived at Colombo, we were not allowed to disembark for three days because of a cholera outbreak, which might unnecessarily put the soldiers at risk. The girls however were whisked off immediately. Cholera or not, Lord Louis was not going to do without his staff. An incident occurred, whilst we were at anchor on that first day, which made the quarantine even more unpleasant. Two stokers, who had had too much to drink, had a disagreement over a game of poker and ended with one knocking the other overboard. Unfortunately, there was a Lighter alongside, which the stoker hit on the way down, breaking his neck and the body was only found, covered in shrimps, three days later as we were finally disembarking. The shrimps were, I understand, collected by the coolies and sold in the market, which put me off shrimps for some considerable time.

While we were in Ceylon, the Fourth Platoons were moved to a Training Camp at Krunagale where we had instruction in jungle warfare. I found out that Iris had been posted to Trincomalee so, on the first weekend, a group of us set out for it, hoping to be received with open arms. I phoned Iris only to be told that she would indeed be coming to a dance at the Trincomalee Club, but accompanied by her old boyfriend and so would not even be able to speak, let alone dance with me. The others in our group all received the same sort of treatment, with the exception of Metcalf, who knew no-one, but met up with a girl on the dance floor, went off with her and got back only just in time to catch the truck home. When we asked how he always managed it, he replied,

- "Because I'm honest. One of the first things I ask is 'Do you or Don't you?' Either I get a slap in the face and walk away, or I get what I want, and I don't waste any time or money in the process".

The next weekend we went off again, this time to Kandi, because we had heard so much about the place. As soon as one started climbing up from the muggy coast the countryside transformed into a lush, clear Eden. There were large dams, known as Tanks, named after the kings who had been responsible for their construction, and leading off these were well-planned and efficient irrigation schemes. Beautifully laid out terraces on steep hillsides intermingled with forest giving way to orderly tea estates, which was a marked contrast from the low country, covered in low grey bush and coconut plantations. John Bradley and I went to see the Temple of the Tooth where a large, straight ivory-coloured tooth, said to be the tooth of Buddha was on display, resting in a glass case. From here it was a short trip to the Queen's Hotel, a large white colonial building built on the shoulder of a hill and surrounded by ornate and manicured gardens. In its heyday, we had no doubt that it must have been impressive, but was sadly run-down and neglected. Whilst there, a bearer asked us if we were interested in a bottle of Black Label Whisky for sixty rupees, which was four times the price of ration whiskey, but which was also very rare and so we tried, unsuccessfully, to get him to reduce the price. Eventually we told him to bring the bottle over, and after inspecting the label to see that it had not been tampered with, we paid for it, poured ourselves out two generous tots and toasted one another - with cold tea. The man had drilled two small holes in the bottom, probably with a fine diamond drill, taken out the contents and replaced it with tea. Furious, we searched everywhere for the culprit but he was nowhere to be seen. One of the other waiters then came up and offered us five rupees for the bottle, whereupon we saw the funny side of things and began to laugh. We took our bottle to the bar and joined some of the other people there, who also saw the humorous side of our sad story and advised us not to let the bottle go for less than ten rupees. However, there were no takers at this price, so we let it go for five rupees, which having mutilated the label, was all we would expect to get for it.

We spent the night in the Officers' Rest Camp, which was very pleasant, and then went to the Queen's Hotel for lunch where we happened to bump into Metcalf, lunching with a very pretty Anglo-Indian nurse. On the way back that night in the back of the lorry, some of the fellows were pulling Metcalf's leg about his nurse, so he reminded us that she had been brought up in England and, what's more, educated at Cheltenham Ladies College. One of the men's wives had also been educated at the same establishment and he promptly took exception to this. We made room in the back of the truck so that the two men could get at each other and fight it out. It was raining heavily and the lorry's lights had gone out and so the fight was very much hit and miss when suddenly the lorry came to a grinding halt with the most terrible clatter. On investigation by torchlight, we found that two water buffalo, one on each side of the road, connected by a rope around their horns, had been coming towards us and the driver, because of his lack of lights, had not seen the rope. One buffalo hit the passenger door and disappeared into the night; the other had been hit by the right hand mudguard and was lying stunned by the roadside. Eventually, it got up and walked away and we spent some time getting soaking wet and trying to pull the mudguard free of the tyre. When we got into the back of the lorry, we found the two fighters squatting there, well-bloodied but quite dry. The lorry refused to start and there was nothing we could do until daylight. At about four in the morning, a staff car with a Major and two Captains turned up and I managed to get a lift back to camp because I was due to leave that day for Shimoga in the State of Hyderabad on a Jungle Warfare course.

The trip to Shimoga was a bit of an ordeal, as I had not travelled alone in a strange country before. I arrived at the northern tip of Ceylon and boarded a ferry boat to the southern tip of India. The following train journey was rather tiresome as I changed trains constantly only to find new challenges or adventures awaiting. On the first half of the Madras leg, I shared with an Indian couple who claimed to be brother and sister but were obviously not, a fact that the man concerned, who was to appear on the same course as me, later admitted to. I then became infested with bed bugs between Trichonopoly and Madras, which at least offered me the sanctuary of an Officer's club in which to delouse myself. At Calcutta, I got off the train with my kit, and while

I was looking round to find where the Rail Transport offices were, three Indian children pick-pockets pounced on me, despite the ineffective Railway Police standing nearby. The urchins were very quick and efficient but I managed to catch one a glancing blow, which sent him sprawling on the platform. The children got away with a ten-rupee note, some silver and my Railway warrant but, fortunately, the bulk of my cash and paybook was in the top inside pocket of my jacket. The pick-pockets stayed nearby not even bothering to move away and when I pointed them out to the policeman, he indicated an office further up the station, turned his back on me and walked away. After regaining control of my temper and sorting out my kit, I walked along the station in the direction the policemen had indicated and found a Military Policeman, who helped me to the R.T.O. office. Here, I was issued with a new warrant and taken off to a mess where I met up with an old friend, Jack Johnston, and a group of Indian and European Officers from the Indian and Ghurkha Regiments, on their way to the same course. I was very pleased to know that there was going to be someone I knew on the rest of the journey and my confidence, which had started to wane, was returning. On the rail trip to Bangalore, there was a crowd of us on the train, some of whom had spoken to people who had already been on the course. The general consensus was that the course was so tough that on each one, up to date, one or two officers had actually died, which stretched credibility a little, or so it seemed.

We arrived at Bangalore in the very early morning so Jack and I decided to walk half a mile up the road to the Great Western Hotel, where we were to stay the night. Bangalore had the reputation of being one of the cleanest and most attractive of the central India towns. The road was wide with large gutters on each side, and the people of both sexes were busy doing their morning ablutions into the gutter for all the passers-by to see. I have never seen such an array of differing nudity in my life. The Indian women I had seen were normally very modest, but these in Bangalore in the early morning were a definite exception.

Next morning we got on the train for Hyderabad, eventually completing the journey by lorry and arriving at Shimoga on a Friday evening. The previous evening on the journey had been very "wet" as far as Jack, a couple of Ghurkha Regiment officers and I were concerned, and we were a little dry in the mouth. Jack was already in the bar, drink in hand, as I walked up unfastening my Sam Browne strap, when a Major tapped me on the shoulder, directed me to an office and proceeded to tick me off for walking into the bar with my Sam Browne on. A Sam Browne is the leather belt worn by officers, when not in combat uniform, with the strap coming across the shoulder to meet the waistband so that it does not sag when carrying a weapon. In most messes it was sufficient to simply undo the strap if not carrying a weapon but if you were carrying a weapon, which I wasn't in this case, then it was required to remove the whole belt. Apparently the only thing that saved me from being kicked out of the Army was that I was not in a proper Army unit. This was given me as a warning and I was told the next time I slipped up on behaviour or discipline, I was out. Whilst we were drinking, another Major walked in, ordered a drink and introduced himself as Harry Bennett, Chief Instructor, but "Harry" off-duty.

-"What are you drinking?" he asked and, before we could reply, he ordered the barman to refill our glasses with "bara pegs" (large tots). He had been commissioned into the Essex Regiment and had served for the last five years with the Ghurkhas before he came to "this bloody dump". He went on

- "I had one of your boys with the last batch - best fellow on the whole course but didn't get on very well with the non-combatants. Watch out for the Major in charge of the camp administration - a fairly short fellow with a walrus moustache".

Jack, with a supercilious grin, told him that I had already had a brush with Major Dennison. Bennett had been addressing Jack most of the time, as he was the senior of the two of us. He now turned to me and, putting out his hand, grabbed mine and said,

-"Forget that non-combatant, from Monday on you won't see much of him".

Gradually, the mess filled up with more instructors and officers. There were only four Lieutenants altogether, two of them were instructors, one was an officer from a Ghurkha regiment and lastly myself. The rest of the Company were either Captains or Majors, with the exception of the three Lieutenant-Colonels, one of whom was the Camp Commandant. When the dinner bell rang, all the officers were directed to their places at the table, with every three officers being attended and served by one bearer, which was to become the routine for the duration of the course. The following day, which was a Saturday, we were given lectures by the C.O. and Chief Instructor in which we were informed that with the course starting on the Monday, the bar would be closed from Sunday until half-term when it would be opened for two days. The first part of the course was mainly concerned with physical fitness and jungle camouflage and within a week, a Sikh Captain had broken his leg falling off a tree trunk and two other Officers were returned to their units as unfit. Just before half-term we took instruction on construction and uses of bamboo rafts, featuring a practical which required us to get the jeep and ourselves over the one hundred yards wide river. The instructors made their own rafts and waited for us on the other side, whilst those of us who got over in the allotted time continued with exercises after hiding our rafts. It was dark when we got back to the river and we had to find our rafts, some of which had been found by the instructors who were acting as the enemy and rendered unserviceable. Less than half of the course members were back in time for the dinner bell and no-one knew what had happened to the others, because we were all placed at different spots along the river. One group arrived back the next morning, just in time to start on that day's exercises and only had time to change into clean clothing, with no time for a proper meal, before starting again.

The course was becoming more difficult as it advanced, but fortunately most of us were very fit. The final test came in the last six days of the course when we were again put into groups of four and given four day's rations and five rounds of ammunition, which we were told we could use only in an emergency. Then we were taken at night, in an enclosed vehicle, and dropped in the bush in the early hours of the morning and, expected to make our way back to camp, some thirty miles away, armed with a compass and a map and without being seen. The local population received twenty rupees if they reported a sighting of us and we had to pay it from our wages.

Luckily there were few people around, hardly any tracks and the forests were teeming with an unfriendly mixture of tigers, rivers in flood and leeches. To add to our problem, we were also warned to watch out for snakes and Panji pits, which were used as game traps. We didn't get any sleep that first night, as our matches were soaking wet, ruining chances of a fire, but once we had got our compass bearings, we made quite good progress, stopping only once for a meal so that by nightfall, we reckoned that we had covered over ten miles as the crow flies. We chose a very dense part of the forest on higher ground to hide the smoke from our fires and escape the mosquitoes. After eating a hot meal, we put out the fire and one person kept watch while the others tried to get some sleep. I was on first watch - from dusk to 10 p.m, and was quite calm, drawing on my Africa experiences that immediately gave me a calmer outlook than my colleagues. Halfway through, when I was wondering what all the fuss was about, I suddenly heard a tiger quite clearly. After peering in the direction from where the noise had come, I was still unable to see it, and so I raised the alarm but our torches failed because they were wet from the continuous rain. For those who have never heard a tiger growl in the darkness, I can assure them it is a most frightening and blood-curdling sound and everyone was on edge. After a while our nerves were unable to stand it any longer and we re-lit the fire by turning the log over, assuming no-one would be looking for us at that hour anyway. We then decided to keep watch in pairs, replenishing the fire as we did so. The tiger seemed to disappear when the fire was lit, but returned just before dawn. We had agreed that if anyone should see it clearly enough to take a shot, he should do so. The Sikh Officer with us said he had shot quite a few tigers but he had never been in such ineffectually close contact or so alarmed by one.

By midday on the second day, we reached a high piece of ground and, finding a climbable tree, were able to pin-point our position in relation to a large river below us, which made us about half-way along the course. We were all reasonable swimmers and our clothes were already soaking wet, so we tied up the matches, useless torches, rations and ammunition in our waterproof capes and waded in. After the river , we had about three miles of swamp to cover, which we decided not to skirt because we did know its size and so spent until midday the next day struggling through. We had a bad time being attacked by mosquitoes and leeches, everything was sodden and we had spent all night standing in the mud. It was with great relief that we finally emerged from the swamp and took a well-earned rest, brewing up hot tea and rewarding ourselves with a meal from our rations. Gradually, as the sun appeared, we were able to dry out sufficiently for us to continue further until, when the moon came up, we reached a small river in flood. We camped on the banks of this river for the night, lighting a large fire and for the first time for several days we had a reasonable night's sleep. The river should not have been a major problem and was the last real obstacle, but it did cause an argument between Major Gates of the Mahrattas and myself, because I refused to be included in a chain crossing the river. I was of the opinion that the current was too strong but agreed to go over first and alone with a rope attached to me. The river was only about twenty yards across but I ended up about fifty yards downstream, the others doing about the same.

We arrived back at our barracks, the second group to do so - Jack's party had beaten us by one and a half hours. Two more parties arrived before dark, and later a report came in that one group had lost an Indian Officer by drowning, and a second man from the same group had been rushed to hospital. The remainder of the men turned up the next day.

This was virtually the end of the course and when everyone was back at the camp and rested, the bar was re-opened and remained so until we left. On the last night a party was held in the mess and after speeches, the Colonel and most of the regular Indian Army Officers went off to bed leaving the rest of us to team up with the instructors, and have a thrash. Major Dennison, rather surprisingly, joined us and as I was leaving, came up to me, held out his hand and said,

-"Congratulations, Lt. Read. I didn't think you would make the course but I understand that you did very well. May I get you a drink?"

I felt like refusing him, but of course accepted and thanked him graciously.

The Carew's Gin didn't do me too much good and I certainly wouldn't have got to the train at Hyderabad if it hadn't been for Jack and the help of a Ghurkha orderly, however, back in Krunagal (Ceylon), among our own troops again, I began to feel much more secure. Everyone was speaking the same language and I realised, for the first time, just how important it is to be able to speak the language of the people with whom you are dealing.

There was, at this time in Krunagal, a restaurant called Elephant Rock. Here we could order quite good curry dishes, and on one occasion a crowd of us had booked a table for eight for the coming Saturday. We could not get drinks at the Elephant Rock so went first to the Club where we drank arrack made from rice and palm wine. When we arrived at the Elephant Rock we were told that a Minister with his family and friends were consuming our meal, and we would have to go away and return much later or go without, but after some discussion, it was agreed that we could sit in the lounge and wait for more food to be cooked. We had all brought our own drink to continue with our party and were being rather noisy, making uncomplimentary remarks about "green men", which was the slang for the local people, which were certainly overheard. Connie, up to this point, had been one of the best behaved in our party but on his way to the loo he saw a rather delightful young Ceylonese lady cleaning her teeth, as was their custom after a meal, and he tried to help her. She screamed and all hell broke loose. Connie dashed through the lounge shouting "Run for it!", for which we needed no second bidding, scattering in all directions. I ran towards the Club and hid in a sisal hedge from where I could see what was going on. A group of people and local police passed within yards of my hiding place and entered the Club and so I left my hideout and walked back whistling innocently in the direction of the Elephant Rock, where I was questioned by a couple of local Military Police. I told them a man had passed me, running along the road past the Club, which seemed to satisfy them and I hired an ox-cart to take me back to camp. The next morning, I learned that Connie had been followed up a track and in order to shake off his pursuer had run through a hedge only to fall down a twenty foot well. The only thing that saved him from being badly injured was the four feet of mud and water at the bottom. He lay low in the well for a while, then, judging it to be all clear, he tried to get out but it proved impossible in the dark. However, the noise he made attracted one of the local men, who threatened to call the police, though when Connie showed him a ten-rupee note, he changed his mind and fetched a rope. No sooner had Connie reached the top, than the man started demanding double the money or he would take Connie to the police and so in the name of good public relations, Connie replaced the note back in his pocket and pushed the man down the well, throwing the rope after him. We had a quiet Sunday but, from remarks heard in the Mess, it appeared that a Minister had complained of officers from our camp assaulting his daughter, and he was not going to rest until the culprits were found.

Sure enough, on the Monday, all the officers in camp were put on an identification parade. Four witnesses were produced separately and succeeded in making the whole thing a farce when they started to argue amongst themselves. I was "identified" by one and accused of shaving off a moustache that I had never had. Connie was picked out and so were John Lawrence and Bradley but no one was identified more than twice and although about twenty people in all were identified, most of them could prove they were nowhere near the place. A court-martial was convened and the four of us were summoned before it. Connie's orderly was asked if he had noticed anything unusual about his officer's uniform the morning after the night in question. The poor man thought he was being reprimanded for Connie's scruffy state and so vehemently denied that there was anything wrong with his clothes and couldn't break his opinion, even under cross-examination. At the end of two days the court closed and two weeks later, three of us, Connie, John Bradley and I, were brought before the Brigadier and given a severe warning.

Three days later, I was on my way with my Platoon to join a new unit, the 4th (Uganda) Kings African Rifles in Burma. It had been decided by the High Command to change from the usual three platoons in each company by adding an extra, on account of the excessive amount of patrol work in the jungle. The Samburu soldiers learnt that I was to lead a new fourth platoon and asked to join me, because I spoke Masai, which is the same as their Samburu language. So it was that the 4th platoon which was nominally a Ugandan platoon, received a high proportion of Samburu soldiers. This, however, was a blessing in disguise because the Samburu proved themselves to be amongst the finest jungle warfare troops, accustomed to the heavy terrain and natural elements with an outstanding courage and cheerfulness.

After a tour of duty in Burma, we went to Assam where, after only a few days, John Bradley and I were finally given a spot of leave. On our tour we had collected three Japanese samurai swords, which we knew might be of value if we could just find the right place to sell them. Calcutta, where we were on leave, was full of American soldiers in search of souvenirs and these Samurai swords, with their handles encrusted with precious stones, fetched one hundred and fifty rupees each. We decided to use the money on a few nights at the Grand Hotel in Bombay, where we met some Ordinance Officers who invited us to a dance in their Mess. There were plenty of girls at the dance and we were told that we would be fine as far as they were concerned, once we had been introduced by Rob the drummer. After a while Rob turned up with two Women's Royal Army Corps girls who were great fun. He then returned to the band and we were getting along well with the girls, when suddenly they announced that they had to go, but would see us later. Rob turned up next with a bag full of drink which he gave me, telling me to take it back to the hotel, while he and Brad went to collect the girls and so I took a taxi back to the Hotel and waited. An hour later I decided that the two of them had decided to leave me out of the party, so I went to bed, only to be woken up by Bradley, in a towering rage. All he could say was "The bloody queer tried to do me" until he calmed down sufficiently to explain that Rob had taken Brad to his place where he had made a pass at him. On being told by Bradley to pack it up, Rob had attempted force, whereupon Brad had beaten him up.

The first full day in Bombay, Bradley fell madly in love with the Maharajah of Kutch's daughter, after they had played tennis together at the Bombay Sports Club. As a result we were invited up to the Maharajah's Palace but unfortunately we were prevented from going there and so joined up with two men staying at our hotel for dinner at the "Kamling" restaurant. It was here that we learnt that the war in Europe was over and the restaurant owner invited us to have dinner "on the house". There must have been about thirty of us altogether and even champagne was produced, free of charge but the wonderfully generous Chinaman and his family would not accept a penny from us. It was a big night of celebration across the world and we had already been invited to another party, which was being held on the top balcony of a seven-storey building. Since it was on our way home, we decided to call in and I was making my way across the room to get a drink when, suddenly, the music stopped and everyone went to look over the balcony. A very attractive Anglo-Indian girl, who was married to an Anglo-Indian officer in the Indian Navy but who had been living with a Royal Naval Officer, had decided to take her own life because the Naval Officer had told her he would be leaving India and would not be taking her, or their child, with him. This episode abruptly ended the party and put a sad damper on the V.E. night celebrations for the end of the War in Europe.

The next day was our last in Bombay so, to pass the time, we went to see the Parsee Burial Ground where the dead are traditionally carried and lain out for the vultures. Despite sky burials being the tradition amongst the Masai when one of their number die, I still found this place to be one of the most disgusting and unhealthy sights I have ever seen. The Masai rely on hyaenas to carry off their dead and they do not leave a single piece, but here pieces of human flesh and bone were picked up by the birds and scattered all over the place. We both felt quite ill and were pleased to board the train that night, to return to Calcutta. That night I awoke to find a baboon, with a leg missing, peering through the train window when the train had halted at a station where baboons and humans competed to beg for food. A large proportion of both humans and animals had been maimed in some way or another and, like the baboons, the humans relieved themselves when and where they wanted, regardless of other people. It was not possible to give these wretched people anything until the train was on the move - and then only by throwing it from the window - otherwise one would have been trampled underfoot. Not all the stations we passed through were like this, but there were quite a number. Although I had always believed that in Africa one saw the worst cases of disease and dirt, they bore no comparison with the human suffering I saw in Central India.

On arrival in Calcutta, we received orders to rejoin our unit, which was on the march heading for Ranchi. We joined them a couple of days later where they had set up camp near a small castle which had been built by an Indian Prince, but was now being used as a prison. Although we were only there for about a month, it was long enough for sixty per cent of the Battalion to get infected with V.D. There were also some nasty knifing incidents over women, a result of some of the

Indians encouraging the women to make passes at the Askaris. They would then trap them and demand large sums of money, which the Askaris would refuse to pay, whereupon the lurking pimps would then set on the Askaris and beat them up. Soon the troops got wise to this and they returned the compliment in double measure, particularly if they had contracted V.D. in the process. Matters got quite out of hand and led to several murders, so it was decided to move on to Ranchi about eighty miles further west.

We arrived at our camp site outside Ranchi at about midday on an exceptionally hot day. We had been marching in temperatures of 110 degrees since early morning and were having a well-deserved rest, when a heavy wind with dust devils blew up. Across the dry paddy fields we could see complete roofs flying in the wind which grew stronger and stronger until, at about three o'clock the skies opened with heavy hail, and then with rain. This weather continued into the early hours of the morning when it was bitterly cold and we could do nothing except try to protect ourselves out in the open until the next morning, in the daylight, when we could see the full extent of the storm. Many of the officers and men were sent to hospital, two Askaris had died of exposure and if we had not been very fit and used to being wet most of the time, many more of us would not have survived. It was after ten o'clock the next day before we finally ate a hot meal, by which time most of the tents were up and our clothes nearly dried by the sun. However, too many officers and men were running dangerously high temperatures for our own medical staff to cope with, and we had to ask for outside help so that many of the men could be taken to hospital. As a result of all this turmoil, we were given a relatively relaxed time for the next couple of weeks, before starting serious training for our next posting to Burma.

Brad told me one morning as we were taking his platoon over the rifle range that on the following Saturday we were going on a moonlight picnic to the Serpentine (a dam outside Ranchi) with a VAD girl who would be coming along with her room-mate. However, it so happened that, on this particular Saturday, an old school friend of mine - Jack - turned up but as he was not commissioned, I could not take him to the Officers' Club, so we therefore decided to ask Valerie (the VAD girl) to find another girl to make up the party. This she did, but unfortunately the girl was quite a lot older than us and rather off-hand and so Jack made a pass at Denise, who was supposed to be my date but she didn't take to him. Denise was a very lively and rather naughty French girl who suggested that we all strip off and swim, and, without waiting for a reply, did so, followed by Jane. The rest of us, all nude in the moonlight, rushed to the diving board to the tune of "Don't Fence Me In" coming from a portable gramophone. I could not get to the diving board and over the side fast enough, as I thought that once I hit the cold water, my over-expressive ardour might be quenched. It did, for a short while, until Denise swam up to me and playfully pressed her wet body up against me. Then the two girls tried to pull Jack under and I had a rest on the diving board. Denise left the other two and swam out of the dam. I watched her and realised she had what can only be described as a perfect body and by the time she reached me I was aroused. She could see this, and as there were no other people near enough to see us, she put her arms around my neck and gave me a long wet kiss, promising that we would get together at the first opportunity. I dived back into the water amazed at her manner for no other girl had ever approached me in that way before.

Shortly after this, I was, proudly, part of the guard of honour for General Auchinleck, one of the most-respected of the British Generals, who was visiting us. From past experience, I knew that it would mean a very tiring day in the sun, with men from the guard fainting if they were not in top form. I was not going to take any chances that night, so my usual bottle of rum was cut down to two drinks and at ten o'clock, I announced that I was going home. Denise asked me if I could drop her off at their mess and when we arrived, she asked me to walk with her to the room she shared with Val. When she invited me in, I refused because of my duties the next day, at which point she became quite annoyed, saying that she had arranged everything just so that we could have the room to ourselves. I was allowed to leave only after I had promised that I would come along with Brad and we would spend the weekend together. Turning down such a generous offer was one of the most difficult things I have ever done.

Auchinleck's parade turned out to be better than expected. After the inspection, he gave us a short talk, when he told us we would soon be going into action again and it would be a different type of warfare from anything we had experienced before, but we were being given this task because commanders had confidence in our ability. We discovered much later that this referred to a sea landing approach.

Among my other duties, I was Battalion Weapon Training Officer and this took up much of my time when the company was not out in the field. As I was sitting down to breakfast one morning, Lt. Selkirk came up to me and told me that an Atomic Bomb had been dropped on Japan and that the 5th (K) Bn. K.A.R. were moving to a camp on a ridge, adjoining "C" Company, which was great news for me as my two old friends, John Lawrence and David Sheldrick were in this Battalion. A couple of days later we went out on field exercises, where I was given the task of attacking a would-be Japanese bunker, using the H.Q. Company three-inch mortars and tank fire covering the approach. When we got into position, I called for a smoke screen from the mortars, followed by high explosive shell fire on the bunker, giving the order to move forward as soon as the first mortar had exploded. The second mortar shell did not fire but the third one landed in amongst my group, a piece of shrapnel hitting the wireless, shattering its components and knocking the operator into a ditch. I gave the order to get down and abandon the exercise but had no contact with the covering fire groups as my wireless was now out of action. No more shells came over, the tank stopped firing and as the smoke lifted, a jeep with the C.O., Duncan Geddes, came rushing towards us. After calling the roll and finding the only casualty was the wireless and a lot of shaken men, I was informed that the mortar charges were believed to be faulty. I was then ordered to take my troops back to the transport and we were able to go back to camp in Ranchi to celebrate the end of the war with Japan. It took me a day or two to realise that my way of life was about to change and I should start thinking about my future. The next few months were a difficult time for Battalion Commanding Officers (and higher ranking Officers) as they had to try and maintain interest and discipline in a cause that was no longer valid. A rift had begun to show between the regular and the war-time soldiers causing the regulars to try and tighten up on discipline and smartness on the parade ground. The others were not interested in "bloody parades and playing at soldiers" and made their views known in no uncertain terms.

One evening, a group of us from our mess and the 5th's mess decided to go and join David and John, who were in the mess drinking alone. When some of the new officers of the 5ths saw our party of six enter, they went to bed probably, I think, because they could predict what would ensue. The C.O. at the time was a new one and not very popular with most of the officers and David in particular. As a result, the C.O's table and chairs were broken up and shoved into the fire which did not seem to achieve the required reaction, so the C.O's tent pegs were pulled out, just far enough to hold the tent up until a breeze came. Predictably, the following day, David, being the Senior Officer, and Phil and John to a lesser degree, got a ticking off from the C.O. They had absolutely no sympathy from us, and most of the hard drinkers in our circle moved to our mess where I was doing my duty as Wines Officer. We had no problems as our C.O., Duncan Geddes, was one of the most respected and widely liked C.O.s in our division.

One night, Connie got drunk and rugger-tackled a Senior Officer on the dance floor of the Ranchi Officer's Club and as a result the Club was placed "out of bounds" to all East African Force Officers under the rank of Major, and Connie was put under arrest. Somehow David, with the help of two others, managed to get him released and a week later the Club ban was lifted but the East African Forces always had to have an Officer on duty at the Club thereafter, to ensure good behaviour. I was on Club duty one day, when Selkirk arrived with two nurses to play tennis, so I joined them for tea. While he was playing tennis with one of them, I decided to sit and talk to the other, Patricia Dowling, a rather quiet but very striking girl of about 23 years with a unmistakable London accent. She did not appear to be very good, or indeed, very interested in tennis, but when the talk shifted to the field hospitals and their duties, it was very obvious who was the most knowledgeable. Over the course of the conversation, I began to become more interested in this very good-looking girl and decided I would like to take her out sometime.

One weekend, Phil asked me to join him for the weekend at his grandmother's home, just outside Ranchi and whilst I was very keen I felt compelled to ask him how it had come about that he had a grandmother living in this God-forsaken country. He explained that his grandfather had been Governor of Bihar and had retired and died there and his grandmother, a very lively and cheerful person had decided to stay on, at least for the duration of the war. The house was large, set in beautiful gardens, with a host of servants to run it, both indoors and out so that even when we sat down to a meal, a bearer stood behind each chair. This was luxury at its highest level and after the rigours and deprivations of war, it was a most enjoyable weekend.

Whilst we were there, the old lady told us of the great parties that were held by the different regiments before the war and so we made up our minds to keep the ball rolling. I suggested that we have a combined party of the 4th's and the 5th's in our Mess but with the arrangements going well, we discovered that the men detailed to invite girls had let us down. Less than half the number promised were coming so Phil and I went to the new East African Nurses Home where we collected four girls: Pat Dowling, Dorothy, Myra and Kay. I was wines officer that night and so did not get much chance to dance, but I noticed with some pleasure that Pat spent quite a bit of time talking to me, when she wasn't dancing, and I was already quite smitten. After the party, I took Pat home and arranged to see her the following weekend but unfortunately had to cancel this as I was on duty, training for the Torchlight Tattoo. The date was changed to one in the following week but this day I was Orderly Officer so I asked Brad to take her out. As I had nothing to do except be present, I had a few drinks in my tent, when some of my friends turned up and insisted on doing my duty so that I could join Brad and Pat. I was certainly unpopular when I arrived and Pat would not believe that I had been on duty, assuming that I just did not care about taking her out. After a few more rums and some smooth talking, I was allowed to take her home in a taxi.

During the next two weeks I was very busy, as the heats for the Divisional Shooting Competition were being run and Col. Geddes hoped our Battalion would win. We did so, and were entered for the South East Asian Command Competition, but in the event we never competed as we were the first Brigade to return to East Africa, and left before the competition began. Christmas was approaching and as we were preparing to leave India, we celebrated our return with a farewell party at Audrey House, a well known place of entertainment in Ranchi. Many people had been transferred, others had gone on overseas leave and there were a number of new faces in our Battalion. I was still Wine Officer and I had asked Pat to the party but she said she would only come if I invited her old boyfriend as well. I had already taken Pat out quite a few times and as we were about to leave for East Africa, thought I would probably not be seeing her for quite some time. After the party, having drunk sufficient to be bursting with Dutch courage, I asked Pat if she would marry me, and a few days later she agreed.

The voyage back to East Africa took about two weeks and was uneventful. We disembarked at Mombasa and immediately entrained for Gilgil, where we arrived late in the evening.

My mother was living in Kigoma in Tanganyika at this time, where she and my stepfather had been running the Greek-Cypriot Refugee camp. Just before leaving India, I received a telegram telling me that whilst repatriating some refugees through Dar, he had had a violent diabetic coma. Unfortunately he had forgotten his insulin and had tragically died. I arrived in Kigoma on leave, prior to being demobbed and was relieved to find my mother in good form, in spite of her bereavement, busy with the running of the camp. Two days after my arrival, she had to escort a batch of refugees to Dar-es-Salaam, so I accompanied her. While there, I received a cable, forwarded from Kigoma, telling me that I had been chosen to command the Uganda contingent to the Victory Parade in London. I also received another cable from my C.O., Duncan Geddes, saying that Derek Watson, my previous C.O., was to command the whole East African contingent to the Parade. Lt. Col. Geddes had accepted on my behalf and wished me to return to Nairobi at the earliest opportunity for instructions.

My fiancee, Pat, was also returning to East Africa from India, so my mother decided to come to Nairobi with me, as she was keen to meet her future daughter-in-law. Pat finally arrived two days before the Victory Parade contingent left but was not coming with us. We managed to get a special license and married in the District Commissioner's office in Nairobi, the night before I left. In Nairobi, I was delighted to see that many old friends would also be in the East African contingent, such as John Lawrence, David Sheldrick, the Block brothers (Jack and Tubby), Fred Seed and many others in other contingents, as well as Myfanwy in the F.A.N.Y.s. The Uganda party for the Victory Parade consisted of Charlie Broomfield, Peter Bess and me, representing the Europeans, Lt. Freddie Mutesa (Kabaka of Uganda) R.S.M, Ali of the 4th Battalion and about 50 other Warrant Officers, Non-Commissioned Officers and men from all the Uganda Battalions. Freddie Mutesa was an interesting inclusion for he was the heir of the Kabaka (or King) of Buganda the largest province in Uganda, and as such was a very important man. This undoubtedly was the reason that he was chosen, for otherwise he was a 25 year-old lieutenant pretty much like myself. He was later to become Kabaka, when his father died, but his brief reign was finished by independence when Idi Amin put him under house arrest. He was helped to escape and fled to London where he died penniless in a boarding house in South

London, not ten miles from where the Victory Parade was to take place.

Charlie Broomfield was an ex-Grenadier Guards Drill Sergeant, and so we had no difficulty in choosing our trainer with him doing most of the training for the entire East African contingent. When we finally set sail, everyone was in high spirits, particularly as most of us had never visited this country, for which we had spent the last few years risking our lives. The contingent was split up into sections with the band put under my control and a more unruly and undisciplined crowd I have yet to come across. They had a very high opinion of themselves until they reached England and saw some of their opposite numbers - only then did they realise how amateur they were. I must admit that as a band they were quite good but when they were asked to play at Edinburgh Castle, they refused unless they were paid individually for the occasion and so I cancelled their going. This raised a storm of protest from the War Office but Derek Watson backed me up and, as a result, the next time the band was invited to Edinburgh, the members were very pleased to go.

Our contingent was encamped in bell tents in Kensington Gardens in London, and John Lawrence and I shared a tent right next to the Albert Memorial. We had only been there a couple of days, when I got up early one morning to relieve myself on an oak tree next to our tent. Immediately a park attendant with a long spike full of used condoms came along and ticked me off for indecent exposure. Just then John emerged for the same purpose so the attendant turned to him only to be told by John in his best King's English to "F... off with his dirty French letters".

On our arrival in England, we had all been given numbered identity cards giving our names and addresses, in case we got lost. For the first week the Askaris could only go out in groups escorted by one of their own Officers or by a European approved by the Army. Readers will appreciate the predicament when I point out that I had never been to England before and did not know my way about. I felt it was my duty to take some of my men to the West End, but, like all the askaris that accompanied me, I had never even seen a tube train or an escalator. I decided to go down the first underground we came to and all went well until we reached the bottom when some of the askaris decided they wanted to go up the other side for a ride, whilst the rest strode ahead to see what novelties awaited them elsewhere. To cut a long story short, I ended up with the R.S.M. Ali and two soldiers out of the original twelve, but they all managed somehow to return to camp before sunrise, having had a wonderful time. I gathered that people picked them up, some were taken home and others were shown around London with some of their hosts being ex-East African who could therefore speak Swahili. After this, I did not bother to take out organised parties again.

There was one unfortunate incident. Two young ladies, one related to a Minister, got the necessary permit from the War Office to allow them to visit the camp and take out troops to show them around the city. Instead of going to the Orderly Room and asking for two men, they picked out the first two they saw, who were on fatigue duties, somehow obtaining permits for the two men and took them home. Unfortunately, the girls must have given the soldiers the impression that they wanted to go to bed with them, because the next day the soldiers were brought back under arrest. Not realising who the girls were, I told the Military Police that I had no intention of charging the troops concerned, since loose women looking for men should go through the right channels or take the consequences. I was very quickly corrected about the morals of the young ladies and put in my place in no uncertain terms. Fortunately, Derek Watson, the East African Contingent Commander, was there and had voiced his views about civilians coming into camp without complying with regulations. The result was that civilians were not in future allowed beyond the gate without an escort, but the whole incident cast a shadow across a time of great celebration.

The night before the Parade, David, John, Myfanwy, some others and I met up in the "Captains Cabin", a pub in the Haymarket, where we found a lot of ex-East Africans. John and I were with a girl and her husband who were from Tanganyika and we got very drunk. In the early hours of the morning, our newly acquired friends hailed us a cab and sent us home and we arrived in camp only just in time to get dressed and go on parade. It was a hot day and people lined the streets by their thousands as the procession made its way through the West End toward Whitehall and Buckingham Palace. From time to time, the parade had to stop to allow other units to join in and during such stops, both civilians and soldiers were fainting from the heat and being taken away. John and I were in the front row carrying the King's Colours and David was behind with the Kenya Regimental Colours. I was on the verge of collapse as we approached the Mall but a quick shower of rain revived us and I can still remember John saying in a very hoarse voice "Thank God for that!"

Although the march was not all that long, what with the drink the night before, the crowds, and the weight of the Colours, by the time we returned to Kensington Gardens I was ready to collapse. Suddenly our Tanganyika lady friend took the flag from John and me, handed us a beer each, and disappeared - still in possession of the Colours. This was highly irregular and before the girl returned, whilst we were on our second beer, it dawned on us that we could get into serious trouble. We had handed over our Colours without a receipt, and to a civilian at that and we were discussing what to do, when the girl reappeared with a friend and handed us two receipts. I still don't know how she managed it.

After a few more drinks, the girls left to collect their husbands and we all arranged to meet up later. John and I made our way to the "Captains Cabin" and on the way there we were approached by a couple of very attractive "street women", who made some remark about the men of East Africa, to which John replied "I see you're not blind". The girl's reply to that was "Oh, they speak English", so we asked them what the score was and were told six pounds for an all night session. To this I replied that we only wanted to borrow it, not buy it outright. After a few more remarks, the girls realised that we were not really interested and were just about to set about us, helped by some others, when a policeman arrived. The policeman ordered them off and they went, calling us every name in and out of the dictionary and the policeman warned us against teasing street girls if we didn't want to end up in hospital. It was interesting to note that these hazards of civilisation were as numerous as in the Bush. Shortly after arriving in London, I had a bit of trouble with the Kabaka of Uganda, as he was in my contingent but could also claim to be a political guest. He at first refused the tent he was given to sleep in, claiming that he should be accommodated in a hotel. He had also begun to miss parades, claiming that he was on political business, until the position became impossible, from a discipline point of view, and I had him relieved from the contingent, except for the Parade itself.

We were in England for nearly a month, during which time we were entertained and paraded in a number of places and on various occasions, at some of which we met members of the Royal Family. On one occasion, the King, the Queen, the two Princesses and Prince Philip inspected the East African contingent. On this particular day I was luckier than most as I was introduced as Commander of the Tanganyika contingent because there was no officer who was actually from Tanganyika present to answer questions about that country. As a result, I had a lengthy conversation with Princess Elizabeth and Prince Philip, answering questions about Tanganyika.

A few days after the parade, a number of us were invited to a party at Hampton Court Palace, where once again we were introduced to the King and Queen. The party was due to go on until 11 pm. and at that time Lord Louis Mountbatten announced that the King and Queen would retire on account of pressure of work but that the party should continue. From that moment, the party turned into a riot, with Mountbatten and General Slim, Commander of the 14th Burma Army, joining in and encouraging everyone to 'let their hair down'. It continued into the early morning and one of my best recollections is of Lord Mountbatten performing a Maori dance.

Before leaving England, the East African contingent held a party at the Dorchester Hotel to return some of the hospitality we had enjoyed. I took my very beautiful cousin Joanne to this and when I introduced her to a great friend of my mother's, Major Cathy Hicksonweed, all she would say was,

-"I've heard that one too many times before. Don't worry, I won't tell your wife!"

My cousin and I had not met before and we were getting on rather too well, but fortunately, the trip to England was short and my time was not all my own.

One of the things I had to do whilst in England was to meet my new mother and grandmother-in-law. We arranged to meet at the War Ministry and spent about twenty minutes looking at each other before I went up to her and asked if she was Mrs. Dowling. She was so surprised that she nearly fell over, as she was expecting me to be black, since Pat had sent a cable saying that she had married an East African. We had lunch together at the Kensington Hotel, then I took her to the station by taxi, paid the taxi-driver and gave him a half-a-crown tip. Instead of expressing gratitude, he flung the money down on the pavement saying that he "didn't need that kind of money". I bent down and picked it up saying "Well, I do!" Pat's mother explained that it was because of the Americans who had so much more money and tried to impress local people by giving large tips. After that, I did not bother to tip any more and I still embarrass my friends when in England by not tipping the taxi-driver. At Paddington station when our contingent left to return to East Africa, we were harassed by prostitutes making claims on our troops for non-payment of services rendered which they called 'board and lodging'. Despite this annoyance, I was impressed by the beauty and age of some of the girls, who looked well-groomed and innocent.

We returned to Kenya on the same ship which had brought us to England. At Port Suez, in the Suez Canal, we were inundated with 'Gili gili boatmen' trying to sell anything from dirty pictures to their sisters for the night. We could not keep them off the ship and we were warned to keep an eye on our cabins as they would steal anything. The problem was solved when someone discovered some tins of ham that had 'blown'. David put a couple of these, opened, on the boat and some over the side and on to another boat. He shouted something and, like magic, the 'Gili gili' men left the ship, climbed into their boats and followed the cans of rotten ham.

First day at school   *Otto and my mother, Lupa Goldfields*

Arusha School - 1932

On leave in the Lupa goldfields, 1941

My brother Norman breaks a leg.

Nairobi Victory Parade Contingent - 1946

Creech Jones Inspecting the Troops - London, 1946

The newly -weds - 1946

Pat, Penny and myself

Victory Parade - London 1946

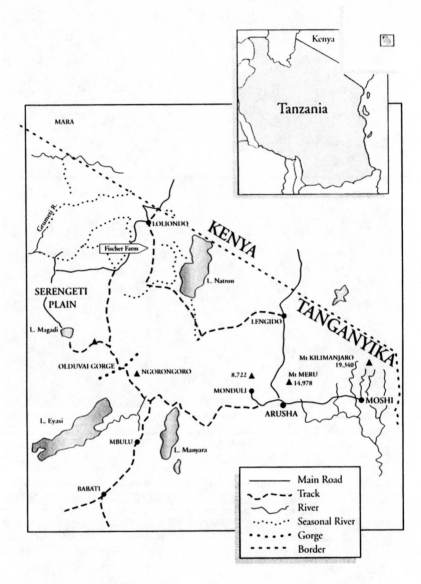

Northern Tanganyika - 1935

Chapter Seven
Veterinary Service,
Tanganyika

Back in Kenya, it took me about two weeks to get my troops discharged or back to their regiments before I got my own discharge from the Army, together with my gratuity and allowance. The whole sum for nearly six years' service came to just under two hundred pounds, with a first class train ticket to return to Tanganyika to find a job.

I had the future to consider but it did not inspire confidence. Like most servicemen being demobbed at the time, I felt a little lost after spending six years of my life with a bunch of good men in unique circumstances, only to find it had come to an end and I had a life to restart. My experience of civilian adult life up until that time had been very limited, as limited as my scholastic qualifications, and brief experience in the "Lands and Mines" department. I had no training for anything in civilian life, very little education, a wife to support and a cupboard full of life experience, but not of the workplace. The future did not look too bright but I knew I must face up to it and knew that with Pat, who was very capable, beside me, things would work out in the end.

There was only one job available and that was with the Veterinary Department in Dodoma - as a livestock marketing officer. Fortunately, Pat was not due for release from the Queen Alexandra's Imperial Military Nursing Service for a few more months, which I hoped would give me sufficient time to get things sorted out before we started our married life together. After spending a week at the Avenue Hotel in Nairobi and five days honeymoon at the Brackenhurst Hotel, Limuru, I set off for Dodoma for an interview, which, I hoped, would result in something to do. On the railway bus from Korogwe to Morogoro, I met a girl who had been in the forces and was now returning home to Tanganyika. She was very depressed as she had gone off to the Forces with her husband, who had then met another girl in Europe, and left her, with no home and pregnant. Now she was going to live with her parents, and was not looking forward to the future. It seemed there were many of us around at that time, and so I offered her my sympathies, listening to her story until we reached Morogoro, where we were to go our separate ways. Unfortunately, the girl, whose name I am ashamed to say I have forgotten, would not let go of me, clinging to me until I eventually pushed her on her train, hanging on to the door until it pulled away for Dar.

I arrived in Dodoma in the early hours of Saturday morning and went straight to the Railway Hotel, scene of my first days after leaving school. At about midday I looked in at the Club, to see if there was anyone I knew and was relieved to see it full, with one of the first people to recognise me being John Harris, who seemed pleased to see me. He took me round and introduced me to some of the people I didn't know, one of whom was a short fellow called Gordon Pevie, who turned out to be the Provincial Veterinary Officer for Dodoma. He told me that I would be working under him and that I should not appear in the office on Monday in my uniform. He had made that last remark in a rather sarcastic manner, and so I replied that I was not yet employed by the Veterinary Department and if, and when, I was, I would take my orders from those I considered my superiors. Furthermore, I told him, neither he nor anyone else would have to suffer the embarrassment of my uniform after that day, as I did not intend to wear it again. I then walked off to the bar where I met up with an old friend, Eric Howe, who was also employed by the Veterinary Department. He said that he had been expecting me, and that I would be working under him but I replied that I doubted if I would be working under anyone in the Veterinary Department, after what I had just said to Mr. Pevie. There was a strange atmosphere for returning soldiers after the war, with the vast majority very welcoming but a few remaining wary of the newcomers' expectations. So it was that, for a while, the soldier's frustrations at returning to Civvy Street were to clash with those people worried about losing their jobs or having their promotion hopes ruined by these strangers in uniform.

Later, I was still at the bar drinking with a crowd of people, when Pevie came up and introduced me to his wife. They were both very friendly and offered to show me the house I would live in if I took up the job I was being offered and so after a good liquid lunch at the Club, Pevie picked me up and drove me out to a tiny little house at Kikuyu. The house was the European-style bachelor quarters normally reserved for newcomers, consisting of a nine square foot bedroom, a sitting/dining room about ten feet by twelve feet, a tiny bathroom and store, a kitchen, W.C. and servants' quarters separately, outside. Pevie was very apologetic about the small size and said that they had applied for a larger house, but I assured him it was bigger than the tents which my wife and I had been used to and, in any case, I could not afford the furniture needed for a bigger house. He then told me that he had spoken to Neil Reid, the Director of the Veterinary Services, who had agreed that I should be awarded six years war increments. The war increments were a system whereby those people who had served in the forces during the war were given the usual pay raises that they would have enjoyed were they to have stayed in their post, which would bring the salary I was being offered to four hundred and eighty pounds a year. I would be Acting Livestock Marketing Officer, on probation for six months, and could take up the appointment without an interview, as Neil Reid already knew me. This meant that if I decided to take up the offer, I could move out of the hotel and into the house immediately. I decided, there and then, to accept and moved into the house with my newly acquired servant, Seweji, the next day.

The house was next door to Pevie's and was about two miles from the office but this did not present a transport problem as Pevie gave me a lift back and forth, and Eric Howe was also only about three hundred yards away. They both had cars of their own and I would soon take over the Market Staff lorry, which I would be able to use in an emergency. On the Saturday night, the Club threw an impromptu party in my honour and on Sunday morning, half of Dodoma turned up to move me to my new home, with offers of just about everything needed for a new house. This kindness lifted my spirits once more.

When I went to the office on Monday, I was given a lecture by Pevie, about the work I would be conducting under Eric Howe. He said I was to forget that I had been an officer in the Army, as most people had had enough of war and soldiers and did not want to be reminded of this period, sentiments I suspected of being Pevie's own feelings rather than those of most other people in the area. I considered he had a chip on his shoulder, which was to cause problems until we had sorted it out some time later.

I spent the next six weeks learning about the cattle markets from Eric Howe and the market staff. Meanwhile, cattle weigh-bridges were being installed at three of the larger markets so that at the end of six weeks, I was told to change the whole system of buying and selling at all the markets in the Province. The cattle would no longer be auctioned but instead graded into one of five grades, weighed and priced, so as to give the seller a fair price. The Somalis and Arab buyers were in the habit of forming rings and depressing the prices to less than half their proper value. The seller could refuse the price and often did, but the country would soon become over-stocked and taxes would not be paid until there was a sudden drought or something and the cattle would be given away to any bidder. If buyers from outside came in and did not join the ring, or were not allowed to do so, the prices were pushed up over the top and the market turned into a shambles. There were then fights, which ended up with knives being drawn and people killed. It was illegal to buy or sell cattle, sheep or goats without a licence or at any other place other than a prescribed market - and then only on a day when the market was officially open. The small local butchers were thus forced to buy illicitly, direct from the farmers. These were mostly local tribesmen, some of whom were becoming traders and this was undermining the whole system.

The stock traders were having a field day at the expense of the farmer and consumer and, not surprisingly, were opposed to any change. They had organised efficient propaganda against the new scheme, which had been going on for some time while a decision was being made. At the end of my six weeks' probation period, Eric ceased to have anything to do with this project and Neil Reid told me to go ahead and implement the new programme on my own, which annoyed Pevie and meant I got very little help from him.

I went round to all the markets, explaining the changes that were to take place and here, once again, my fluency in Kiswahili and knowledge of other African languages saved the day for me. I started by weighing each animal at the three weigh-bridge markets before allowing them to be auctioned and when they were being sold, I would call out the prices. The Somalis first threatened me, then tried to bribe me, in an attempt to bring me into line before changing their tactics and offering realistic prices at these particular markets. At first things started slowly as by refusing the system, no animals were sold, but finally at the end of a week of little business, everyone came round to the system and sales picked up. Once I was able to estimate weights accurately to within five per cent, I introduced the new system at Mwitikira Market. At first all the traders refused to buy but I could buy for the "Bully for Britain" drive, a system sponsored by the British Government to buy cheap beef for its ration-starved population, and so trading continued anyway. The traders attended the next three markets, still buying nothing, but then the butchers started bidding. This was the cue for the Somalis to lodge a complaint with Pevie, the gist of which was that I had messed up the arrangements and so was now allowing the unlicensed buyers to purchase direct. When I returned to Dodoma the next day I was approached by an Arab trader, Abdullah

Makhel, who told me he had broken away from the other traders as he believed the new rules were just to both buyer and seller. He told me about the complaints lodged against me and said he was prepared to say in public that they were lies and that he could get some of the other Arabs to come forward if necessary. The Arabs had obviously decided to change their views and this turned out to be very helpful, as Abdullah was the largest of the Arab buyers and very highly regarded.

I had to report to Pevie about what had happened and was quite sure I would be looking for another job shortly. He, however, had had instructions from "higher up" to back me, as long as I kept within the law, but he had seized on the complaint that I had allowed unlicensed dealers to trade. I was in an aggressive frame of mind and challenged him and his Somali friends to produce evidence to support the complaint. Hard words followed between us, during which I suggested that they take legal action against me and refused to discuss the matter with him and the Somalis unless all the traders and the chiefs were present from the areas concerned. One of the chiefs had gone to the District Commissioner and thanked him for all the help the farmers were receiving from the Government in getting fair prices for their cattle and when this information was passed on to Pevie, nothing further materialised.

After the showdown with Pevie, I regained my confidence, and the job became sufficiently challenging for me to derive genuine pride from the sense of achievement it brought. By the end of six months, he and I were on the best of terms, my contract had been confirmed, I had pushed in the teeth of a Somali who had attempted to knife me, and I had gained acceptance for the system of grade and weight throughout the province.

Four and a half months after I returned to Dodoma, Pat, my wife, was released from the Army Nursing Service and came to join me. I was away at the market on the day she arrived, but Gordon Pevie picked her up in her Captain's uniform and took her to his wife, Enid, where she stayed until I returned from safari the next day. Pat had made an immediate, favourable impact in Dodoma, as she was young, good-looking, very capable and a good nurse, in a place where there was a shortage of trained nursing sisters. My mother had given us a lot of her household surplus to help us set up home. She was now living in Tabora, where she ran a ladies' dress shop with two Polish refugees as helpers and so did not need so many of her household possessions. Despite this help we still needed cash to buy a car and now that we had been given a bigger house, it needed more furniture. Also, Pat wanted to go home to see her family in Great Britain as she had not been back for some time, and this required cash too. Pat was only too pleased to carry on working part-time at the local hospital and seemed to love Tanganyika and its people from her very arrival. I arranged that I did the Dodoma Market on Mondays and would be camped out at a market, such as Ruaha, where there was good fishing and shooting, on Saturdays. Friends who wanted a break from Dodoma would bring Pat out, spend the night in my camp, where I would have everything laid on - fishing and shooting on the Saturday evening and all day on Sunday - and all return to Dodoma on Sunday evening. We managed to arrange about one of these weekends every month and the party usually consisted of Pat and me, and two or three other couples. The weekends became very popular, especially with the younger and more recent arrivals. Most possessed guns or rifles, which they did not yet know how to use proficiently and these weekends gave them the opportunity for good practice.

I was made an Honorary Game Warden, because of my continuous travelling and experience, which meant that I would be called out, from time to time, on crop protection control, and also, during a famine, I would be asked to shoot game, at Government expense, to feed the local population. This was very useful, as I would have my two elephant and one rhino licences for both of us, and if I shot a good one, this would be on licence but if it did not come up to regulation size, it would be booked down to crop protection. Few people know about the license system in the Colonial Administration and in these times of popular outrage against the hunting of animals, I believe it deserves an explanation. After the war, Government expenditure was as tight as ever, and the salaries of Government officers were very low, particularly for the unqualified. These areas were teeming with game before the onset of mass poaching, and so a system of hunting licences was devised by the Colonial Administration, which was a popular way, especially amongst lower-ranking officials, of spending local leave and adding a little to the salary. The Major Game Licence entitled he holder, with the permission of the Government, to shoot two elephant and one rhino, both of which had to be over a certain size. The Minor Game Licence allowed one to shoot small game for the pot and there was a freely available bird license, which, as the name suggests, was for shooting game birds, again for the pot.

It was on one of the crop protection calls, just outside Dodoma at a place called Nkungi, that I was asked to go and deal with a rhino that was chasing the natives out of their *shambas* (gardens or smallholdings) and was becoming dangerous. Pat was seven months pregnant at the time, but insisted that she came with me on the shoot. I tried to dissuade her because of her condition and the type of country I would be working in, but she insisted. We went off, after a report had come in one Sunday that the rhino had, that very morning, chased a woman from her sorghum field and very nearly caught her. We drove to the watering place, then had to follow the spoor on foot along the rhino tunnels in the Mitunduru thorn. It was impossible to move through this type of bush (similar to a thick mat of "wait-a-bit" thorn) except along game tracks. I was leading the way, followed by the guide with a spear, then came Pat and behind her my veterinary guard-cum-gun-bearer, who was an Ndorobo tribesman. We had been going for about an hour, when I was tapped on the shoulder. The Ndorobo wanted us to stop and listen. We heard a rhino crunching grass, quite clearly, about fifty yards ahead to our right, but the wind must have changed, because suddenly the crunching stopped and the animal charged. The first thing I saw was a dark wall of thorn bush, moving towards me. I fired twice at the wall, and it changed direction. I still had not seen the beast but I turned to see where the others were. Pat was up a thorn sapling and, although she had climbed about eight feet up, she was in fact no higher than three feet off the ground because the sapling bent over under her weight. The guide was nowhere to be seen, whilst the gun-bearer was standing guard beside Pat, with my 7.92 mm, which was almost useless against a rhino. We got Pat off the sapling by pulling it over just a little further, and she walked back some distance with the Ndorobo, whilst I searched for the rhino. I found it about thirty yards from where I had fired at it. It was stone dead, with a bullet through its heart and another through its kidney.

The next day was Monday, the Dodoma market day and cattle were abundant, but there were no traders. I asked the market master where the traders were, as all their cattle brands were ready in the wood fire. One of the traders said that they had a *shauri* (problem) to discuss with me and were waiting for me under a tree, a little way off. I asked the trader what the problem was but he would not say. Things had been going so well recently, so any setback would be a great disappointment to me and I walked over to the tree, expecting trouble. Even my staff, with the exception of the market master and an Asian named Akbar, seemed aloof and off-hand. I was met by Sheikh Maji Hussein, who then proceeded to give me a dressing down about taking the mother of an unborn child on a rhino hunt. I tried to excuse my behaviour, but this got me nowhere. When I told them that Pat was none the worse for wear and was at the hospital, nursing the sick whilst we were sitting talking, I was told to expect a delegation from the elders that evening, to see for themselves. Only then were we able to get on with the market. That evening, true to their word, three of their elders turned up with their senior wives who had gifts for Pat. It was a most embarrassing situation, but indicated their caring concern.

The Dodoma district, at that time, consisted of Gogo tribesmen, but it had a belt of land stretching from Hanetti in the north, round the eastern boundary of the district, to Zoisa Gulwe, Chipogoro, Loge, areas to the south and along the Ruaha River, which was Masai land. They are a mixture of pastoralists and farmers who are relatively quiet these days but according to the diaries of the explorers that passed through the area, were once a very fierce bunch. Among the Ruaha Masai were two exceptionally wealthy men, one of whom, it was said, owned about thirty thousand head of cattle and the second, an old man called Ole Hau, who owned over ten thousand head. As their contribution towards the war effort, someone had persuaded the Masai to sell off ten per cent of their herds and these animals were to be walked to the Leibigs factory at Athi River, just outside Nairobi in Kenya to be turned into "Bully for Britain". The idea was good but how could one stop the Masai from selling an animal at one market and buying another at the next? The Masai liked to have their wealth on the hoof and, if they need to have money for a particular purpose, they sell an animal. The purchase or debt is paid and the balance consumed in drink. They seldom keep coins because coins do not themselves increase whereas they set great store by, and boast of, their herds, their colours and the behaviour of individual animals. A man's prestige, which is of paramount importance to him, is judged by the size and condition of his cattle. This was sure to happen, unless they could be persuaded to bank their cash from the sale of the cattle. I was handed the problem and told to solve it.

The first big market day in my Masai area was at Chipogoro, where I held a meeting with the local Masai. Ole Hau was present and so I explained the procedure and told them all about the Post Office, and how they could go and collect their interest every six months, whether there was drought or rain, explaining that this could save them from starvation in a bad year. One elder asked why he should keep his money at the Post Office, instead of home. I pointed out that at the Post Office it would gain interest and there was no chance of it being stolen. Another elder said that I was lying, for how could shillings increase in the Post Office in a box? The only explanation I could think of was that the shillings in circulation were all female, and when put in a box with male shillings, they would breed: "Why then" asked one of them, "do you not give us male shillings as well as female ones?". I replied that only the King had these male shillings and he would not let them out of his control. The meeting broke up but about an hour later, Ole Hau turned up with a fat sheep and told my servants to slaughter it for my food. Meanwhile, I had gone off with the gun to look for guinea-fowl for the pot, but when I returned, I found Ole Hau outside my tent, with two other elders, roasting mutton, Masai style on sticks over a fire. He announced that the grazing was poor and that most of the cattle were a long way from Chipogoro, looking for grazing, otherwise he would have brought me an ox, but, in the circumstances, the best he could do was give me a sheep. I thanked him and offered him and his two friends a glass of squash. We then sat round the fire and ate roasted mutton, well into the night, talking about the droughts and how the Masai happened to be on the Ruaha, so far south. Then the old man started to talk about the male shilling. Was it true what I had said about the male shillings? Could I, as a special favour to him, get him a male shilling? I replied that I could not get him a male shilling, as all these came from the King of England's land and had to be returned at the end of each season, but I would put a curse on myself, if his did not increase by the end of the six month period. How was he to know that I would not cheat him? At the end of the six months, I had to promise to get the mobile Post Office to bring the "parents" and the "progeny" to show him. When the time came, he meticulously counted out nearly twenty thousand shillings in bags, which he then handed back to the Post Office. Then he counted nearly two hundred and fifty shillings in sumunies (fifty cent pieces), which he wanted to take away with him, but I persuaded him to leave them for six months, when he would find that they had grown into shillings and there would be even more sumunies as well. Others came forward and slowly the Post Office Savings in the area was launched. I was now accepted as a true friend and received a sheep on each of my visits, but I never managed to get away without being pestered for a male shilling.

As I had tried to explain earlier, Ole Hau was not, by any stretch of the imagination, a poor man, yet he could neither read nor write. He had a vast family of sons and relations, apart from several followers who were ready and only too pleased to be given something to do. One evening, when the cattle were coming in to one of the old man's manyattas (cattle enclosures), he noticed that three animals, out of nearly a thousand, were missing. He summoned his elders and asked them where the missing animals were but no one was able to give him a satisfactory answer. Men were sent off in different directions to seek information and search for the missing animals.

I was at the Kikombo market, which was about sixty miles from where the cattle had gone missing three days earlier, when I suddenly saw Ole Hau hiding behind a bush, waving to attract my attention. I walked over to him and he explained that there were three of his stolen cattle about to be put up for sale. He did not want to be seen at the market, as the thieves would run away if they saw him, and he needed my help to catch them. He described the three animals in great detail, two were old cows, both brown with white markings, and one was a young black steer with white markings on the legs. I promised to do what I could and indeed the animals came for auction early and the culprits were arrested. This illiterate old man, who was probably nearing his seventies, had missed three cattle out of a thousand, and had followed their spoor, covering a minimum distance of sixty miles, on foot in three days.

After I left Dodoma I was told that the old man was persuaded to take money out of his Post Office Savings Account to buy a car, and he used to visit the big towns more and more, on drinking sprees. The car eventually crashed and the driver was killed. The old man returned home, where I heard he died shortly afterwards. He was still a wealthy man as his herds were being cared for but he had nothing left in his savings account!

On one of my safaris to the southern area, at Chipogoro, an old man with a bald head and a little grey moustache, came up to me, asking if I was going to the Ruaha river on this trip. When I said I was, he asked, "Do you eat suru suru fish?" I had never heard of the suru suru fish, so he promised to let me have some later that day if I gave him a lift to Ruaha, about twenty six miles to the south. I did this and I had just got settled in my camp on the banks of the Ruaha when, at about tea-time, the "suru man" turned up carrying a net. He told me that he was about to catch my dinner and he would like me to accompany him so that I could see the great danger he faced in order to catch these fish. The Ruaha crocodiles are renowned for killing humans and cattle and no-one would approach the river except at shallow fords, in case there was a crocodile lying in wait for prey. The crocodile often lies in wait for its prey in shallow water and, when the sun is in the right position and the prey's shadow falls on the water, it whips its tail at terrific speed and knocks the prey into the water. When we reached the spot the old man had chosen, he asked me and my veterinary guard to remain about twenty yards from the river's edge. He went into the adjoining bush and came back with lengths of wild vine and two thin sticks about twelve feet long. He wrapped some of the vine around his waist and gave one of the youngsters the remaining vine and one of the sticks. Then the two boys, with the net and the sticks, went into the river. They walked and swam, one at each end of the net, whipping the water from time to time and talking non-stop, to the far end and back. This took about ten minutes and as the net was being pulled out, two large crocodiles were spotted behind the fisherman. The net had thirty-one trunk fish caught in it, which apart from the mouths that give them their name, all looked like one pound trout in shape and size. The old man gave me ten and told me that if I could get him a couple of old lorry tyres, from which he could extract the cord for making a larger net, he would supply me with fish every time I camped on the river. These fish were very good eating and had less bones than a trout. They have a very small mouth, which is round like an elephant's trunk, and will not take bait of any kind, as they feed on plankton in the muddy shallows.

That night, I was expecting Pat to arrive with friends from Dodoma and so for a surprise, I gutted the fish, cleaned them well, put a little garlic butter with mustard, salt and pepper inside them, wrapped them in newspaper, mud-packed on the outside and placed them in a hole, covering them with hot ashes. They were delicious and from then on, I suspect, most of my visitors to Ruaha came to sample my fish dishes and not just to see me. Apart from the fish, I would shoot a hippo about once a year and, rendered down, this would give us enough good quality cooking fat for twelve months, in addition to meat protein for my chickens, and dried meat for the dogs. On this same trip, I had to shoot a hippo in camp, the first night, as it took a dislike to my visitor's tent. It frightened them so much that, even after it had been shot, we had to move all their beds into our tent and have a watchman on guard.

Just after the war, in a small town the size of Dodoma, a certain amount of resentment was felt against the ex-servicemen who came back and took over jobs with a higher seniority than those who had been carrying out the work for the duration of the war. In many cases they had to train the ex-servicemen, some of whom had become quite senior with years of experience in how to handle men, and resented having to serve under people who, had they been in the Army, would probably have been their juniors. Pat and I, however, did not experience much of this resentment and within six months or so we were being invited to join the social round. Dinners were held once a month, with a number of families getting together for a meal where we would have drinks and toasties at one house, soup at the next, the main dish at another, and so on. At all the houses we played some game, usually ending up by making "cardinals" of those who had not qualified. This game consists of a memory feat, the forfeit for failure being to drink a full glass of your choice and Pat, who had drunk very little before marrying me, volunteered to become cardinal on sherry and port. After about the fifth attempt, she made the grade, but then the effects of the alcohol took over. We lived out at Kikuyu, three miles out of Dodoma, on the Veterinary farm, and Pat insisted she was going to walk unless I took her home immediately. We set off in the car but, before we had gone very far, we had words so she decided she was going to walk home. I left her in the pitch dark, then took a turning which brought me back along the same road, but behind her and when Pat saw a car, she thumbed a lift, not knowing whose car it was. When she realised it was me, all she said was, "You'll pay for this!" She was asleep within minutes of reaching home and remained in bed all the next day and to the best of my knowledge, Pat has never touched port since.

On the Monday Pat went back to work in the morning but was brought home by Doctor McGregor just after lunch with a high fever. This was her first attack of malaria and Dr. McGregor treated her with a new drug, which had replaced quinine. She was running a temperature of between 103 and 104 degrees and when, on the fourth day, this temperature had shown no signs on subsiding, I asked Dr. McGregor to give her an injection of quinine. However, all he said was that he knew what he was doing, that she was having the correct treatment for malaria and that, in any case, if she had quinine, she would probably lose the baby. I maintained that if she did not have some quinine they would both die. So I consulted Dr. Dickshit, an Asian, who came and examined her and immediately prescribed a quinine injection. This was administered at around ten in the morning and by six o'clock in the evening her temperature had nearly returned to normal. The next morning Pat had her first meal in five days and I had lost one doctor and found another. The baby arrived four days early, weighing just over six pounds, and so I suggested we called her Penny Dickshit Read, but Pat would not hear of it.

In that first year as a livestock marketing officer, because of the aftermath of the war, I was pushed in at the deep end. Very early on, a severe famine developed as the dry season continued well beyond the normal time and, even when the rains did come, they were a failure. The traders tried to force the prices down, knowing that the farmers had to sell their stock in order to get cash for food and markets that normally dealt with one hundred, were handling five hundred head and over. The traders refused to buy and some ran out of cash, and something had to be done. It was decided that I would take over a large piece of land, where there was good grazing, at a place called Makutapora. There was no water so bore holes were sunk and ample water brought to the surface and this water was later to become one of the main sources of supply for Dodoma Town. The Native Treasury, which dealt with the financial matters in the Dodoma area, now financed me in the purchasing of immature and poor-condition animals, which I bought at the markets, and so began my first experience of ranching. Although we lost a few because of their poor condition and the distance they had to travel to reach the ranch, the scheme was a success and gave a financial boost to the Treasury.

On one of my safaris during this period, when I was accompanied by Pat, my staff banged on the roof of the lorry to tell me to stop. A small child had been seen, apparently abandoned in an ant hole by its mother, but the child was already dead, so all we could do was hand the matter over to the local authority. However, shortly after this, on another trip, returning from the Kintinku market late in the evening, we found a little boy of about two years old, running along the road crying. This was in an area heavily infested with game and so we took him to the nearest chief, who later told us that he had been abandoned to the hyenas by his parents, intentionally, since they had no food. On many occasions, the Wagogo would come up to me and admit to crimes they had never committed in order to be taken to jail, so that they would be fed, such were the effects of the drought..

I had to do some official shooting of game on these trips and the meat was used for famine relief. During this famine, I was asked by the District Commissioner to go and clear the Nkungi water haffier of elephant as the Wagogo tribesmen were unable to water their stock. Haffiers are man-made water storage pans, which are common in black cotton areas. This haffier was situated about eight miles out of Dodoma, in a small open vlei (glade) surrounded by thick Mitunduru thorn bush. When I got to within half a mile of it, all I could see apart from the thorn bush was what looked like reddish-brown ant-hills, some of which were moving. The game scout who accompanied me had been down the day before and thought that we should go no further as the elephants were very thirsty and would be aggressive. The numbers certainly frightened me so I had to stop and think carefully about the situation since they were not the relatively tame park elephant.

I was in an old military open-bodied Dodge truck with two-wheel drive. This vehicle seemed fairly safe and looked reasonably formidable, giving one a false sense of security and so I told Asumani, the driver, to move along the track slowly whilst the game scout, a veterinary guard and I stood in the back. I had my Rigby .416 and my double-barrel .450, both powerful rifles known as "elephant guns", loaded and held by the veterinary guard. The game scout was at the other side of the lorry with the standard game department rifle, an equally-powerful single-barrel .404. We reached the edge of the vlei without much happening, only having to stop occasionally to let a slow animal pass. However, this made the game scout over-confident and when we got to the end of the vlei, an old bull would not move out of the track fast enough and the driver went at him. The game scout fired, breaking his front leg, which earned him a severe reprimand, as we always teach our rangers to shoot to kill, if they are going to bother firing at all. I got off the truck to shoot the wounded elephant, when suddenly its younger mate came trumpeting back in a full charge. I managed to get two shots into it before it collapsed into the haffier, and then returned to dispose of the first wounded elephant. By now the elephants had gone and the Wagogo were already taking water and bringing their stock to drink. Before I left, the tribesmen had started cutting up the old bull and the game scout was left to oversee the removal of the tusks, which would be sold to local licensed traders.

I was negotiating with the Public Works Department to send a vehicle down to remove the élephant from the haffier when I got a message from the District Commissioner that a complaint had come in that I had shot an elephant and left it in the haffier to pollute the water. I could not accompany the District Officer who went with the removal vehicle, as I had a market to attend to. I discovered later that, when they got there, they found that the game scout had had great difficulty in recovering the tusks from the old elephant and had refused to allow anyone to start cutting up the other one until the tusks were removed. This meant pushing the floating elephant to the end of the water course and removing the tusks when it was pulled to dry land. The District Officer had to wait for over two hours before the job was completed and the local tribesmen were allowed to cut up the carcass. I had many requests to go and shoot rhino and elephant at Nkungi when the famine was over but the only thing I shot there was duck for the pot.

On my previous monthly market round of Kintinku Kilimatindi, Manyoni, Ikasi and Iseke, Steve, the District Officer at Manyoni, asked me to leave out the Kilimatindi, Iseke and Ikasi markets and accompany him to Simba Nguru where there was a small settlement well to the south of the district. It was the Government's intention to see what could be done for these people who had lost most of their stock because of tsetse fly and who were now starving and dying of sleeping sickness. This sickness, essentially a brain infection, is carried by some types of tsetse fly and can be fatal if not treated properly, which in those days involved a series of unpleasant lumbar injections. These flies also carry tripanosomisus, which can kill untreated cattle, and much of the modern tribal distribution of Tanzania can be traced to whether the pastoralist tribes can take their cattle into a specific area. A track was being cut through the bush so that a vehicle with badly needed food and medical supplies could get through and I arranged my markets so that we would have one whole day to get there, two complete days at Simba Nguru, and a day to return to Dodoma for my attendance at the market there on the Monday.

Simba Nguru lay about thirty miles beyond Iseke, the nearest trading centre, where the track ended. Here there were two Somali shops, a few water-holes about twenty feet deep and a Roman Catholic Missionary who was their only other visitor and who had started visiting the place about once every three months. The reports of the predicament of the Simba Nguru settlement came from the settlement itself, via Iseke. However, no one knew how many people were involved, although it was said that a large proportion of them were game and honey hunters.

Steve (the District Officer) and I left Manyoni in my Ford lorry and were accompanied by the Administration lorry with the men, the Safari Vet and guards. With the food and medical supplies and an extra two tons of maize meal, oil, beans and salt, we eventually reached Iseke after a four-hour drive, where we were told that the track was through to Simba Nguru and there was a guide to show us the way. This guide, who walked in front of the leading vehicle, told us that the settlement had been continuously harassed by elephant and rhino and people had twice been attacked by lion. Rhinos put in several dutiful appearances to prove the point.

We started seeing a great deal of game about ten miles out of Iseke and I have never seen so many Greater and Lesser Kudu either before or since or such fine specimens of Sable Antelope. Indeed the place was teeming with game of all kinds because none of the hunting safaris had, as yet, discovered the area. In the afternoon when we were about twenty miles from Iseke and had stopped for a break beside a square cairn under a large baobab tree, we noticed the trunk had been written on at some time in the past but the words were no longer legible. The guide told us that it was said that a European, probably a member of one of the early exploration parties, had been taken ill, eventually died and left behind here, buried under the cairn. Steve took down all the details and, after further investigation, discovered that the grave belonged to Elton, who was with Speke on their travels to find the source of the Nile in 1862. On the return journey he went down with malaria and had died under this tree. Subsequently, the Administration had the grave properly done up with a memorial in concrete, with a chain surround, but the elephants uprooted and broke it down as soon as the Sikh mason had left. The local people said that this was the dead man's spirit at work, as his resting place had been disturbed.

From here onwards, the track became worse as it became a mass of dried, black, cotton-soil potholes made by elephants' footprints during the wet weather. The whole area was seething with tsetse fly, buffalo fly and the small honey flies which attack one's eyes in search of moisture. It was getting very late and we were about to strike camp for the night, when we came to a river. The small settlement was within sight just upstream of this spot so we made camp under a large, wild fig tree about a hundred yards from the main river bed. We had shot a young male Greater Kudu earlier on for the pot and the smell of the meat attracted hyenas, which spent most of the night disturbing us with their mournful yowling. I had done some of the hardest and most uncomfortable driving I have ever done and was feeling exhausted when one of the staff had just come back from the river-bed and told us that if one dug away the sand at a spot in the river just below the camp, there was good, clear, sweet water. An immediate attack was made with spades and, in no time, there were four holes the size of a bath-tub. The top one we reserved for the kitchen and drinking and the other three were used for a very welcome and refreshing bath under the cool and starry night sky. There were midges biting but they were hardly noticeable after the day's attacks by other insects. We made a large bonfire and after a couple of beers and a typically large safari meal of tinned soup, fresh green beans, potatoes, Kudu liver and kidney and fried eggs, we turned in for the night.

It appeared that the Simba Nguru settlement consisted of about forty families, numbering just over two hundred men, women and children, trying to scrape a living out of the soil. The crops, with the exception of the last season's, had been quite reasonable, but sleeping sickness had killed a number of people and trypanosomiasis had taken its toll of the cattle. Most of the original farmers had left in the past three years for other areas. The Ndorobo who frequented the area, and who were hunters, had saved the lives of the remaining families by providing them with game meat, but now they too had moved on. Steve issued out the food we had brought and I went up river and shot two buffaloes for them. Then in the afternoon we had a baraza (meeting) with the self-appointed headman who had been our guide and a dozen elders. When Steve told them that they would have to prepare to leave the area and be settled at Kilimatinde in the new clearing, they would not contemplate it. All they wanted was food, medicine for themselves and their cattle, and no further interference from the Government. Later in the afternoon, they were sent off to think things over and the Government Tarishi (district runner or policeman) was sent with them to try and persuade them that it was in their best interests.

Steve had two elephant licences which would soon expire, so we took a walk into the bush where we could hear elephants breaking down trees. We had not been walking very long when we came to a bend in the river and saw a herd of about fifty females and calves in the river bed itself. The larger ones were digging holes with their trunks, drinking and watering their young, then covering up the holes before leaving. We just sat on the bank and watched fascinated, while herd after herd came in to drink. When it began to get dark, the bulls came to drink with one of them was carrying over sixty pounds of ivory a side. Steve had never shot an elephant before and became very excited when I told him the size but the Ndorobo who had come with us advised us not to shoot it as it was too small. They said they would show us far bigger ones the next day. This was good news as far as I was concerned, as it was getting too dark for shooting and I had not brought my own rifle along but one I was trying out for someone else, a double-barrelled .475. Fortunately, I had cause to try it out that night on a hyena that was being a nuisance in our camp, only to discover that one of the firing pin tips had broken off. Although we went out again, early next morning, we saw nothing worth shooting.

Later in the morning, we had another meeting with the tribesmen, but the answer was still the same: "We do not want to move from this place". They also refused to name a headman but said they would improve the road from the grave. Steve replied that that would not be necessary as no one would be visiting them. "What about food and medical supplies?" they asked. They were told that a Government representative would be with them in a few days time to make arrangements for those who wanted to leave and the meeting was closed. When the Government transport did arrive, about eighty per cent of them moved and the rest moved under their own steam within the year. Four years later I took a hunting party into the area and although the road had been improved by hunting safaris, the area was completely deserted of human habitation and the still abundant game were very shy, because of the hunting safaris that had been shooting in the area.

When the rains had been going on for about a month and the area around Hanetti was very green, there were a number of large water pools inhabited by different kinds of duck and geese. I had my camp set up under some acacia trees, about five hundred yards from the creamery. I was sitting having my tea before going out to shoot a bird for the pot when a safari outfit with a lorry and two safari trucks turned up, drove about two hundred yards further on and set up camp. There were seven people in the party, including two hunters and long before the first tent was up, seven guns were at work on the birds. The place sounded like a battlefield. Within minutes, all that could be seen were animals and birds fleeing in all directions. I had always made it a rule, whenever I took out a hunting party that I would never allow any shooting within a mile of the camp. I was later invited to have a drink with the party and learned they were an Italian group led by two very young and inexperienced hunters and, happily for me, they left very early the next morning.

Once, while I was shaving outside my tent, an old Gogo tribesman with two grown-up sons came to report that, about three miles away, a leopard had pounced on his young daughter while she was relieving herself during the night. The girl was dead and had been partly eaten. The leopard and the remainder of the body was in a clump of bushes surrounded by tribesmen and the leopard was frightened and very aggressive. I took my Masai veterinary guard, Soito, with me and found the hut from which the girl had been taken about a hundred yards from the clump of bushes. A number of people had heard the girl scream but no one had ventured out to help her and, when at last there were enough men gathered, it was already getting light. By the time I reached the spot there was a group of about a hundred very excited people surrounding the thicket and I had great difficulty in persuading them to keep quiet. Indeed, I had to threaten the local chief that I would leave them to deal with the leopard themselves unless they kept absolutely quiet and still.

When all was reasonably peaceful, Soito, who had a borrowed spear and knobkerrie, and I with a double-barrelled 12-bore shotgun, did a quick reconnoitre. The dense thicket, which was about half an acre in extent, containing a couple of large trees, was fortunately isolated from any other bush by open grassland. We started to approach and just as we were within a couple of yards of the thicket we heard a growling sound like the noise made by a cross-cut saw. The leopard was obviously in a very nasty frame of mind and every time either of us moved, the blood-curdling growl would come from the centre of the dark patch of bush. There was no visible movement, however, and we could not see anything even though we had walked right round the clump, peering in every few yards. There was one place where we could see about eight yards into the thicket. Lying on my back, with Soito protecting me from attack, I ordered the tribesmen to throw stones into the centre of the thicket so as to precipitate movement, which would enable me to get some idea of the animal's position. However, this did not have the desired effect and only succeeded in triggering off noise from the tribesmen all over again, so Soito and I pulled out for a rest to re-establish quiet and make a plan.

After some discussion, we decided it was no good trying to get help from the Wagogo, so Soito found an old blanket which he wrapped round his left arm and in his right hand he took a sharp *panga* (machete). I stood guard as he bent down and hacked away at the bush and with each stroke, we could feel we were getting nearer and the tension was mounting. Suddenly, about six yards away, I saw a slight movement which looked like the leopard's tail and tracing the dark object to where the head was, pressed my knee on Soito's back to stop him. The leopard began to move into position and gave me a reasonable view of its head and I fired a single shot and waited for the attack. With the second shot the leopard slipped a couple of feet where it was caught and suspended in the branches. The tribesmen still would not enter the thicket until we had pulled the dead leopard out. It was a lovely dark forest leopard, its only blemish being a newly healed arrow wound in its right leg. The child was about seven years old and her left shoulder and part of her stomach had already been eaten. The arrow wound in the leopard's leg must have incapacitated him so he had become a village follower rather than an effective game hunter. To end the whole affair, the girl's father demanded ten shillings for showing me the leopard.

On my way to the next market at Gulwe it started to rain and the road grew worse as we approached. We finally reached the Gulwe River a little after two in the morning, the river was in full flood and it was still raining. The market was about a mile away on the opposite bank and it was ten o'clock before we could get a rope across, a necessary precaution because most of the market staff could not swim. The lorry would certainly be unable to cross the river for at least another two days - if then - and even if it did get over, it would never negotiate the fifteen miles of black cotton soil to Kintinku. It was one of those days when nothing went right. We could not get the cattle in the pens as the owners would not go out in the light rain and then, when we eventually got them in, the Somali and Arab traders refused to cross the river. I felt like closing both these markets but could not do so as the area was still suffering from the after-effects of the famine. The last animal in the ring was sold just after three o'clock and I waded across the river to collect sufficient kit for a one-night stop at Kintinku. Then a small staff contingent and I set off on foot, eventually reaching

Kintinku station five hours later. The rain had stopped, yet the station was full of people and it transpired that there had been a couple of man-eating lions in the area and a woman had been killed in the last forty-eight hours. The station, with all its lights on, was considered to be the safest place and when I turned up with my rifle, I was made most welcome. They expected me to go and look for the lions there and then. Apart from the futility of the idea, I was in no state to hunt anything, let alone two man-eaters! I had had no sleep or food since the night at Hanetti and had just walked fifteen miles over rough, muddy ground while being eaten voraciously by mosquitoes. The stationmaster, an Asian, produced a pot of very sweet tea, which was welcomed by both Akbar Walimohamed (the market master) and me. We could not get a fire going as everything was too wet and we were all too tired and so the six of us in my party moved to the western end of the station and tried to get some sleep on the wet ground. The cattle market was situated a few hundred yards away and we could hear the corralled cattle calling. The lions were also aware of the potential and roared throughout the night, and seeming to come closer and closer as time went on. Some of my men kept pointing into the dark, saying they could see them. I began to wish I had not left Soito behind and started to get jittery like the rest of them, when out of the semi-dark dawn, a figure appeared. It turned out to be Songiek, my Ndorobo game scout.

- "Suba Oljore Lai, (Hello my friend). Why do you, a man of respect, sleep out here on the wet soil, when the Asian station master has a good dry bed and a warm wife that you should have?".

-"I sleep out here because these people you see are worried about the lions and they think I can protect them".

-"But they should know these lions; they have lived here since I was a young man and have never done anyone any harm", he replied.

-"I am told that they have killed a woman in the last couple of days".

- "That was not here. That was Kilimatinde, up the escarpment.

Now, I have found a very large elephant, that will take four people to carry each tusk, but we must move fast as it will be moving on with the rains."

I spent the next hour trying to persuade Songiek that we would have to forget the elephant on this trip, as I had neither the time, inclination, nor the correct rifle. He eventually saw my point and, instead of hunting elephant, stayed to help at the market. He was in fact quite right about the lions, as Ndorobo inevitably are, as the woman had been killed some way off. The lions we saw were local opportunists, attracted to the presence of cattle and any stories of man-eaters was rumour and imagination.

We sold some eight hundred head of cattle that day and afterwards caught the goods train down to Gulwe. The river was still up but it was not raining and a camp had been set up with hot food and a proper bed. I didn't like the idea of wading through the river, so I arranged with the train driver, a man called Miller, to stop the other side of the bridge and let us off and we had only about half a mile to walk to camp when the most wonderful smell of roast beef assailed us. There stood a camp table, complete with a bottle of Indian Pale Ale, brewed in Dar-es-Salaam, the best beer East Africa has ever produced, in my opinion. Seweji, my Safari servant was not a particularly good cook but he excelled himself on this occasion. He had made my favourite roast meat on the open fire accompanied by sweet potatoes in their jackets and rice pudding. A good meal, a good bed and good comfortable drive back to Dodoma finished the trip off very nicely, and my overall feeling was that it was all well earned by all.

Chapter Eight
Cattle Markets, Groundnuts and Safaris

One day, on my way to the Kongwe and Pandambili markets, I came across a convoy of five lorries stuck in the black cotton soil near the Kenya-Sungwe river. It was already late and there was no question of me getting past the vehicles blocking the road, so I decided to camp a couple of hundred yards away, on higher ground. Seweji reminded me that we had no fresh meat and said there was a herd of impala not far away. I answered that I did not feel like impala - but he pointed out that the others in the party also had stomachs and could do with some meat after a hard day. He suggested I could then go and get myself a duck, guinea-fowl or yellow-necked spurfowl, with which the place was teeming, but first he needed an impala, and added that if it was a good young one, I could have some liver for breakfast. I did as I was bid and then went to one of the pools and shot two fat, knob-nosed geese. I was returning to camp when a European approached me. He turned out to be Jimmy MacIntyre, one of the Lupa men, in charge of a lorry convoy going to Kongwe.

-"What are you doing here?", he asked.

I was about to reply, when he stopped me, saying,

-"My men are starving for meat and I haven't got my rifle. Be a sport and shoot something for us, before it gets too dark."

The place was full of impala, so I shot them a big male. Jimmy returned with me to my tent, where he stayed the night, after sending for his bed and a bottle of Scotch to be brought from his camp. I learned from him that the British Labour government had approved, and was going ahead with, what became infamously known as the "Groundnut Scheme".

After the war Britain was short of many commodities, one of which was cooking oil, and the oil from groundnuts, or peanuts, were considered to be a particularly good quality. Tanganyika was also in need of foreign revenue, and so the Government of the day decided, without consulting local or specialist knowledge, that three large planting schemes in Tanganyika would be a good thing. Finally, the areas of Kongwa, Irambo and Mtwara were chosen, few people know why but rumour has it because some local African farmers had a few groundnut plants growing in their allotments. However, instead of getting decent farming equipment and specialist consultants to survey and prepare the scheme, the British Army were called in and put to work using military equipment, so as to save money on labour and equipment.

Jimmy was not very happy about his predicament, as he had to return to Nairobi for yet another load of equipment but next morning we managed to get all the lorries out of the black mud and went the long way round through Mpwapwa to Kongwe. I left him to set up his camp and went on to the market, where there were only a few animals for sale, however there was an elderly European present who seemed to be taking an unusually keen interest. As most white people, with the exception of Government officials, usually avoided the markets, I began to be curious about him and when he talked to my Asian market master, I asked if I could be of any assistance. He introduced himself as Thomas Bain, adviser and consultant to the Overseas Food Corporation, the Organisation that would be attempting to grow the groundnuts in the nearby Kongwa region. He told me that he farmed nearby in the mountains and would probably be supplying Kongwe and its expatriate staff with all their fresh supplies, suggesting that if I co-operated with him and gave him help in buying the right type of cattle, he would make it worth my while. I pointed out that I could not do the actual buying for him, as I priced the animals, but so long as he got authority from the Veterinary Department at Mpwapwa, I would give him all the assistance I could. I also told him of Jimmy MacIntyre's arrival in the area, and he wanted to know where Jimmy was setting up camp but I could only explain where I had left him, and so he got into his car and drove off in the direction I had given.

After closing down the market for the day, I visited a Masai friend of mine who was having a spear made for me by one of the old Masai Wakwavi spear-makers. There were very few traditional blacksmiths left and their handiwork was becoming valuable, although the quality was not as good as those made in Birmingham at a quarter of the cost. The next morning I collected my Masai friend and took him to Pandambili with me so as to visit the spear-maker after the market but unfortunately, he still had not started on my spear, which often took over two or more years to complete. The old man explained that he had many orders, and had to travel a long way for the ironstone and that the youngsters, who worked the bellows for the fire, were lazy. He showed me his factory, which consisted of a smelting pot made of clay, air-fed by a large hand-operated wood and hide bellows, and a heap of iron ore, which is the material used in traditional Masai Spears. In another room was a fire with smaller bellows, similar to the others, where three men were shaping *simis* (machetes) from pieces of old railway sleeper. They worked on proper anvils, using modern hammer heads, but besides them were the traditional tools of their trade including home-made tongs and earthenware pots containing water, which were the crucibles in which the ore was smelted, pieces of sacking and sheepskin gloves. On another occasion, I had tried to visit this same place with Pat, but was not allowed anywhere near the factory because women were not permitted to see the men working, believing that it would make the weapons become weak, like women, and so would fail to give men confidence when using them. The interesting thing about spears and their role in Masai life is that whilst the spears are incredibly important, the craftsman who make them are not. A Masai will be able to identify his spear amidst a pile of twenty identical copies, such is his devotion to it, but the Ndorobo who make them are lower caste Masai. The reason for this is that the Ndorobo are not cattlemen, spending their time making spears instead of tending their herds, and as such are not considered to be real Masai.

Apart from my livestock marketing job, I was manager of the Dodoma Experimental Farm and when I returned from my Kongwe safari, it was reported to me that hyenas were eating the young maize cobs there. My reaction was that I had never heard of four-legged hyenas eating maize before but perhaps, by some chance, could the culprits be two legged hyenas? The crop assistant who was making the report said that I should take a look at the field before making any further comment. Having seen the field, I realised that the destruction was indeed being caused by real hyenas - and a large number of them- that had destroyed most of the twenty-acre field leaving it fit for little else other than silage. That night, a couple of friends and I sat up in the field and waited for them. We shot five, but there were many more and a few nights later I was called out and told that the hyenas were now attacking the pigs. The hyenas had broken down the sty and a whole pen of seven fully-grown porkers was missing. The hyenas had been chased away when I got there but one of the porkers had been found, badly mauled, four others were found with no injuries and the remaining two were later discovered hiding in a nearby shed. The next day I had to go on safari but before leaving I gave instructions for a petrol *debe* trap to be baited with pieces of meat. This trap consisted of a four gallon petrol or paraffin tin, with the square top cut in the shape of a cross. The sharp points towards the centre of the cross were then pushed down, and a piece of meat tied inside to the bottom of the tin. The cut flaps stop the hyena from withdrawing its head, and in the dark it is blinded and makes its objection heard, bumping into everything in its way until the waiting watchman disposes of the hyena. On my return a week later, no less than seventeen hyenas had been trapped in this way and the remainder got the hint and moved away.

Not very long after the pig episode, two workers from the abattoir that I was occasionally doing some work for, were coming back from town in the early hours of the morning, very drunk. They had difficulty in clambering up the bank of a sand river next to the abattoir and presumably fell asleep in the river. The hyenas smelt them and all that was found the next morning was one foot in a shoe. Up until this time, there had been a small section of the community in Dodoma who disapproved of my methods of controlling the hyena population but after this incident an order was issued that hyena poisoning would be carried out for a whole week under veterinary, game and police control. Volunteers were called to assist in the operation and nearly all the able-bodied Europeans in Dodoma offered their services so that by the end of the week, together with those I trapped, over fifty hyena were accounted for in the Dodoma-Behuana area.

Every three months I had to arrange the Kondoa-Irangi district markets, which I did not look forward to as there were only a few small cattle produced for sale. The people would appear at one market, refuse to sell, do the same at the next and so on, until the last market, by which time the animal would have lost weight and the price would be down. They would then beg for the original price, with long hard luck stories about how ill their children had been or how the crops had failed so they now had no money to buy food etc and it was all rather gruelling.

There was, however, some light relief for on this particular safari, Pat was not working and I had taken her with me. Our first stop was at a place called Farkwa where there was a large Italian Roman Catholic Mission and I was arranging our camp, when a European appeared on a motor-bike, introducing himself as Father Valentino who insisted that we break the camp and stay at the mission. Eventually, after much discussion, we agreed to go to the mission for dinner, which was served in what I can only assume was the Sisters' mess. We were given what Father Valentino called his "Farkwa Wine No.1", which was clear, like gin, but definitely much stronger. Pat had just one but I had managed three when food was placed on the table. It was one of the best chicken stews I have ever tasted, served with home-made pasta, followed by a delicious, fresh fruit salad with cream, accompanied by home-made red wine which was named "Farkwa No.2". After coffee, just as we were about to leave, Father Valentino produced his trump card, a golden liqueur, which was called "Valentino Specials" and tasted very similar to a smooth Curacao. Like the wines, it had a kick like a horse and whilst I was no novice to drink, the combination got the better of me. I only just managed to do the mile long drive to our camp, but to our surprise we both woke up the following morning with clear heads. As a result of this, when I was due to go to the area again, my boss Gordon Pevie volunteered to come with me, with the aim of testing the Farkwa water of which I had talked so much. After lunch and some three Farkwa No. 1's, he overshot the small bridge at the bottom of the hill and it took me, the priests and the help of some fifty local people nearly three hours to get his box-body International on to its wheels and on he road again.

.From Farkwa, Pat and I moved to the guest-house, one of the better guest houses it must be mentioned at Kondoa Irangi. Having settled in, we were told that there was a cobra in the lavatory, which had already spat at a child, which was enough to put the lavatory out of bounds for us. We had just begun our evening meal when two European women arrived and asked if we had any objection to their sharing the next room, as they had no camping equipment. We raised no objection and the ladies joined us for a drink, introducing themselves as Jane and Mary. Mary was dark, petite and feminine with long hair, and was rather shy whilst Jane was a tallish blonde, with short-cut hair, wearing a safari suit with bullet pockets on her well-developed chest. She never stopped talking about her elephant shooting escapades and told us she was looking for a large bull elephant and did I have any idea where she could find some. The relationship between these two women was quite obvious and I do not think they were trying to hide anything but what fascinated both Pat and me was the way Jane tried to be male in everything, including mannerisms and speech. Also, it seemed odd to us to go to the trouble of travelling over five hundred miles on the pretext of looking for elephant to shoot, when she has already established that they had them on their doorsteps.

After we had all had another drink, the two women went out into the bush, with their loo rolls, and when Jane was out of the room, Pat turned to me and asked me to go out with her, so she could have a pee, as she was wary of the cobra squatter in the toilet. Pat had never 'peed' squatting on the ground before and she felt Jane would laugh at her if she asked them. She was having difficulty as there was nothing to hold on to, so I told her to hold on to my leg, when I suddenly felt a warm trickle down my safari boot. Needless to say, the story of this trip to Farkwa and Kondoa spread around Dodoma and if anyone wanted to draw a blush from Pat after this, all they had to do was mention Kondoa, Irangi or safari boots.

On our return journey, we were held up twice by the floods caused by heavy seasonal rain. We eventually reached the Kelema River, a large sand river, half a mile across and there seemed to be no possibility of crossing it. Eight vehicles, of different sizes, in front of us had already set up camp on our bank, while on the far side there were more vehicles marooned. As we were going to have to camp there for between two to ten days, I contemplated moving back and off the road, when a voice from behind me said "What do you think you are doing here?" It was my old friend Albert Levy, the veterinary stock route inspector who I knew was working in the vicinity of Kelema village, but that was on the opposite bank. We went down to Albert's camp, where we stayed for the next two days, and met another old friend Fujo, which in Swahili means 'nuisance'. That's exactly what he was too, but a very likeable nuisance, for Fujo was a white Bull Terrier belonging to a man called Tomlinson, who was in the Administration at Mbulu. Unfortunately, Tomlinson had to be taken into the Mental Hospital at Dodoma, where he was being treated. One day when he seemed to be quite sane, he somehow managed to get the keys to his cell, locked the Doctor in his cell and walked to Dodoma station, where he terrorised the staff and passengers of a train before he was taken into custody again. The medical people at Dodoma could not cope with him so he was sent back to England and so Pevie inherited his dog and, when he went on overseas leave, Fujo was passed on to me. It was difficult for me to cope with him, as I was on safari most of the time and, if left behind, Fujo would attempt to kill any dog that came onto the farm - so he was passed on to Albert, who cared for him until Fujo died of fly, some two years later.

The following day, one of the lorries, driven by the Asian owner from the opposite side of the river, tried to cross and was doing very well, until it slid off the concrete drift. The driver managed to get out and swim ashore about half a mile down river, but the lorry, complete with its load, completely disappeared into the sand, never to be seen again and so we camped out a little longer. Finally, the level of the water started to go down quickly, and the following day we crossed without any difficulty and returned to Dodoma.

I took part of my local leave in Tabora with my mother, as Pat was paying a visit to England. My mother had started up her dress shop but it was not going too well and she needed a little moral support, of which Tabora was distinctly lacking. Tabora was famous for three reasons: Firstly, most of the old explorers, like Livingstone, Stanley, Speke, Burton etc. had used Tabora as an inland headquarters, secondly, as the Tabora mango fruit is the biggest and best, and thirdly, for the number and extraordinary behaviour of its lions. One evening, my mother and I had gone up to the Club for a drink and to see some old friends. As we entered, we heard roars of raucous laughter from the bar, and a voice shouted "Ma Fish, (Fischer) you must hear this one!" It transpired that a man, whom I will call Tom, had been drinking rather a lot and as Tom's home was not very far from the Club, he preferred to walk. It was recounted by some of the regular members that Tom had gone home after a fairly heavy evening but had only been gone a very short time before he returned to the Club, where he sat very quietly. When one of the men, Neil McLeod, said that he was going home, Tom approached him for a lift as far as his house and so Neil obliged and took him home. Three nights later, Neil asked if anyone had seen Tom since that night but no one had, so they went over to Tom's house to investigate, where they found him quietly reading a newspaper, without a drink, adamant that there was nothing wrong. After a little persuasion, Tom agreed to come to the Club, on condition he was packed off home after three drinks, "Doctor's instructions" he said. At the bar he overheard someone say that something would have to be done about the lioness which was keeping the whole town on tenterhooks by appearing in unexpected places. Tom asked if anyone in the Club had seen it and was told that most of them had seen it, at some time or other during the last few days, on the golf-course. Tom immediately ordered drinks all round and announced that he would not be going home after his third drink after all. He then told them that on the night he left the Club, he was walking home on the far side of the golf-course when, in the moonlight, he walked up to within five yards of a lion. He had tried to shoo it off but the lion would not move and so he started to move back towards the Club, sure that the lion was following him, only for it to suddenly disappear. This incident had convinced him that he had succumbed to delirium tremens. ("D.T.s") and caused his sudden resolution to be more sober.

Upon my return to Dodoma, I still had a week's leave left when I heard a report that a special elephant I had been after for over a year had returned to a water-hole near Bahi, where it had been the previous year. I went to Bahi, where I picked up Legesana, my tracker, and set up camp, half a mile from the water hole. There were only two trees of any size near the water hole and we chose the smaller of these in which to build a hide-out platform which we completed the following day. It was reported that this particular elephant watered every second night, and it was due again on the night the platform was completed. My veterinary guard, Yusuf, wanted to accompany Legesana and me in the hide-out and I reluctantly agreed, not knowing how he would behave and so we finally entered the hide just as it was getting dark. I gave Yusuf the torch and told him to switch it on after I had fired the first shot and not before, and that, until then, I did not want to hear a sound from him. At about half past eight, two females and a calf came, watered and went in the opposite direction, downwind. When they got scent of our presence, they turned to face us and stopped for what seemed a long three minutes, then turned and continued their safari. The moon was up and the light was quite good. Two more elephant appeared out of the bush, about three hundred yards away, but the clouds covered the moon and they could not be seen until they were close enough for their rumblings could be heard. Eventually the cloud cover moved on to reveal hulking across the illuminated plain, the old elephant we were waiting for. Everything then became dark again but the two elephants were near enough to be seen reasonably well, passing about thirty yards to our left and taking a drink before heading back the same way as they had come. The younger one approached the tree near to the one we were in, and began playing with it so that we could clearly see the tree moving back and forth before it was pulled down. I was ready to fire but only if it came to our tree despite the animated Yusuf, who was nudging me, pointing to the elephant, trying to encourage me to shoot it.

About a hundred yards behind him, stood another elephant - the one I was after. However, the tree falling down was too much for Yusuf so he shone the torch at the elephant and this frightened them off and we heard the whole herd breaking through the bush in a general stampede. Legesana had lost a bonus of two hundred shillings and I thought I was about to see a murder committed when he hit Yusuf on the head with the butt of his rifle and was about to repeat it when I stopped him. The following morning, Legesana and I picked up the spoor of Bahi (the name I had given to the elephant) and over the next two days, I must have covered over fifty miles with Legesana looking for him, spending our nights in trees, taking turns to stay awake. Some elephants came to the water, but nothing with tusks big enough to shoot. Bahi had disappeared and he was not sighted again for over two months, when he was seen near Kilimatinde. When I dropped Legesana off at Bahi he told me that, if I wanted to shoot his elephant, I should bring with me only Soito, my Masai guard, since he did not want to go after big animals with a woman! Then he turned to Yusuf, saying that he had better thank the *musungu* (European) for saving his life!

Just a year, and two elephant later, I was at the Bahi market when Legesana came running up to me with a large grin on his face and a request to discuss a small matter with me in private. We walked a few yards away from the cattle ring and he told me that the elephant Bahi was in a thicket about two miles away, waiting for me to shoot him. I was not to tell anyone or take anyone else with me and I could get no more out of him until we were in the car about an hour later. Then he told me that he had been following Bahi for the last two days and that there was another *musungu* from Manyoni who was also tracking him. That morning, on his way to market, Legesana had again picked up Bahi's spoor and suddenly came upon him so he had shot him in the leg to stop him getting away. I was horrified but I said very little until after I had killed the elephant and put it out of its agony. I do not think Legesana ever understood why I got so annoyed with him despite my attempts to explain how much pain the animal had suffered. As far as he was concerned, it wasn't my pain, so what was all the fuss about? After this, Legesana never told me about any good-sized animals.

Dodoma market was always held on a Monday and the same old faces were usually there. One of these was Forte, the Greek butcher, who always brought his cattle at this market and he was the only European to attend regularly. On this particular Monday, however, there was an extra European present, in the form of Mr. Thomas Bain who was there to buy cattle for the Groundnut Scheme at Kongwe. I asked to see his licence and I told him that he would have to get one from the Revenue Officer before I would let him buy any cattle. This didn't please him very much although he did go and get the licence. I could see that he was very annoyed when he returned so I went over to him and explained that I couldn't allow the licensing laws to be broken, especially with the Somalis watching for me to make the wrong move. The Somalis considered that Bain had no right to attend the markets and that he should buy from them and, to make matters worse, both the Somalis and Arabs had tendered for this particular contract, only for it to be given to a complete outsider, so they felt somewhat bitter. On the other hand, had they been given this contract, it is likely that they would have tried to use it to break the grade and weight systems, to give the unscrupulous buyers control over the farmers. Bain asked me to do his buying for him but, as on the previous occasion, I had to say that this was impossible. However I agreed to keep an eye open for him and give his buyer a helping hand, provided Bain got the necessary permission from my department, which he did, and I became a regular visitor to Kongwe.

Three months later it was Christmas, and Bain asked me if he would be permitted to give my wife a radiogram. I pointed out that neither my wife nor I were allowed to accept gifts of this nature, however, I went on to say that I realised it was his way of showing his appreciation for the help I had given him. As Bain made bacon and ham, I accepted a ham and an invitation to stay with him and so whilst on my next trip to Turiani, where my brother Norman farmed, I spent a night with the Bains and had a very good time. Next morning, a box containing some ham and sausage was put into the car and, just as we were leaving, Bain gave Pat a box of chocolates, which was found to contain a hundred pounds in twenty shilling notes. So, on the way back, I thanked him but asked him not to do it again. He insisted that I should get a bonus for money I was putting into his pocket, so I told him that when I left the veterinary department to farm on my own, if he still felt the same way, he could help me then. Five years later, when I started farming, I wrote to him asking for a loan of five hundred pounds, which I would return within one year but received a letter back saying that I should approach my Bank instead.

Kongwe, the first of the three great Groundnut Schemes, was forging ahead. It was 1947 and I was running at least three markets a month in the area, and had come to know quite a number of people working on the Groundnut Scheme. Nearly all of them were ex-service men and a large proportion of their equipment was ex-Army surplus. The men were generally known by their Army rank, both officers and N.C.O's and some of them had even been promoted for their work on the "Kongwe battlefield". I was continually being invited to stay but I preferred my own tent and camping staff and would usually only go over for a drink or meal in the mess. There was one occasion, when Pat was with me, when I managed to seize up my engine about sixteen miles from Kongwe, on the Dodoma road. A lorry with a winch was sent from Kongwe to pull me out and it towed me all the way to the Kongwe workshop where, a young officer greeted us and asked us if we needed any assistance. I told him what had happened, whereupon he transferred all our luggage to his car, told a sergeant to look after my car, and if he was unable to get it going by morning, to organise transport for me to the market. We then left for the mess where we were given a fully equipped tent. After a wash and change we went over to the mess where the officer introduced us to some people, including Alan Bobbitt, who had been one of the Warrant officers training us in the Kenya Regiment. The sergeant who was looking at my car came to tell me that something was wrong with the distributor and I would need a new one. When I told him the engine had seized up, he told me to forget all about it and that when I returned from the market, my car would be ready.

I woke up next morning with a hangover, only to find a driver and vehicle waiting for me. I arrived back from the market at about six in the evening and there, outside our tent, was my car, tuned up and ready to go, with a note, gummed to the steering wheel, suggested I drive slowly and change the oil at the end of the first thousand miles. The engine, radiator and battery were all brand new! How was I going to pay for all this? Fortunately both Lewis (the officer) and Jack were in the mess when I got there and so I thanked them both for everything and asked how much I owed for the car.

"Nothing" came the reply. "But there are still one or two things that need doing, so when you can spare it for three full days, we will do them," added Jack.

It transpired that Jimmy was the man who had seen me stuck and had the lorry sent out to rescue us. He had told the workshop about the time I had helped him out, and this was his method of repaying me but there was just one small favour Lewis asked of me. He and Jack wanted to become members of the Dodoma Club, and wondered if I could help? Apparently, a few hotheads had got drunk down there, created a scene at the bar and were made to leave. On the way out, they intentionally damaged three saloon cars in the car park before leaving and so membership of the Club, for Kongwe personnel, was therefore closed for the time being unless they were recommended by either a member of the committee or a long-standing member. Luckily, at the time, I fell into both categories and having told my story, got them both accepted.

On the whole, the people who were at Kongwe were a very pleasant and acceptable crowd but, like all large groups of people away from home ground, some were inclined to be a bit uncontrollable at times and, of course, there were the misfits. I always got on very well with them, since they were all ex-servicemen like myself. Unfortunately for the Groundnut Scheme, the people at the top were also ex-Servicemen who knew little or nothing about business, farming or local conditions and were trying to run things like an Army organisation. The whole project turned out to be a complete and very expensive fiasco and had to be abandoned as a groundnut producing venture, not only at Kongwe but also in the other areas at Irambo and Mtwara. The Kongwe scheme was later turned into a Ranching Project, with local Europeans to manage it, which proved to be one of the few Government Agricultural success stories. In view of the size of the original Groundnut Scheme, which was being paid for by the British taxpayer, a railway line was laid from Masagali to Kongwe, a distance of about twenty miles. This was done long before there were any groundnuts to transport and has since been abandoned. It was said, and I believe it to be true, that where the railway ended and before a station was built, an area on both sides of the track was cleared. On one side, cement was stacked, and on the other, fertiliser. When the time came for fertilising the fields, cement was used, and it was only when the builders ran out of cement, that it was discovered this had been used on the fields. I understand they had great difficulty in harvesting the groundnuts that year.

Another incident occurred when they were collecting sand in the Kinyasungwe dry river bed. One of the veterinary officers, who worked at the research station Mpwapwa, had lived in the area for a considerable time, and driving by at night, noticed all the large earth-moving machinery left in the river bed for the night. He warned the people concerned that this practice was unwise, as when it rained higher up, the water swept down in considerable flood but was told "not to teach his grandmother how to suck eggs!" Shortly afterwards, the work force arrived one morning, only to find the river in flood, as predicted, and a large number of the heavy units submerged. Some of the units were recovered but in unworkable condition and others are probably still embedded there. One of the things that the Scheme did do was to turn Mpwapwa into a thriving small town. Although the Groundnut Scheme as such was not a success, it did help the country by bringing technicians to East Africa, and a great many of these people still remain in the various independent countries on the African continent.

I was driving along the Iringa-Dodoma road, in the bright sun of a late afternoon, when I heard a very distinct roaring noise. I looked to the right, where the sound appeared to be coming from but could see nothing. As I was crossing a dry river bed - about a hundred yards wide - the noise seemed to get louder and my market staff, on the back of the pick-up, started shouting. As I cast around to find out what the shouting was about, I saw a wall of brown water and trees, at least ten foot high, like a dirty wave, rolling and roaring towards me. When I put my foot hard on the accelerator, luckily the wheels did not spin and the pick-up dashed across the river-bed and up the bank on the far side, getting splashed as we continued up the bank. I went about one hundred yards further along the road before stopping to look back at this phenomenon, and was thankful we had not stalled. I had two Somali cattle traders with me and they both got out of the car and started to pray, while the market master and I approached the river on foot. There was no sign of rain up river, or for that matter, anywhere else but it was obvious that, in the upper reaches of this dry river bed, great destruction had been done as there were large miombo trees, some at least forty feet tall and livestock of all types intermingled with the still rising, swirling water. When we returned to the car, the two Somalis told me they thought this was a warning to them not to contest the census that I was to carry out that night. The Government had decided there was to be a general African census throughout the country and I was to deal with the Somalis, who objected on the grounds that they were not Somalis but Isakia, who came from Asia, and were not therefore Africans. The two men I had with me were the Somali Traders' Community representatives and I was asked to take them to the District Commissioner who, at the time, was Jock Griffiths, where they would put their case. I was told that the Somali census would be postponed for the time being. The two Somalis then asked me to join them that night at the 'end-of-Ramadan' feast, as they wished to pray and thank me for delivering them safely from the river hazard. Being strict Moslems and on a sacred fast, they had no intoxicating liquor and I was persuaded to try some *Murungi* (miraa) a small young plant also known as *qat*, which at first has a bitter astringent flavour and works as a stimulant. Because of this, I was able to remain at the feast until daylight without feeling tired, but I was unable to sleep the next night either.

The next day, I had to attend the Hanetti market fourty miles north of Dodoma. Fortunately, there were only a few head of cattle for sale, as the rains had started and most of the cattle had moved away from the permanent water-holes to dry areas where the grazing was better. On my way home, I saw a small herd of Kudu and one male had a lovely spread, (that is to say a good head with a large distance between his horns) and so I decided to bag him. Greater Kudu in this area were very shy and would nearly always make for the *Mitunduru* thorn thicket, which this herd did and so I followed, as much to shake off my hangover as to get the Kudu. I had not gone very far when Yusuf, my Veterinary guard, tapped me on the shoulder and pointed to the animal through the thicket. I fired and the buck went down and I made my way up to him through the thicket. He had not, as I thought, been shot through the heart, but through the spine and was very much alive. I was about to finish him off, when I noticed the look he gave me, as much as to say "What harm have I done you?" I killed him cleanly, but I never forgot the baleful expression he gave me, and this has put me off shooting for fun ever since. I still shoot for the pot, to save others or destroy pests but never for the sake of shooting for record heads or sport.

On one of my trips to Ikasi, one of the Catholic fathers asked me for a lift, which I was pleased to give him. Unfortunately, I was in one of the old Army Fords, which has the hot engine situated between the driver and the only passenger seat. The father was wearing old, rubber-soled shoes, which I don't think he had ever taken off and the smell in the hot cabin was soon unacceptable. When we got to Ikasi, he told me that he would be staying the night with a friend for which I was very relieved - I could not savour the thought of surviving the smell all night in a tent. Unfortunately, thinking that he was well set up in the area, I asked him round for a drink that evening but when he turned up for the drink and supper, he asked if he could sleep on the floor in the tent, as his friend was away. He was an extremely pleasant man, who liked his drink and was very worldly in his outlook but by the next morning I had decided that if I ever saw him again, even in the desert, miles away from anywhere, I would pretend I had not seen him. My tent stank for days and even now, fifty years later, if I see a hitch-hiker wanting a lift, my first thought is "What are his feet like?"

It had been raining heavily in Bahi, and the pools in the swamp had filled up, allowing the large Barbels (cat fish) to come out of hibernation. These fish, which in this area grow up to sixty pounds in weight, spend about four months hibernating in the hard, dry mud until their dried, black cotton soil casing softens with rain and they are able to swim away. At this stage, the fish are very vulnerable, as they are weak from the effects of hibernation and the water is very shallow. It is at this time that the local fishermen have a plentiful food supply, cutting the fish up and drying them by smoke and sun. The duck and geese were also starting to come in and, within a week, the whole country would be green as the small pools join up to form larger pools, thronging with bird life. The Bahi depression of some one hundred and fifty square miles, changes from a quiet desert to look like a game park, but no vehicle, except the train, will be able to move in this paradise until the rains are over. Its ecological rhythm is, I believe, rather similar to that of the Etosha Pan in Namibia.

I only just managed to finish the group of markets in time to get to Manyoni, from where all the market staff, traders and all our vehicles had to be railed back to Dodoma. On arrival at Dodoma station, I was greeted by Pat, with a new Ford pick-up.

- "Where did you borrow that from?" I asked.

-"You!" was the answer. "And George Kipris (the garage owner) has taken the other one, at the price you agreed".

That evening at the Club I was asked if I would shoot some duck for a party to be held over the weekend. A young vet, Peter Lake, asked if he could come along with his dogs, two Labradors, of which he was very proud, and boasted about their breeding. The idea sounded good so the next day Pat, Peter, his two dogs and my spaniel Winston set off for the Mwitikira market in my new car. The market finished early so, after a quick picnic lunch, we went to a swamp nearby for some duck shooting. Peter turned out to be a good shot and, from where I was, I saw at least eight birds drop. Between Winston and myself, we had recovered all five of mine, which I dropped in the car with Pat before going over to see what Peter was doing. He had four birds by his side, another five were in the water and the two dogs appeared to be playing with some others in the reeds. Peter tried everything to get them back but the dogs would not move from the water until he eventually gave up in despair and Winston was sent in, adding another six birds to the nine we had already collected in a very short time. We then moved round the swamp and got another eight, but this time the Labradors were not allowed out of the car. Peter moved to Mbulu after this, and I am told that he did eventually get his dogs trained but Winston had never been trained and I assume he retrieved by instinct.

The roads along the railway line, both east and west of Dodoma, were now impassable because of the rain, so all the markets along the line had to be reached by rail. On my way back from the Gulwe market, when the train stopped at Kikombo station, a delegation of tribesmen asked me to assist them by shooting a leopard, which was worrying their small stock. They said it was on a goat kill at that particular moment, less than five hundred yards from the station. The Station Master told me that there was another train due in less than two hours so I had no alternative but to let the train go on, bearing Seweji, my kit and all. Sure enough, in a small thicket of light bush, was a leopard up a tree, keeping watch over its kill, which had been partly eaten. At about fifty yards, I put a bullet straight into its brain; it was the easiest leopard I had ever dealt with and within half an hour of my arriving in Kikombo station, the leopard was being skinned under Yusuf's supervision, and I was about to sit down to a curry lunch with the Station Master.

The grade and weight method of marketing cattle had been well established in the Dodoma district. It was approved by the seller, because he knew he would get a fair price for his stock all the year round, as the traders (buyers) could no longer form trading rings and it was decided that the rest of the Province should adopt this system. I was asked to go to Singida, to organise the local veterinary people, administer the construction of new market arenas and set up the organisation for weighing and grading for which I would have to train another officer. Pat was now pregnant again and suffering badly from morning sickness but even so she wanted to go on this safari, which would last about ten days. On our arrival, we went direct to the Singida Hotel, which was exactly as it had been in 1933 when I stayed there with my parents on our way from the Lupa - the same old open drains (as mentioned in my book "Barefoot over the Serengeti") ran through the middle of all the rooms and so forth. The only difference was that it had previously been owned by Germans, but was now owned by Greeks. One look was enough for me, and Pat felt the same way, so we went to the Jacob's house, hoping to camp there, but they insisted that we stay with them. It was already getting late and we had come a long way; all we needed was drink, a bite of something to eat and a bed. Tea was produced, as the Jacobs did not keep liquor in the house. They were an Afrikaans family and Dannie was one of three brothers, all in Government service, who worked as a stock inspector at the time. Mrs. Jacobs was a qualified teacher and I believe very good at her job but cleanliness in any form did not appear to be one of her attributes. To add to our nervousness, she had something wrong with one of her middle fingers, which she kept covered with a finger sock, tied round her wrist. This finger sock looked as though it never came off and seemed always to find itself in the stew or soup. Mrs. Jacobs had a young African helper in the kitchen, who worked in an old Army trench coat, which was so sodden with grease and filth, that I am sure it could have genuinely stood up on its own. Next morning early, I looked out of the windows of our bedroom and called Pat to come and look. A lamb had been slaughtered and was hanging by its hind legs on the wall. The kitchen helper was squeezing the intestines, thereby removing the excreta, and plaiting the intestines into long strips. Every now and then, he would wipe his hands on his trench coat and continue the operation. Whether or not the plaited intestines were washed before being produced fried, with eggs, for breakfast, we did not know but Pat took one look and asked for only an egg. I was persuaded to try some, which was well cooked and I found it quite tasty but one had to try and think of something other than the trench coat and the finger sock.

After breakfast we went to look for Albert Levy, who was to build the new market corals. No sooner had we got away from the house than I stopped and Pat left her breakfast behind. Albert's first words when he heard where we had spent the night were,

-"You won't be wanting to go back for another night, I take it?"

The Jacobs were so genuinely kind and glad to have us to stay that we could not let them down, particularly as they had killed the sheep in our honour. We did, however, organise a safari with Albert for the rest of our stay, and were probably more fastidious about the cook's hygiene practices than we had ever been before, thanks to our recent lessons in cleanliness about the home.

Chapter Nine
The Ndorobo and The Mbulu

I decided to spend the second week of my local leave with a group of Ndorobo in the Kibaya area, as I had always been interested in and fascinated by these people and was keen to learn more about them. The Ndorobo, who are the bushmen and honey hunters of Eastern Africa, do not cultivate land or keep stock, pay no taxes and are very difficult to contact. Every now and then, one of them had broken away from the group and taken up employment, but these were very few. They were in great demand because of their superior tracking skills, in fact it was said that if anyone wished to become a successful professional hunter, the two most important requirements were an Ndorobo tracker and a good rifle.

They can live for days without food, but normally feed on game meat, fruit, wild plants and honey, which they collect themselves and sell to the Masai. They were at one time the chief weapon makers to all of the Masai, but by this time the weapon-making groups had broken away from their old clans and become weapon makers to different clans of their tribe, such as the Orgunono, Olgonombesh, Ilolilash and others. They remain in one area, keeping their bellows and smelters so as to continue their trade and keep livestock, occupying something of a middle territory between bush Ndorobo and Masai. The true bush Ndorobo operate within a certain area as a clan, and are very jealous of their territory, fighting any other clan that dares to enter their area. There are now different branches of these people, who are known by different names, depending on which tribe they originally come from. The group that I went to stay with were from the Masai tribe.

The Masai legend says that before the Masai started practising circumcision, there was a great famine and this particular group of Ndorobo, who were part of a Masai clan, broke away from them because despite being workers employed by the Masai, they were not being fed by them and yet were still providing sustenance for the Masai by killing game. One day a very attractive young Ndorobo maiden was about to go into the bush with one of her Ndorobo lovers to look for tubers. Her mistress, who was a Masai, called out to her saying,

-"You are to look after the pot on the fire and when it is ready you must go and fetch water, while I attend to my lover".

The Ndorobo girl replied that she was going into the bush with her lover, and took no further notice of the Masai's orders.

When she got back, she was beaten by the Masai in her village. The Ndorobos then held a meeting and decided that it was a waste of time working for the Masai, as they got nothing but abuse and had to feed the Masai and themselves as well. So it came about that the Ndorobos, by mutual agreement, became the owners of all the wild game (except eland and buffalo, which they shared) and would go and live near it, and the Masai would stay with their herds of cattle, sheep and goats and if they wanted anything from the Ndorobo, they would have to pay for it. When the Masai decided to be circumcised, they brought the honey from the Ndorobo to make the beer for the celebration. The Masai then proceeded to get very drunk and, in this state, tried to circumcise their young men. They were not very adept and, to this day, have the 'ndelelia', the piece of skin hanging below a Masai moran's penis. The Ndorobo had to complete the procedure for them, for the rest of the youths and all the circumcisions done by the Ndorobo healed up without trouble and the new morans were left with a neat 'ndelelia' which gave great pleasure to the women. The circumcisions carried out by the drunken Masai, however, went septic and became very swollen and the Ndorobos were called in to repair the damage. This they did by completely removing the foreskin, leaving no 'ndelelia' and bleeding the swollen area with the use of a suction horn. In a short while, the swellings disappeared and the Masai recovered and from this time, the Ndorobos carried out these tasks for the Masai for payment.

I arrived at Kibaya and set up camp about twelve miles out, while my contact man, Legesana, went to try and discover the present whereabouts of the tribe. He turned up the next morning to tell me that we would have to move on about twenty miles, where most of the game was. Once again the contact man went off, leaving Asmani, my driver, and Seweji, my cook, with me. I left the two servants to set up camp, while I tried to get some meat for the pot. The area was mainly bush and thickets, with occasional scattered clearings but near the river bed the country was a little more open with large trees, some of which were huge wild fig trees. I advanced towards one of these and as I approached, a very large black snake slid off into the river. I was watching from the bank to see if I could get a better view of it, when I sensed danger behind me and, as I turned round, I saw two buffalo approaching me about thirty yards away. My movement must have frightened them, as I was charged instantly by the younger of the two. Fortunately I had my .306 rifle at the ready and was able to get a shot in between the eyes. The buffalo dropped a few yards away and his mate disappeared into the bush. As I approached, the fallen buffalo started to move his head and I realised he had only been stunned and so I fired a further two shots and returned to my position behind the fig tree, until I was sure he was dead. Still a bit shaken, I walked back to my camp.

I was having a cup of newly brewed tea and Asmani, the driver, was trying to skin part of the buffalo, when Legesana, my contact man, walked into camp. He said that he had heard the shots and had come back as the Ndorobos would certainly want to investigate them. Asmani, after collecting enough meat to last us for a week, came back and left the contact man at the kill. It was dusk when Legesana came to tell me that the Ndorobo were cutting up the buffalo and thanked me for allowing them to have it and now one of the Ndorobo had agreed to see me.

Legesana and I were sat talking, when suddenly he turned and listened. I heard no sound but Legesana said they were calling him. He went off and reappeared about ten minutes later, saying "Follow me". I was about to pick up my cigarettes and matches but Legesana would not let me take them. I was asked to sit on a log in a small thicket, about a hundred and fifty yards from my camp and Legesana then addressed me in Masai, asking what it was that I wanted from his Wandorobo brothers. I started to reply in Kiswahili but Legesana stopped me, saying my brothers were present and would prefer that I spoke in a language that they could understand. It was not all that dark, but I could not see anyone, however I continued in the Masai language, assuming that the people I wished to see could see and hear me talking. I said that as a *layoni* (child), whilst living at Olgosorok, I had an Ndorobo weapon-maker friend, whom I had not seen for a long time. I had heard through Legesana that his clan of the Oldorobo had been having a difficult time because of the drought and that I hoped they would agree to my living with them for a few days and helping them by shooting some game. Later on, I said, when they found some big elephant, they could let me know and I would come and shoot a bull and let them have the meat. I would pay them in rupees or livestock. Suddenly there were two people sitting opposite me and a voice came from my left, and as I turned to look towards the direction of the voice, I saw a small man standing there. I had not heard them arrive.

The man asked me how they could be sure that I would pay them if I shot a large elephant and how they were to know that I was not just catching them for tax. I told them to ask Legesana who knew me and I told them that I would find it easier to speak in Kiswahili, since we spoke a different dialect of Masai. After they had their chat with Legesana, I asked him to tell them that if they came for me in the morning, Legesana and I would spend the next two or three days and nights with them, shooting game for them without expecting anything in return and if, after that, they began to trust me, we could discuss the other matter.

-"Why don't you come and shoot buffalo for us now?" asked the younger man, sitting in front.

Legesana then stepped in and spoke to the man who was sitting closest to me. I could sense that he did not like the idea but it was decided that we would meet at a point further down river, the following morning. As we were about to leave, the younger man said,

-"Give me lighting sticks". I handed him the box of matches in my pocket and his friend then asked for his. After promising to have some for him next day, they departed as they had come, one moment they were there, the next they had gone.

The following morning, we met up at the place arranged. After greeting one another, I was signalled to follow, which I did in silence as it was understood that one did not talk whilst hunting. Within fifteen minutes my guide stopped and pointed to a dark object no more than thirty yards away. It was quietly grazing and as it moved forward I recognised it as a buffalo. At the same time, the Ndorobo signalled that there were five altogether and pointed to their position up wind, which meant that they would either stand firm or stampede into wind away from us. I shot the first one in the head and then saw one that was about to disappear and gave it a shoulder shot. They both went down about two hundred yards from where they had been hit.

The Ndorobo had disappeared with the second animal and was heard signalling to his clan. I was about to go over but Legesana stopped me, saying "Wait until he calls us". We were standing over the first buffalo, when he turned up, followed by four others. The Ndorobo then told me that the other one was dead and pointed to its position. In no time they had set to work. Men, women and children appeared but they were rather nervous about my presence. A fire was made next to each kill and bits of meat were laid on the naked flames, on skewers whilst certain pieces of meat, offal and congealed blood were being eaten raw. The excreta and undigested food were scraped off the offal, which was eaten raw and unwashed. One young man asked why I was not eating and Legesana explained that I did not eat raw meat, which raised a laugh and, to a certain extent, was the first sign of acceptance by the clan. Legesana advised me that I should now be prepared to eat some meat with them so he called to one of the women and told her to cook a piece of meat, which he had cut and put on a skewer for me. When she brought it to me it was filthy, but at least it was cooked. Within the Ndorobo, it is the custom that when someone brings you food, you share it with them, so I cut a piece from the outside and gave it to her, then took a piece for myself from the inside and so on.

Most of the meat was cut into strips and laid on grass, bushes and makeshift trusses to dry. By noon, all the meat had been laid out and I suggested to Legesana that we might now go back to the camp. He pointed out that if we left them they would disappear and we would probably never see them again. He said that as we had made great progress with them, it would be inadvisable to leave until my acceptance was properly established, which he thought might take a couple of days. Having got so far I was determined not to give up, so I agreed to stay.

To get away from the clinging smell of crowds of meat eaters for a while, I suggested that we might go hunting again but my offer was declined as the meat was still too wet and heavy to carry. Instead I moved to the shade of a tree up wind a little and slowly, in ones and twos, the others joined me. I made numerous attempts at making conversation but my questions were met with a silent stare or were answered by Legesana. Gradually some of the others started answering my questions and Olemoijo asked why I was called Debe, which was my Masai name, and so I explained a little more about my childhood. As darkness approached, the women and children came to sit by their men.

Throughout the night, we made small talk and slept as we were, sitting up. I told a couple of stories to try and bring them out but with little success, although about a dozen men and women did move closer to listen. In the early hours of the morning I nodded off and lay back against a low root and when I awoke, a young girl of about sixteen had moved up to within a foot of me. From then on this girl hardly moved away from me until the time came to return to camp. Just before dawn, Olemoijo said that we were about to go hunting and that if I did not want to carry anything, I should leave it with my girl. She grabbed my greatcoat and empty water bottle and when I told her to give me the water bottle, Legesana said she would fill it and bring it to the next kill. I still insisted on doing it myself, as I knew she would fill it with the first water that came to hand, clean or otherwise.

We were led first to a small herd of elephant with calves, but I refused to shoot one, as they were all too small. I found it difficult to convince them that I would not shoot an elephant just for the meat, as I only had a certain number on my licence, a rule applicable also to rhino, but I could shoot anything else for them. By midday I had shot two zebra and an eland and I had filled my water bottle from a little spring. In a very short time "my girl" (so called) had arrived, with others, carrying partly dried buffalo meat. We were a good five miles from our previous night's stop and I can only assume that these people knew exactly where the elephant would be and moved there until they heard the shots. The girl walked up to me and, without saying anything, showed me her hands. Legesana said,

-"She is showing you that she has washed her hands and wants to know what meat you want cooked", so I pointed to the eland's fillet which she grilled and brought to me.

When these people wished to relieve themselves, the men did so where they sat or stood up, sometimes using the urine to wash their hands. The women would walk about five yards from the nearest person, spread their legs apart and lift their short leather skirts. I did not see any women wash their hands with their own urine but this did make me wonder what the girl had used to wash her hands before cooking my meat.

I once again selected a spot up wind under a tree for my sleeping quarters and was sitting there when some of my new friends turned up. They carried a leather bag full of honey on the comb and something else wrapped in fresh leaves. When it was opened, the girl picked out a section of whitish honeycomb filled with embryo bees and pushed a piece towards my mouth. I could not refuse to take it without being insulting but I had eaten this kind of honeycomb before, with my other Ndorobo weapon-making friends, and I found it quite palatable. After eating about three mouthfuls, I took a piece from the leather bag with honey in the comb. I asked why they did not eat the honey and was told that the whole bagful was mine, as a gift, to seal our friendship. From people who possessed so little, this was indeed a gift.

That evening they asked me to tell them some stories and, after telling them a couple, I asked them to tell me one of theirs. Oleteyanga, who until this moment had not spoken a word in my presence, started:

-"Namansi went out hunting with his new buffalo hide sandals. He was recognised among his people as the best sandal maker and this was the best pair he had ever made. He was very proud of them. Game was very scarce and, after the second day without seeing anything, he was very hungry and tired, when he came upon a Masai Elder leading a fat sheep along a path. He decided to skirt around the Masai, through the bush and get in front of him, where he dropped one of his new sandals and went and hid in the bush. The Masai, seeing the sandal, picked it up, admired it, looked around for the other one, but could not find it, so he threw it in the nearby bush and continued on his way. Namansi retrieved his sandal, then skirted round the old man and dropped the second sandal. When the old man found it, he tied his sheep to a tree and left the second sandal while he went back to retrieve the first one. Namansi, meanwhile, retrieved his second sandal and the sheep, carrying it off into the bush, where he slaughtered it. Whilst he was skinning the dead animal, a Masai turned up and accused him of stealing it. He admitted that this was the case and, as there was too much meat for him to eat on his own, suggested that he should join in and have a good feast, to which the Masai agreed. When he had removed all the stomach contents from the rumen, he informed the Masai that he would go to the river, wash it out and fill it with good Ndorobo medicine. He should not be followed as a Masai could not see his medicine and when well out of sight, he filled the rumen with air, tied it to a tree and started to whip it with a thin whip, at the same time crying out,

"It's not me but that Masai over there in the bush".

When the Masai heard this, he took to his heels, leaving the sheep all cut up and cooking on the fire. After eating his fill Namansi hid the rest of the meat. He then took the large pot which had belonged to the Masai and filled it with the contents of the rumen, to within a few inches of the top and covered it up with honey. He took this to a Manyatta where there was a circumcision ceremony about to take place, and sold it as good fresh honey. The children dipped their fingers into it, but when they had finished the honey, an elder smelled the rumen contents and chased the children accusing them of farting".

Oleteyange then looked at me and said,

-"You see my people are so very much cleverer than the Masai". They all broke into roars of laughter, rolling on the ground with excitement, even though they had all heard this story many times before.

No sooner had Oleteyanga finished his story, when another fellow started up:

-"A long time ago, when the Ndorobo still lived and hunted in small family groups, this family saw some bees entering and leaving a hole high in a tree. The man told his wife to tie up his axe and calabash on a long rope and throw the rope up to him when he reached the hive. As he tried to catch the rope, he slipped and fell to his death. The woman was left a widow with two young boys. As time went on she found it more and more difficult to find food for her small family. With tears in her eyes, she turned to her two sons and asked 'What are we to do for food?' The younger of the two boys, who was the cleverest, said,

'If you can plait a long piece of catgut, I will tie it to a piece of wood to make a bow. I will then make an arrow like the Masai use for bleeding their cattle but I will put the poison from the Morijo tree on its tip. We will then stalk the animals and as soon as we get close enough, we will shoot the arrow into the animal's body.'

Their mother did not believe that this was feasible but it was worth trying. As soon as the bow and some arrows were made, the boys began to practise, soon discovering that one arrow which had a broad flat tail was going straighter than the rest. So, with this arrow, its tip poisoned, the boys went and hid in a bush near to some grazing buffalo. When a lone cow came in range, they fired their arrows into her belly. The buffalo searched for the source of her pain, but the boys were safe up a tree by the time she had located them and after a short while, she moved away, collapsed and died. From this time on, the family improved on their weapons and never went short of food again. One day an Ndorobo from over the river came looking for meat, as he had seen the boys making a kill. The mother refused them saying that they never came to help when her husband died, and even when he was alive, they wouldn't allow him to hunt on their side of the river. 'Now go back to your own area' she ended. The strangers made plans to kill the two youths and move over the river. However, the mother found out and warned her sons of the plan. The boys took up a position on either side of the ford in the river, at the only place one could cross, and they shot and killed the two Ndorobo leaders as they were coming across the river.

The mother was too old to breed and the other group had no men of mature breeding age, although they had plenty of women and girls and so the mother and her two, now grown-up, sons were invited to cross the river and join the other group for a feast on an eland. The offer was accepted and the two young men became the new leaders of both groups. It was from this group that the Ndorobo learnt how to use the bow and arrow."

These stories went on into the early hours of the morning; no sooner had one finished than they started another. It started raining, and did not stop until about eight in the morning, and so the Ndorobo took off what little clothing they had on and continued as though nothing out of the ordinary had happened. The meat was turned as soon as the sun came up and instead of collecting clean water from the spring, they scooped up muddy water from the nearest puddle. I was, by this time, dying for a cup of tea, a bath or at least a good wash with soap and water, and a shave. I had been able to keep my teeth clean by using a twig with a chewed brush at the end, but the rest of me stank worse than a polecat and so I announced that I would have to leave my friends later that day but would shoot for them walking back in the direction of my camp.

My "shadow girl" then summoned enough courage to ask how long I was going away for and what she was to do whilst I was away. I told her she would continue to do what she had always been doing. Legesana then spoke in his own language, which I did not understand. He explained to me that when the tribe had a guest of importance, he was given a helper to do his chores and she had been given to me, and would always be ready to carry out my wishes.

We did no more shooting, as the rain had complicated the meat-drying process and they already had meat sufficient for the group. Under the improved relationship, I was escorted back to my tent, but did not get any help with the loading. It was arranged that as soon as a good elephant was found, I would be told. No sooner had I got into the car than they disappeared from sight, and within a few seconds it was still and silent, as if they had never been there.

I had no need to go back to Dodoma until the following evening so I went as far as Kibaya and stayed the night in the rest camp. I enjoyed the luxury of a hot bath, out in the open, a pot of tea and a good dish of goat curry and rice. I felt a different man and rather pleased with my success, as I had, I thought, made the first step towards an inroad into an Ndorobo clan. Not many Europeans had succeeded in doing this and whilst a lot of effort and patience was still required if

I was to progress any further, I was very happy with what I had learnt.

A few days after our safari ended, Legesana told me he did not want to continue his work with the Veterinary Department, as he wanted to go back to his people. I persuaded him to get a transfer to Iodines as a game tracker, as he would then be with his people most of the time. Iodines is probably the best known authority on African snakes, a cultured and eccentric man who lived at this time in Tanganyika, working for the Veterinary Department. There are several books about his life and work. Legesana did this for a short while and then he just faded away and was not heard of again until 1952, when he came up to me at the Naberera Market, wanting his job back. I had no job for him at the time, but was able to employ him as a gun bearer about a year later.

I continued my studies into the various ethnic groups of the areas in which I was working, talking to local people, traders and farmers as I progressed through the markets. My childhood had been one of cultural juxtapositions, shifting between Masai and European cultures with ease and fascination. I believed that once I understood the traditions and belief systems of the people with whom I came into contact, then the less chance there would be of misunderstanding and conflict. It is a creed that I still hold true today.

I learnt that in the Mbulu District, there are four tribes called the Barabaig, the Wafiomi, the Wambugwe and the Iraqw. The Barabaig occupy the lowland area to the south and west of the Mbulu Highlands and as far north as Endabesh. They are semi-nomadic, related, I believe, to the Pokot in the north west of Kenya and although a very small tribe, were considered the fiercest warriors in Tanganyika and even the Masai treated them with respect. They are unlike most other tribes in that all of their wealth is owned by the women, and it is the women who have the choice of husbands. It is the custom for the women to demand proof of their chosen mate's masculinity with the highest proof being to kill a man from another tribe and present the removed penis as evidence. In the case of a female victim, the breasts were removed. It was also acceptable to kill single-handed an elephant, rhino, buffalo, lion or leopard. Each one of these qualifies for the addition of varying numbers of fine cat-gut strands called Simnyeks to be added to a hereditary belt, worn round the waist. The highest number of strands, five, are given for killing a human and these are presented to the warrior by the girl. I have seen some belts over six inches in diameter, which must have contained at least five hundred strands.

While I was in the district in the late 1940's, these ritual murders were still being carried out, although the authorities were doing everything they could to stop them. The warriors would hide in the bushes near an infrequently used footpath and, when an unsuspecting person went by, they would be clubbed on the head from the back, their pertinent parts removed and their bodies left to rot on the path. One can't help suspecting that this was easier than hunting a wild animal, which could retaliate and which had a more highly developed sense of hearing and smell.

The young Barabaig girls were dressed in a cowrie corset, like a one-piece swimsuit of leather, decorated with cowrie shells with a small hole at the bottom, joined with thin gut thread. This remained on the girl until she married. If she became pregnant before marriage, she would normally be made to abort, otherwise the girl would, by tribal custom, be killed, however, these days, she is made an outcast and is unlikely to be taken as a wife. The people are tall and slim, attractive, unruly and totally unpredictable. If they take a liking to you, you can do no wrong - if the reverse, it is advisable to leave the area.

The Wafiomi inhabit the country south east of Mbulu, round Ufiomi Mountain and below the Rift Valley escarpment from Gidas. In the north they border the Masai, to the south lies the Kondoa district, to the west are the Iraqw and the Barabaig and to the east lies the tsetse fly belt - what is now the Tarangire National Park. They are, I think, a cross between the Wambulu Sandawe and the Barabaig with their features and language similar to the Mbulu, but their customs seem to be more like those of the Barabaig. The tribe is a small one and they have a mixed agricultural economy of livestock and cultivation. During the early nineteen twenties, a number of titled and wealthy white men bought land in the area from Mount Ufiomi to Masakaloda, building themselves elaborate houses with large gardens. Most of them came from Europe or the United States and had local managers or partners keeping an eye on their properties. They came out every winter with their friends and girl-friends and sexual orgies were reputed to take place with local African girls sometimes coerced into joining in. The late Chief Dodo of the Wafiomi tribe told me that he had taken part in these activities and said that in his opinion, although the black women on the whole were best, any white woman who had no inhibitions was by far the better. This comment was made to me by a man who had a considerable number of wives and reputedly a wide range of experience with both black and white women.

The Wambugwe are the smallest of the tribes. They live to the east of Mbulu on the flat ground below the Rift wall and along the south eastern shore of Lake Manyara and are hyena worshippers. The legend is that the hyena live with them as pets, copulate with them, and so reproduce their witch-doctor clan. Their dances were said to go on for four or five days, during which time the young men and women copulate with each other and with hyenas. I have heard of hyenas being shot near the area and found to have on them bead and cowrie necklaces and wooden combs. These people keep a few cattle and goats and cultivate a little millet, rice and cotton, hunting game in much the same manner as the African Hunting Dog, by chasing the animal in a large circle until it gets tired, and when the first chaser gets exhausted, another takes over. This can go on for several hours until they get near enough to the animal to kill it.

The new Tarangire National Park used to be their main honey and game hunting ground. Unfortunately the tribe is now dying out because of sleeping sickness, syphilis and famine. No livestock culling was necessary in this area since it was carried out effectively by nature. The Iraqw people, who are normally referred to as Wambulu, occupy the

Mbulu Highlands and are blessed with fine features and semi-straight hair like the Somalis of northern Kenya and Somalia. At one time, they must have been nomadic, but became surrounded by other tribes in the Kainam Murai area. They were obviously not strong enough to defend themselves and their stock from the Masai and the Barabaig, and in order to survive, they took to building their houses underground, with the cattle, sheep and goats living in with them at night. The houses have a small entrance into the side of a hill, wide enough to take about two head of cattle at a time, and tall enough to take the largest animal in the herd, Mbulu cattle are known for their small size. Once inside, the area widens out and there is enough room for quite a tall person to stand upright. Some of these houses can hold as many as one hundred head of cattle and still leave enough room for a large family to live in comfort. The walls are lined with strong split olive logs, the roof is framed with wild olive and sealed with branches and grass, then covered outside with soil and planted with grass for camouflage. I have often stood on the roof of one of these houses and not realised I was doing so as there is no wood or thatch visible except at the entrance. It is also very difficult to set them on fire, which is an important advantage. These houses take a tremendous amount of effort to build, when it is remembered that the heavy olive wood logs have to be carried by hand over as many as five miles. Such a home is a major asset to the family. However, the custom is that if there is a death in one of these homes, the whole family has to vacate it for good, and it may never be used by any member of the tribe again. The family becomes "taboo" and only people present in the house at the time of death may associate with them. A relation may leave food in the bushes but will not touch a container that the family have touched or looked upon so that they become untouchables and outcasts for three years. This custom is severe and has been the cause of a number of suicides. It is thought that the custom derives from an outbreak of bubonic plague some time during the mid-nineteenth century, and is called Mitimani.

The compulsory culling that we conducted in the area was made difficult by a custom called Quasara. Unlike other tribes, the Wambulu did not believe in slaughtering a healthy animal in good condition when they have a ceremony or celebration and instead, would search the herds for an animal in poor condition to make a Quasara deal. This meant that the recipient of the animal would agree to repay the owner with a calf of a certain cow. The cow might not then have a calf of the correct sex, which would mean another cow would have to be agreed upon, and this claim could go back for three or four generations of tribesmen. Sometimes it took the tribal elders two, or even three, days to make a decision on a single case.

The Wambulu, like all African tribal peoples, believe in witchcraft but probably to a lesser extent than most other tribes but rainmaking, on the other hand, they believe is controlled by the Nade family. The story goes that years ago, during a great drought and famine, a man with a donkey, his wife and a small child appeared at Kainam and begged for food and water. The local people asked him why they should give him, a stranger, these things when their own people were dying. "Kill the strangers, and let's eat the donkey" they shouted. The man ignored their remarks and addressed a very old blind man lying on the ground. "Old Man", he said, "Tell these silly children of yours that I am here to bring them rain, so that they can grow crops and feed their people". Whilst he was still speaking, the old man got up and walked towards him, holding out his hand. Then the old man turned towards the people of Kaiman and told them that he had dreamed that a man called Nade would come with his donkey from Iramba and save them. Then the old man turned into smoke and disappeared into the clouds and the stranger was given a place to sleep, water and dry arrowroot to eat.

That night it rained all night until the water holes were filled and the rivers were running in the luggers. Nade was given land and cattle by the tribe and help to build a house and so it is that the Nyeramba family have 'controlled' the rain in the Mbulu country ever since. Each year they receive large numbers of cattle, sheep and goats to bring rain to some part of Mbulu and whilst modern knowledge is capable of predicting the rainy seasons with a degree of accuracy, there are many Mbulu who still believe that the Nyeramba have the ability to summon rain outside of the seasons.

All of these insights into the cultural beliefs and tribal values helped me considerably in my work. As long as I retained respect for their value systems, then I retained respect for the people, and this respect was invariably returned by those with whom I came into contact.

Chapter Ten
Tsetse, Ritual Murder
and Rinderpest

Pat, my wife, was very popular in the District and with her knowledge of medical matters was very much in demand, especially amongst those people who had young children. In 1949 there was none of the comprehensive back-up of social services available to people in Western countries today, doctors and hospitals were many miles distant, sometimes over impassable roads and were only used in acute emergencies because there was no ambulance service. People were very much left to their own resources and relied on friends for support when necessary rather than look to the Government to provide every need. One effect of this was to create a close-knit society and even today, with ex-patriot Europeans who were in the 'colonies' spread all over the world, it is easy to strike up an immediate friendship with someone who has lived in Africa.

As soon as I had got the grade and weight system of selling cattle on a reasonable footing, I began a compulsory culling scheme. This scheme was to effect the reduction of the existing stock population in the over-populated Mbulu Highlands and to reduce the numbers of cattle, donkeys, sheep and goats by forty per cent within two years. We hoped to achieve this by sale and redistribution and by bringing into use new grazing areas, which were being cleared of tsetse fly. The plan was for the District Commissioner and I to visit every sub-chief, explain the reasons behind the culling and how the plan would work and the benefits for the tribe as a whole. The plan had already been fully discussed with the senior chief and so once we had been assured of the co-operation of the village headmen, the sub-chiefs and I took over the management of the scheme. Each animal for sale had to be branded, special markets had to be arranged and I had to make sure that fair prices were paid. I was empowered to buy on behalf of the Government, where necessary, and to arrange transport to a resale market, which could be as far as five hundred miles away. Considering that the scheme was politically unpopular, yet compulsory, the exercise went relatively smoothly with very little unpleasantness, largely due to the co-operation and good ground work done by the headmen and sub-chiefs. Other schemes of this nature, instigated by the Colonial Government in the neighbouring countries, were not so smoothly accepted and some took years to be adopted by the naturally conservative inhabitants.

When we had left Dodoma, we had brought one servant with us, James, a Mnyasa who had at one time worked at Government House for Mark Young, who was the Governor. He was a very superior servant, in both senses of the word and considered anyone below the rank of a District Commissioner too inferior to acknowledge. I never understood why he condescended to work for me but whilst at Mbulu he had to have an assistant to do the more menial tasks, such as cleaning the saucepans or going on safari with me when I went on my own. This assistant was a young boy of about sixteen, an Mbulu called Sakta Ama, who not only became a very efficient safari cook, and later my head servant at home, but he also became a good friend. He stayed with my family for twenty-six years and only left me when I had to leave Tanzania.

One day James told Pat that he thought it was most improper for her to do all the chores for our daughter Penny and that we should employ an ayah. James said he had already found one for her although we did not realise at the time that the ayah, who was a very pretty young lady, was in fact James' girlfriend. The idea was not a bad one as Pat was unwell and had to live in Arusha while she underwent medical investigation until it became necessary for her to have an operation which kept her away for eleven weeks. I therefore had to have Penny with me but since I was on safari most of the time, an ayah was a necessity. After a while, James found Mbulu too far away from the centre of things and he left to take up a job as barman at the Arusha Club.

During the period when Pat was in Arusha and Penny was just two years old, I had to do a market in the Katesh area. Bill Timms, who was buying cattle for Tanganyika Packers, and I were camping half a mile away from the Government guest house, in which were staying a Canadian anthropologist, Gordon Wilson, who was studying the Barabaig people, and his family. His wife Evelyn asked us over to dinner and I left the ayah and my new safari servant Nade to look after Penny. It was the last day of the market and there was a lot of drink and money available, the ayah decided to enjoy herself and left Penny, without telling Nade. When he looked out of his tent, the girl, who was supposed to be sitting by the fire in front of the tent, was nowhere to be seen, so he went and sat there until we returned. He told me the girl had gone off without telling him some time before and when I went into my tent to check on Penny, she had disappeared. Adding to the trauma of her disappearance was the fact that I knew the area was well-known for killer leopards which were regularly taking sheep and goats, and sometimes children, out of the houses. I got into a panic and went out and called all the market staff to mount a search for the ayah and Penny. I was convinced that Penny had been taken by a leopard and that the girl had run away in fright. Not only did the market staff turn up to search, but all the traders and their staff as well. The ayah was found in less than ten minutes in company with a man and she would have been lynched had not Bill appeared carrying Penny, whom he had found fast asleep. When the girl had left, Penny had got out of her safari bed and got into "Uncle Bill's bed". My relief verged on hysteria. The girl left our employment and I never left Penny at night on safari again.

Shortly after arriving at Mbulu, I went on a Safari with the District Commissioner, a Scotsman named Gordon Scott. He was on his way to the southern part of the district and I thought it was a good opportunity to get to know that particular area. Gordon and his wife Barbara were good company and the four of us got on well. The first night we spent at Dongobesh, where we met Roger Austin and his German wife, who held obvious anti-British sentiments. The next day we went to the Government rest house at Dabil, which consisted of three beautifully thatched rondavels in a very pretty setting from where Gordon and I went to have a *baraza* (meeting) with the Elders. He set about sorting out their various problems and at a suitable time I was introduced to them. After our meeting, Gordon suggested that we might go and meet the Lundgrens, Carl who was Swedish and his German wife, Irmgard - who were running a farm for a British oil millionaire called Dick Cooper and his new American wife, Marjory. At this time the Lundgrens, with their little son Nils, were living in a small flat-roofed *tembe* hut made of mud and wattle, waiting for their proper concrete house to be completed. Both Carl and Irmgard had spent some time in a British prisoner of war camp, because of their German connection and were somewhat quiet and reserved in the company of British ex-servicemen whom they did not know. After a few awkward moments, however, the reserve evaporated and we had a good party, which lasted until the early hours, sowing the seeds of a good friendship between the Lundgrens and Pat and me. It was daylight when we returned to the rest camp, where we had a hasty breakfast before going on to Katesh on the southern slopes of Mount Hanang. We were both feeling rather ill from the previous night's festivities and were looking forward to a good afternoon's rest but this was snatched from us when the local chief turned up, with his district police, to report a double murder at Balangda Lalu. This was about twenty miles away, through the bush, so we set off in my Ford pick-up, Gordon, myself, my new veterinary guard Geao, two regular policemen, a district policeman and the sub-chief, and left Gordon's lorry and crew to set up camp. The going was very slow and hot and both our cars were consuming too much water and we had, in addition, the discomfort of the little bush flies which were clustered round our eyes. Eventually, the district policeman asked us to stop near a dry river bed where we left the car with Geao and another man we had picked up along the way. After walking about a mile down river, we heard voices in the thick bush in front of us and as we rounded a bend, there, lying on the footpath, were two black bloated bodies. The body of a woman of about twenty-five in an advanced state of pregnancy lay nearest us and, it seemed she had been hit over the back of the head before having her breasts removed. About twenty yards further on, was the body of a man who had been murdered in the same way and had his penis and testicles cut off. They had been collecting salt from the salt pans and were attacked on their way home. The victims turned out to be from the Nyeramba, a tribe of the Singida district, who were ambushed and murdered by the Barabaig tribesmen for the Simnyek belt of a wedding.

The Simnyek is a belt of very finely-woven animal sinews, to be attached to leather buckles at either end, that is presented to a girl's future husband when he proves that he too had made a kill, generally producing a man's penis and testicles as proof. These belts come down through the generations and earn extra strips according to the value of the kill offered by the male, so for instance a human will be worth five strips, elephant four, lion three, buffalo or leopard two etc. Although the girl makes the Simnyeks, she is also the one who decides on the amount of strips that she is worth. Thus, if she likes her suitor, she will ask for something worth only two strips, but if she is not keen, then she may ask in excess of twenty. The man may refuse to contribute that many but to do so is very degrading and in a matriarchal society, such as the Barabaig, would lead to him becoming an outcast. The only honourable way out is for the man to be too slow in accumulating his kills so that the girl can then negotiate with another suitor. Unfortunately, with humans having the highest value, and them certainly being easier to kill than elephants or buffaloes, then there is a high incidence of murders in the area because of the Simnyek custom.

After carrying out lengthy investigations and arranging for the bodies to be taken to their people, we left to return to Katesh. On this relatively short trip, I saw more guinea fowl than I had ever seen, before or since, with flocks of thousands in every direction. The people who lived in the area said there were always plenty, but there seemed to be more than usual that year. We shot half a dozen for the pot and arrived back in Katesh after dark, very tired, thirsty and hungry.

The next morning, the serious business of investigating the murders began with a meeting of all the chiefs, sub-chiefs and elders, presided over by the District Commissioner. *Barazas* are nearly always held under an accommodating tree and so it was here, when Chief Chonya, the overall chief of the Barabaig, was told about the previous day's murders. He initially proved to be less than co-operative, as he often was, until the stakes, financial or otherwise, were raised. It was not until Gordon suspended him and had the sub-chief arrested as an accomplice, that Chonya promised to find and arrest the culprits. The Chief's and the Barabaigs' attitude was one of surprise, like what was all the fuss about? After all the victims were only Wanyeramba and Chief Chonya was far more interested to know when the next cattle market was to be held, so that he could sell some ill-gotten cattle. Gordon advised me to tell the local people that all markets would be cancelled until the murderers had been found.

The next day we inspected the tsetse clearing around Masacaloda and went on to Gidas, where there was a market in progress. Here I saw eight native albino men, the most I have ever seen in one place which interested me and I made enquiries. They all came from the same family, were all very cheerful but badly sunburnt and suffered from the strong light in their pale blue eyes. When I told Pat about them later, she suggested that we help them by giving them brimmed hats and sun-glasses as a result of which we came to know them quite well. Albinos often congregate in the towns because if they remain as individuals in their villages then they can become ostracised from the village life.

We left very early next morning for Basotu in my pick-up, while the Administration truck went on to Haidum to make camp. Basotu was a Crater Lake, one of many in the vicinity, some of which have fresh water, others alkaline and some saline. When we had done our work, we went to the lake's edge and whilst we were eating our lunch under a large fever tree, our sub-chief turned up with two men in handcuffs, escorted by two tribal policemen. They turned out to be the murderers but did not appear in the least perturbed. During the interrogation, when Gordon asked them why they had murdered the woman and old man, one replied,

-"Because these Nyeramba trash always come and steal our salt".

We continued our safari to Haidum, putting the two accused in the back of the pick-up with one policeman to keep an eye on them. Haidum was an area of land set aside for reclamation from tsetse fly. Tsetses exist in large numbers across East Africa, and numbers continue to grow, as I write. As a result of the effects of sleeping sickness on people and "tryps" on the cattle, large amounts of cash, time and effort have been spent trying to eradicate them so as to open up certain areas for those people starved of suitable grazing lands. This would be done by clearing swathes, of a few hundred metres wide through the bush and, in extreme cases, spraying the areas with insecticide. When the flies have been hatched, they must feed on blood almost immediately, but cannot fly much further than 100 yards, and must remain in the shade, or they will die. Hence the clearing of areas which would then be opened to settlement and, because of the Veterinary Department's interests, I was to play a considerable part in the scheme. From Basotu, we went due north, following a Survey Department track which was only just passable. The countryside was mostly park-like with wide expanses of red oats grass, which was packed with wildebeest, Zebra, Kongoni, Eland, Thomson's and Grant's Gazelle and a herd of buffalo. When we arrived at our camp we found Dick Ludbrook, from the Tsetse Department, at the Survey camp next door, who came over to join us for a sundowner and several more drinks, only to suddenly become morbid telling us he was convinced he had cancer. Next morning we went over to Dick's for a breakfast of young wildebeest steaks - an excellent steak and remains one of my favourites - charcoal-grilled, with an egg on top and slices of bacon. We were relieved to find Dick very cheerful in the daylight and he seemed to have forgotten his fears, which were not mentioned again that night at his camp. Sad to relate, about two years later, when he lived in a house near my mother, he shot himself with a .416 rifle, leaving a note of apology for my mother, explaining he was taking his life before his cancer got the better of him. The autopsy proved there was no evidence of his suffering from cancer at all.

When I got back to Mbulu, I received a report that there was a Rinderpest outbreak in the Endagikot area. I was on my own in the Department and had the big culling programme well advanced, so I needed help because if the Rinderpest scare proved to be correct, all the cattle in the district would have to be inoculated immediately. I cabled the Provincial Veterinary Officer, Newland, at Arusha for help and was sent a newly arrived veterinarian from Edinburgh University called Sparks. Of course he could not speak a word of Kiswahili, had no experience of Africa, or a Rinderpest inoculation campaign, but through the Government's hierarchy system, he automatically took over as the man in charge because of his degree, even though he was sent to help me. Unfortunately, he was not put in the picture before leaving Arusha - it was assumed that he would know exactly what to do and would be grateful for local advice and help. As soon as I had confirmed the outbreak, I sent Sparks with the local veterinary guard to meet with the chiefs and organise the construction of the inoculation crushes. Meanwhile, I provisionally declared the area under quarantine, which stopped all movement of livestock until the Rinderpest was officially confirmed from the laboratory at Arusha. This had to be signed by a qualified veterinary officer before it could be implemented and Sparks duly arrived the next day with a lorry, camping equipment and the necessary paraphernalia for the campaign. He spent the night at my house and I told him what had to be done, suggesting that I should start him off and work south until Jacobs, the experienced Stock Inspector, arrived, when he could move north. He seemed to fall in with these plans but the next morning, he walked into my office and asked who had confirmed the disease to be Rinderpest. When I told him I had, he asked me what my qualifications were and under what section of the Ordinance I was empowered to place a quarantine order on the area. I tried to explain the need for proper precautions and the necessity for acting quickly and decisively but he would not accept my reasoning. He sent a cable to Arusha cancelling my quarantine request and told me he would go and check himself that it was really Rinderpest. I suggested that he take his inoculation party with him ready to start work as he would find that it was correct, and in the mean time, I would send Jacobs off in the other direction. I was very politely told to mind my own business and get on with my own job, a suggestion with which I was more than happy to comply. He went off to diagnose the Rinderpest and I sent a cable to Arusha saying,

"Sparks taken over the Rinderpest campaign. Advised me to keep out of it. I suspect major balls up. Propose resume survey Saturday if no change of plan. Await your instructions."

This took place on Wednesday and on the Friday morning we received two cables. The one to Sparks told him I was in absolute charge of the Rinderpest campaign in the Mbulu District, my instructions were to be followed and he could declare the area a quarantine zone, on my advice. My cable told me to cancel the survey for the time being and get the campaign going immediately, for which I was to be in charge and responsible. To give him his due, Sparks seemed relieved to have the responsibility shifted, as he had quickly found out that, without local knowledge, his Edinburgh University training was inadequate in the field, in this particular case.

Next morning we started the campaign in earnest and by midday we had inoculated and branded over a thousand head of cattle. I then went to see Jacobs and was pleased to find that he had completed one area and was ready to move on to the next - it was a delight to see such a well-organised campaign. Sparks was with us for an initial three weeks for the campaign but was then told to stay on at Mbulu to help me with the culling, which pleased him and we got on well. He was eventually replaced by John Pettifer and by then everything was ready for the culling cattle sales to start, with the cattle sorted and counted, those for sale branded, the owners' objections and complaints listened to and resolved, and the Rinderpest quarantine lifted. It was now up to me to see that the sales went ahead efficiently and the owners got a fair price.

The first market to be held was at Dongobesh. I was advised to take a sergeant and six askaris (policemen) with me, which I believed to be the wrong thing to do, as I did not anticipate any trouble and parading armed and uniformed policemen would, in my opinion, give everyone, particularly the Somali traders, a bad impression. The Somalis like most cattle traders the world over, would buy for the lowest possible price they could get away with. Luckily the District Commissioner, Peter Bell, agreed with me and arranged that he or Gordon Scott would unofficially turn up on the day of the market to see how it was progressing. I stayed in the rest camp at Dongobesh the whole of the day before to give people a chance to talk to me if they wished, organising a meeting with the traders, who promised to co-operate, before moving on to the local area chief for a drink of millet beer with him.

When it was time to return to my own camp, the chief accompanied me and at the river, on the way to the rest camp, I saw one of the most beautiful young Mbulu girls I had ever seen. She was about eighteen years old and was wearing a beautifully beaded Mbulu skirt and a braided choke necklace. Like most Wambulu women she had very fine features and broad shoulders and fine breasts with a beaded strip round her head, above her eyes and ears. I was looking at her, wishing that I had a camera, when the chief asked

-"Do you like my choice for you?"

-"What do you mean, for me?" I asked.

He told me that she was to collect water and wood for me and do any other chores. I did not like to upset the old man by telling him it was unnecessary as I had my own staff and so when he had left, I sent for my Mbulu adviser and consulted him about the girl. He told me that once the Mbulu chiefs got to know their Government officials, they chose a pretty girl to do his chores, if they liked the official but if they did not like him, he was given an old man or woman instead. In this case the girl turned out to be one of his daughters, which made the situation most difficult, as I did not wish to upset the Chief before the next day's opening market. Once again, I consulted Geao about the delicate question of where she was supposed to sleep. He grinned from ear to ear, and suggested that if I wanted her to sleep with me, she would be pleased to do so, but if not, she would go home before dark and there would be no offence either way, so long as I did not forbid her to come back. She would turn up whenever I returned to Dongobesh and if she was ill or otherwise occupied, someone else would stand in for her.

On the first day we sold nine hundred head of cattle and everything went smoothly, with the sole exception of a man who wanted to force his own animals in before the others. He could see the first animals were in far better condition and he wanted his to follow and obtain their high prices. I did not have to take any action as the Chief immediately saw what was happening and the matter was sorted out on the spot.

The next day we sold the balance of three hundred odd head, and moved on to a free market at Dabil and Katesh. The culling programme had started and I was pleased with the first results. Later on, Page Jones, the Provincial Commissioner, and the Director of Veterinary Services, Neil Reid, came to visit the markets to see how they were running and how the culling programme was turning out. During that first month the only trouble I had was at Karatu, up in the north where one of the European farmers tried to make me buy his cattle at a price he wanted. As this was not my job, I refused to do so but he made a bit of a fuss about it, threatening to report the matter to higher authorities. I told him to go ahead but nothing further was ever heard of the matter.

One of the most useful and important men I had in my team, who was also a good friend, was the Market Master, a man by the name of Ali Leseko. Ali was half Mbulu and half Masai, about six feet five inches tall, and very well built. His father had been a soldier in the German Army and his mother was an Mbulu woman. Ali was born at the end of the 1914-18 War and my book "Waters of the Sanjan" is based on his father's life. Not only was he well educated, but also intelligent, with a very pleasant personality, but, if he became ruffled, he could turn into a very formidable character. I can remember one occasion, at the Basuto market, when the Somalis tried to play him up, he warned them about three times to stop breaking the rules and to behave properly in the market but they took no notice. In fact, one of them told him that if he didn't do what they told him, they would `fix' him at which he immediately turned around and challenged the lot of them. There were about eight of them at the time yet not one of them had the courage to move. So Ali, after consulting me, closed the market but announced it would be reopened the next morning. Without the help of people like Ali, Geao, my senior veterinary guard and my servant Sukta, the culling programme would have been a very difficult undertaking. Ali was well thought of by the market staff and highly respected in his own area, so much so, that just before Independence, when the paramount Chief of his area was chosen, Ali's name was put forward for consideration, but he declined to stand. Shortly after Independence, he resigned from his job as overall Market Master Supervisor of the markets and took up farming in the Arusha area.

Geao, who was an Mbulu tribesman from Kainam, had the reputation of being very fierce because, as a youngster, he had, single-handed, killed a lion to save one of his neighbour's cows. He was very knowledgeable and knew nearly everyone in the hierarchy of chiefs and elders. It took us about a year to really get to know one another, but after that, I found Geao could provide any information I needed and would let me know if there was anything underhand going on. Geao remained with me throughout my stay in Mbulu and when I left to become a cattle buyer, he was very keen to join me. However, he had prospects of a good pension, with other privileges, in his present employment, so it would have been unreasonable for him to leave Government to work for me.

For some time, the area around Tarangire, to the east of Babati, had been infested with tsetse fly, coming in from the east and north slowly pushing the human population down towards Gallapo on Mount Hanang. Meanwhile, a verbal battle had been raging for some time between the Game Department, who wanted the area declared a Game Reserve, and the Administration, who felt that the area should be kept for settlement. A belt of cleared land, to keep the tsetse out, had been created some seven or eight years previously but it had not been kept cleared and the tsetse were near the Bugiri Mountain range, close to the road and Lake Manyara. A working party was appointed in Mbulu to look into the situation, consisting of John Percy (Administration), Robert Collet (Department of Agriculture), Du Frere (Tsetse) and me (Veterinary), together with a representative from the Game Control Department. Once the culling scheme was under way, it was felt that the survey, which had been delayed for some time, should be started.

The five of us left Mbulu and set up a base camp at Babati for ten days, approaching the area from the south and entering behind Mount Hanang. When we reached our intended camp site close to one of the springs, we found a hunting party camped there illegally. Outside the camp were two leopard skins, which had been salted and laid under the tree and that same night, more traps were set up and hides constructed by the hunting party. Another kill was made by one of the American clients, who was very proud of himself but the rest of us believed that shooting a trapped leopard was unethical. The hunter in charge came under criticism from us but there was no laws broken as poaching had yet to be outlawed and so we moved the whole party on.

At the springs near where we had camped, eighteen families were still cultivating the land, but although it was good land and was doing well, the families themselves were all suffering from malaria and sleeping sickness. That first night, elephants, buffalo and a variety of smaller animals came to the waterhole beneath a good moon and we were royally entertained by this natural theatre for a few hours before putting in for the night. The following day, we approached the area to the north where the Tarangire River flows and where the present-day lodge is situated. We didn't get very far as we only had two wheel drive vehicles, but the game in that area was prolific, including Rhino, Buffalo, Elephant, Eland, Oryx, Kudu, Impala, Grant's Gazelle, Zebra, Reedbuck, Wildebeest, Warthog and Bushbuck. We also saw a single gerenuk, much to the amazement of the Game Control Department, who had been insistent that they did not live there. All these other animals were in vast numbers and in the swamp we must have seen the best part of a thousand Reedbuck, the largest group I have ever seen in my life. The number of animals was unbelievable with a prolific birdlife too, and they were so tame that you could drive close to them without frightening them. There were also large numbers of all the cat family, including more leopards than I had seen for a long time, numerous cheetah and plenty of the smaller predators like Civet cats, African Wild Cats and Lynx.

At the end of three days we were forced to return to our base camp, as we could not get any further without four-wheel drive vehicles and back in Babati, we received a message to say that Robert Collett's wife was ill, so he had to leave us. There was also an invitation for us from Carl Lundgren to have a meal and some drinks at his house in Ndareda, some twenty miles away, which we declined as we had to leave the following day, suggesting instead that he and his wife come and join us for a drink. Carl is a good fellow and a great friend but he is finicky over his eating habits and unfortunately, this being the rainy season, there were a number of Stink Bugs about. These relatively unknown bugs are small, about the size of a ladybird, that when frightened or disturbed emit an awful stink that can be enough to make one vomit. They are a regular scourge in the rainy season across East Africa, sometimes appearing in huge numbers. One of these got into his whisky and Carl, who had already had several drinks, immediately passed out. Irmgard, his wife, had to drive Carl the twenty miles home, in the pouring rain, on a bad road, for which Carl has never forgiven me. This insect is one of the nastiest flavoured bugs there are, and I have known people unable to eat for two or three days once they have had one in their food.

Next morning we moved camp to a place called Kwacuchinja, a fairly short distance away. The move took us all day and we didn't reach camp until after dark because of the sticky black-cotton soil on the road, which had already been badly churned up by the East African Railways lorries plying their trade along that route to get between Arusha and Dodoma. After inspecting our new campsite in daylight, we decided to move on to where the present-day lodge is, from where we did a lot of walking in all directions and while we were here we saw some nineteen Rhino in an area of less than one hundred acres. It was the largest number of Rhinos that I, or any of us, had ever seen in one group, scattered all over the area, and for some time after, while flying over that same place, I would see many similar groups of Rhino. It was here that we found a large baobab tree, from which we saw smoke coming out of the top and found eight poachers living inside and something like sixty tusks and Rhino horns and a huge amount of meat and dried skins, all in this one tree. The poachers were arrested and handed over to the Game Department, together with all their trophies and after that, the Game Department took a real interest in the area.

I did not agree with the rest of the party that the area should be turned into a Game Reserve, convinced as I was that it was not going to be properly managed, as was the case in many other Reserves. I felt that it would be far better utilised for human habitation, provided that the clearings were redone and maintained, and the area was finally cleared of tsetse. Fortunately, I was proved wrong, as the whole area was eventually made into a Game Park, to become one of the better ones and today Tarangire is considered to be one of the best small parks in the whole of East Africa.

We were driving along the road one day, Geao sitting in front with me, when we came across a group of Mbulu Elders who had had a considerable amount to drink. I had to brake very fast, as one of them decided to go across the road, then suddenly realised that the others were still on the other side, so turned in order to return to them, and in doing so, tripped and fell over. Fortunately, I was able to stop about three feet away from him and the others dragged him away, all in a heap, falling over one another as they did so. As we continued our journey, Geao sat beside me roaring with laughter and so I asked what he found so funny. He answered by giving me a rundown on the Mbulu drinking parties, which are sometimes in aid of some ceremony, but sometimes they're for no particular reason. One person decides to make some beer and when word gets out that beer is being made in an adjoining village, others decide on a "back-up" so that they can come back to their houses and continue with the "booze-up". These parties sometimes last three or four days and both men and women take part, drinking until they collapse and as soon as they are capable of movement again they continue to drink. When the beer has been exhausted in one house, those who are able to do so move on to the next. A considerable amount of illicit love-making also takes place and Geao is of the opinion that a lot of the children are conceived at these parties, as it is here that the woman can have a child by the person she chooses, not necessarily her husband. Certainly during my stay at Mbulu, I found that the Mbulu were as hard a bunch of drinkers as any Tanganyikan Africans. When I asked Geao whether or not the husbands of the women who went off with the other men at these parties approved, he replied that sometimes they do, sometimes they couldn't care less, and at other times they may get a little bit upset and a little fight might take place, but nothing serious. We drove on for a short while in silence, then he turned to me and asked

-"Why did you not keep the Gausmo's daughter at Dongobesh in camp for the night? Lots of Europeans do. That was a special honour that the Chief gave you."

I immediately replied that I hoped the Chief did not expect me to take the girl to bed. He said,

-"No, you weren't expected to but if you wished to do so, she was all yours for the taking. The father would have probably been very happy if you had done so. Did you not like her? Was she not good-looking enough for you?"

_"She was indeed very good-looking", I pointed out, "but I'm a married man. I do not think it would be wise in my situation."

Geao laughed.

A little further on, we saw a young woman digging in a field next to the road, with a small child lying on a skin on the grass nearby. Geao asked me to stop as she was related to him and had obviously had a child just lately and he would like to speak to her. After a few minutes, I went and joined them and I noticed that the handle of the hoe was very short - about two feet long. Geao introduced me and then we returned to the vehicle whilst Geao explained that she'd only just had the child, which was about four weeks old. I said I thought it was a little early for her to start working again in the fields but he pointed out that this was not the case, she was back at work with her hoe and bent right over so I asked Geao why the handle was so short, since the normal size was about five feet long. I was concerned that this must give the woman terrible backache. Geao said,

-"No, not at all. Firstly the woman is used to it and secondly, and more important, she can carry on with her hoeing, whilst at the same time having sex with her boyfriend if he so wishes, by just lifting her skirt!".

He then unleashed his great laugh, thinking it was a great joke.

Geao was now in a talking mood and would not stop. He asked

me if I knew Peter, the livestock officer who had occupied my house before I arrived at Mbulu. Apparently my servant at the time, Sakta, had been working for Peter as a gardener helper. Peter had a one and a half ton lorry which every weekend he used to take out to a spot about ten miles from Mbulu, where he would pick up an attractive young Mbulu woman and take her back to his house for the weekend. He would then put her in a bath and help her scrub herself down, then they would settle down to a meal and drink and when they were both feeling merry, they would proceed to the bedroom, where they remained until the early hours of Monday morning. Peter seldom took out the same girl twice, although it did happen once that he took one girl out for four weekends running. When he went to pick her up on the fifth weekend, she was not there but her brother was, and he told Peter she would come and see him at a later date. Peter was insistent that she should not come unless he came to pick her up again and thought nothing of it. He never saw the girl again, but her father appeared one day and demanded compensation, claiming that Peter had put her in the family way. Peter was not to be fooled without the girl being there and demanded that the girl be brought, be properly examined by a doctor and, if the child was born and was obviously of mixed race, then he would take responsibility for it, but not otherwise. Fortunately, shortly after this, he was transferred and the matter never arose again. When I asked Geao if she ever did have a child and whether it was half-caste, he replied that she was never pregnant, but her father thought he was onto a good thing. This was, in those days, a very costly pastime for Peter because it cost him Shs. 20/- for the weekend (the year was early 1949), and Shs. 20/- plus her meals and drink, was quite a lot of money then. One thing in his favour was that the district had a reputation for having a low rate of venereal disease so he had little cause to worry but he was certainly not the only person doing this sort of thing. The Mbulu girls were particularly attractive and had caused the downfall of many a District Officer and District Commissioner.

The next story that Geao told me was about a man called John, who was in the Public Works Department. He and another fellow called Grey, both had the same girlfriend at Babati and on one particular occasion, John went to Arusha for the weekend, but during the previous week, Grey had lost his girlfriend and since John was away, he decided to 'shack up' with John's girl. For some reason or other, John decided to come back early and when he arrived he found his girlfriend in the house just before evening. She had obviously been to bed with someone as the bed was ruffled up and she was wearing only a *kanga*. Whilst they were arguing, Grey, who had been to Shere Mohammed's *duka* and had had quite a lot to drink, returned with more drink and goodies for the girl. She then told John to go away, as she no longer wished to be his girlfriend which led to Grey and John having a scuffle until John pulled out a knife. Seeing this, Grey quickly tried to escape through the window but as he was going out, John shoved the knife into his backside and Grey had to be rushed to Arusha for treatment. All the local Africans in Babati thought this was a terrific joke as did all the Europeans and the story had spread like wildfire.

Geao started to laugh again and didn't stop until we met up with Peter Bell, the District Commissioner, a short distance from home. He told me that Pat, my wife was confined to her bed, very unwell with bad stomach pains, and that I should go and find out what was going on. Unfortunately, this was in the rainy season, the roads were very bad, and all I had was my Ford pick-up, which had to be mended before I could take Pat into Arusha. The following day, having fixed the car and made a cover over the top and put a mattress in for her to lie on, we set out for Arusha with the Veterinary Officer, John Pettifer and his wife Rosemary, in convoy with us.

It was already dark when we reached Mto Wa Mbu, about 65 miles from Mbulu and for a stretch of some four miles, the whole road was completely under water, with cars strewn all over the place, stuck in the mud. John, at the time, was not used to driving in these conditions, but I could not stop for the night as we had no mosquito nets and Pat, although fairly comfortable, was causing us concern. I had little choice but to brave it and drove on slowly with John loyally following in my tracks. Although I managed to drive right through to the other end, John got stuck one hundred yards from the end of the floodwater. We had had to stop and help move other vehicles out of our way on the way up and it was now after midnight. The water was at least two feet deep the whole way through so I took the car up to a small rise and there we made ourselves some coffee and settled in the back of the pick-up, with all four of us squeezed into the back, leaving a reasonable space for Pat to sleep in. Up to this time, John and I had treated each other with a certain amount of reserve as neither of us knew the other too well, but that night the grumbling, the laughter and the numerous mosquitoes succeeded in breaking the ice.

By midday we were in Arusha and Pat was taken straight into hospital, where she was operated on two days later. As this was a fairly serious operation, she was advised to stay in Arusha for some time for observation purposes, and so she did some work as a nurse at the Arusha School, subsequently being called back to nurse at the school during the term time.

On one of my safaris, while visiting Carl Lundgren, I was introduced to his boss, Dick Cooper, who was out from the U.K. on holiday. Dick, a very gentle and a very rich man, had a house about three miles west of the Lundgren house. He owned a considerable number of shares in oil which, at the time, were making good money and had built a very attractive and imposing property with a beautiful flower garden overlooking a large valley. It was open most of the year to Dick's friends, for although he used to go there for two or three months of the year, his friends used it whenever they wished. When he did come out, he used to bring with him different friends, including girlfriends, as he had never married but eventually he married Marjorie, an American girl. She had been very good-looking when he first brought her out but by the time I met her she had already been married to him for two or three years and had unfortunately become addicted to gin.

Carl had mentioned to Dick that I spoke the language and knew a good deal about the Masai people and, as Dick himself had been very interested in the people of Tanganyika generally, he asked Carl to bring me to meet him. With two other guests, Gordon Scott the District Officer in Mbulu and Jimmy Stewart, a vet, I arrived to find Dick and his wife having an argument about the photographs in the house. Although he had agreed to remove certain personal photographs she didn't like, she was in too much of a state to know what she wanted and was being obstreperous. We stayed on to supper, while Marjorie continued to behave badly and then she suggested that she showed us the house. When she reached her room, she got hold of Jimmy and tried to force him onto her bed. We decided that the time had come to leave. The following morning, Dick came down to Carl's house to apologise for Marjorie's behaviour, followed by Marjorie who was reassuringly sober. Dick and I went off for a drive and had a very interesting discussion on things in general and the Masai problem in particular. This was the beginning of a great friendship and I came to know Dick very well after this. I found out that he had done a considerable amount of good for the area, including the stocking of the Babati lake with six different types of Tilapia, which had all thrived. On one occasion, Dick was stopped from fishing his own fish because he didn't have a licence. The fingerlings had been flown out from the United States, so anyone who fishes in Lake Babati today can thank Dick Cooper for being able to do so. In his day, Dick had been a great hunter but by the time I met him he had given it up, although his house still contained many of his trophies. He was still very keen on duck shooting and it was while on a bird shoot at Lake Giddas in the Mbulu district that he slipped and fell and drowned himself in four feet of water. Before he died, he had told me that if ever I wanted to go into a business of my own, he would be only too pleased to help me. This he said in front of Marjorie and when, a little later on, I told him I wanted to get a farm in Oldeani, he was delighted and offered me any financial help that I might require. Whatever other faults Marjorie had, she kept Dick's word to me, because when I did in fact require a loan for my Olmolog farm, she ensured that I received it.

Marjorie did not come from a rich family in the States, and I think that the money Dick lavished on her went to her head, so that after his tragic death, she went completely out of control. The tragedy was that when Marjorie was sober, she could be very amusing and was a fun-loving person but unfortunately, as time went on, the times when she was sober were few and far between. Marjorie used to spend a lot of time in Arusha with Jimmy Price, who was originally an automobile engineer, but, like Marjorie, had taken to drink, which got the better of him. As a result he was sacked from the Ford Motor Company, then the Usagara Company, and finally did irregular casual work. He and Marjorie were well-suited as drinking partners, he had no money and Marjorie had plenty. It was fortunate for both Marjorie and Jimmy that the barman of the New Arusha Hotel was "Fupi", a well-known character at the time. Fupi had been awarded the MBE whilst at the Arusha Hotel and when you asked him what the initials stood for, he replied "Mingi Bar Experience". (`Mingi' in Swahili means `lots'). Whenever Marjorie and Jimmy got over-drunk, they would just throw their money and jewellery about the place, Fupi would collect it all, take what was owed to the bar, and meticulously hand over all the rest. On one occasion, when Jimmy was working for me up at Olmolog, he received a large sum of money from me for repairing some farm machinery and went straight into the bar. He started flinging money around and eventually ended up with nothing, having had two hundred and fifty pounds when he started, which in those days was a great deal of money. Fupi managed to collect all the excess money for him so that Jimmy was not short the following day.

One day, a tall American, Rab, who had originally come out on a hunting safari and was now hunting alone, brought a friend along for a drink in the New Arusha bar. Whilst Rab was talking to other friends, Jimmy, a very short little man, went over to talk to the newcomer and opened the conversation with,

-"I see you're wearing leather boots in the bar. I don't like to tell you but it is the greatest insult you can give in this country. You ought not to come into the bar with your boots on, as you might cause a riot."

By now Rab had joined them but did nothing to interfere and waited to see what the outcome would be. Jimmy then persuaded the stranger to go round the corner, remove his boots, and come back into the bar and no sooner had he returned than Jimmy excused himself to go to the Men's room but instead he just let loose in the boots. By the time the American discovered what had happened to his boots, Jimmy was nowhere to be seen but unfortunately for Jimmy, a few days later the American walked into the bar, complete with boots, and who should be sitting at the bar but Jimmy, who immediately burst out laughing. The American was not amused and seized Jimmy by the scruff of the neck, Jimmy shouted for help but not a single person moved to his assistance. The American turned round and said

-"What can I do with this little rat? I can't hit him."

So someone suggested that he flung him out of the window. The fall wasn't very great - about nine feet - and so he did just that. This had no effect whatsoever and Jimmy was back in the bar a few minutes later, complete with bruises, begging a drink from the individual who had thrown him out!

Mbulu was a station where the average couple, like ourselves, probably had one guest a month at most, but on this particular day, first Pevie, who was the Provincial Veterinary officer, turned up on a district inspection, and then Carl Lundgren and Marjorie arrived from Babati. As we had only one guest room, I put Marjorie into our room where there was a double bed, Carl and Pevie had the guest room, whilst I slept in the sitting room. Marjorie started by being difficult and insisted on having gin instead of tea, even though it was teatime. After a considerable amount of gin, which had to be replenished from the local shop, she started an argument with Carl, who was her manager, about his treatment of his dogs. The argument went on and on until it became quite boring and Marjorie was on the point of collapse. We decided to put her to bed as she was incapable of going herself, but having got her into bed, she insisted on either Gordon Pevie or myself staying with her. This nonsense continued for some hours until we eventually told Carl to look after his boss and the next morning she woke up as bright as a daisy. Things got steadily worse for Marjorie and, sad to say, one night she went out for a walk from a small hotel and was found dead a few hours later, having presumably just keeled over.

At the meeting of the Mbulu Development Council, it was noted that the onion seed business that had been introduced to Mbulu towards the end of the war was now coming up against political intrigue. Imported seed of the Bombay Red variety was now coming in from overseas at a much lower cost and of a much better quality than the Mbulu seed, the price of which went down. The Mbulu were however not prepared to accept this, as only a few years previously they had been persuaded to grow more and more seed. A meeting was held by the District Commissioner with the Development Council to explain the situation to the Mbulu. If they could not compete with the import market in both quality and price, they would have to cease production of onion seed. The crop they had in hand would be purchased, but at a lower rate. Unfortunately, a rumour then started that the prices were deliberately being kept down by the Administration, and so the Mbulu people, decided that they would move out of the onion seed business. When the market righted itself, and they realised that there was good money to be made, it was too late, as other growing areas had been found.

It was time also for the Haidum Tsetse clearing and settlement area to be inspected. A great deal of work had been done there and it was time for certain parts to be resettled. This would mean that the Development Committee, of which I was a member, would have to go down and allocate land to families from other areas and help to remove them, which was a tricky matter as some of the area was claimed to be the Barabaig tribe's land and it had to be properly allocated. All this would take a long time, so Peter Bell suggested that we should leave on a Tuesday, clear all the areas and sort out the problems and end up at a dam near Lake Basuto, just outside the Haidum area, where we could camp on the Friday evening. That would allow us to do some sand-grouse shooting on the Saturday, attend the Basuto Market, which was small, and then go duck-shooting on the lakes. Basuto is the name of the main lake but there are about twenty other lakes in the area, all of them very rich in bird life. John Pettifer, my immediate boss, would also be in the area, and agreed to join us in the afternoon, for the duck-shoot.

Peter took over control of the bird-shoot and we all took our different places, Peter Bell, John Pettifer, another District Officer and me. We were all placed at intervals around the lake. Peter was on my right, the other D.O. was further down, and John was on my left, about a hundred yards from me. Birds were flying over continuously and when a flight of five birds came over us, I heard John declare the last two birds and with two shots bring both down within twenty yards of him. I fired two shots at the remaining birds and one dived into the water and was retrieved by my dog Winston. When another lot of birds, about seven in total, came over, John immediately shouted he would not take any of them and would leave them to the rest of us. I had not reloaded, so Peter and the other D.O. fired four shots and brought down just one bird, which was retrieved from the water by Winston. The birds were now coming fast and, as they came over, John declared. I shot only two more birds and I don't think Peter or the other D.O. did any better but we all watched John, who amazingly would declare whichever birds he decided on and he would bring them down within thirty yards, every time. There was not a single miss, neither did he wound any bird. At the end of the shoot, we collected twenty-seven knob-nosed geese. The next morning, we went out grouse-shooting and got a large bag of sand-grouse but John would not shoot the sand-grouse, as he felt it was unfair to do so. Although I've been out shooting birds with numerous other people, I've never known anyone quite so accurate as John and during the seven or eight years that I knew him, I never saw him wound a bird, or use a round of ammunition which failed to bring down its target.

However, with a rifle it was an entirely different story. At Kwakuchinja one day, John saw some eland at the side of the road and so he turned to me and said, "You know, I want to get just one eland. I've never shot one in my life." So I offered him my rifle, as he didn't have his own with him. He must have fired six rounds at this eland and hit with every round but his shots were all over the place despite the eland being no more than two hundred yards away and, in the end, I had to kill it myself.

Later on, as we all did in those days, John took out his licence to kill two elephants, with the idea of improving his financial position. When his leave came. he asked me to go with him up to the Murai Mountains to help him shoot an elephant as his licence was soon to lapse. On the first evening we saw a fairly large old male, on its own on the opposite side of the ravine and so I took over the hunt. I was carrying a .416 while John was carrying my .450 No. 2 double barrel, both high calibre weapons, ideal for shooting elephant. When we got to within fifty yards of the elephant, I showed John exactly what to do and where to fire, and when he fired, I fired also. The elephant was going across our front and I was uncertain about John's capabilities of shooting with the double barrel, because I had suggested that he went for a heart shot in the shoulder whilst I, for safety's sake, took a spine shot in the back but the elephant went down immediately. On inspection, John's shot was found to be about four feet to the right of where it should have been and on getting close to the elephant, we realised that it was still alive, so I finished it off with a shot in the brain. After this, John and I took lessons from one another, me for the shotgun and John for the rifle, both of which require a lot of practice in judgement. John improved considerably but I failed to make much progress.

On our return from our week's safari around the countryside, we undertook to distribute around the station the birds that we had shot.

Pat and I took our bag to a new veterinary stock inspector on the stock farm at Ndegicot, some three miles out of Mbulu. Whilst we were having drinks, it got dark and the dogs kept running into the house and hiding behind a sofa but when we searched all round, we couldn't find anything. When it was time for Pat and me to leave, we went out to the car and as we opened the doors, suddenly saw a large leopard hiding behind the car, which ran off into some bushes. Soon after we left, the front door having been left open, a normal custom on a warm evening, the dogs suddenly came tearing in, followed by the leopard, which came right into the house. The owner got hold of a Dietz lamp which he flung at the leopard, the only thing he could think of at the time, but unfortunately, the paraffin went all over the floor and set the room alight. They managed to extinguish the fire without too much trouble, but the leopard came back twice within the next half-hour, determined to get one of the dogs. The stock inspector hid himself in a corner and waited with his shotgun and sure enough, within a very short time, the leopard came straight in the door and as it stopped to look around, he was able to shoot it.

Not long after this, I was at Endabesh in the Rest Camp, after holding a market. I had shot myself an impala on the hillside, which had been gutted and skinned and part of it was strung up in front of the rest house, in a mosquito-netted section of the building. The door, unfortunately, did not fit too well and during the night I heard a growl. I shone my torch onto this veranda section, and there, eating my impala, was a leopard. As soon as it saw the light, it disappeared and did not return. On another occasion, I was at the Endulen market, sleeping in a tent. I had some meat tied up on a tree in front of the tent, about two yards from my flap. I was awakened during the night by a sound and looking out, saw a leopard eating my leg of mutton! This time I did not hesitate and shot the leopard on the spot, the intention being to protect my property but I gained a very good skin trophy in the process. I feel it important to mention here that as a youngster, like most in East Africa at the time, I was very keen on shooting and I used to go out shooting as often as possible. Now, however, I have absolutely no desire whatsoever to shoot, and I am keen on the conservation of our natural resources, which are in such jeopardy. Ideas have changed and this new knowledge about the ecological process and our part within it have meant a great deal of people have changed accordingly.

Pat, my wife, had of late been spending quite a bit of time in Arusha, where she was working as a nurse at the Arusha school. This was very convenient for her, as my mother was Matron of the school, and Pat was, at this particular stage, still needed to be operated on from time to time and so it was much more convenient for her to be in Arusha close to the doctors.

I had just left Pat in Arusha and was on my way back to Mbulu, climbing the Kilimatebo escarpment, when the second gear in my Ford pick-up stripped. Fortunately, a lorry with a driver that I knew had just come up behind me, thankfully with a good rope and he was able to tow me into Karatu, where I stripped the whole gearbox down and repaired it sufficiently to get back to Mbulu the next day. As this was a very expensive fault, I decided that the pick-up, although very comfortable, had to go and in its place I would get something heavier and more solid and so, with some local leave due to me, I decided to take the pick-up into Arusha and see if I could get a reasonable price for it. Fortunately for me there was someone else who had a similar one, which had done him extremely well, it being a very good car on reasonable roads but not in mountainous areas. He offered me an acceptable price and I went straight over to the Motor Mart and bought myself a Bedford one and a half ton bare chassis. I got the garage to fix a box where the seat normally went and drove back to Mbulu sitting on the petrol box, which was not as uncomfortable as it sounds, although the wind disturbed me, as there was no windscreen. It took me all day to drive the hundred and sixty miles back to Mbulu and I had fortuitously bought myself some good dust goggles before leaving Arusha, otherwise I would never have been able to make the trip. The next day, I started planning the construction of the body and cab. After the drawing-board stage, I got hold of Shauri Duankai, who was not a carpenter but who was a useful assistant and he and I went to Babati where we were able to buy the timber that I wanted for the cab. The cab took me some five weekends to build, as I had to use the vehicle in the meantime, and the completed body was finished after just three months. This vehicle remained with me for the next five years and the body, although not as smart as some, did not give me any trouble whatever.

I had a very fierce turkey gobbler, which had been the only male in a hatch of eighteen eggs, brought up from Arusha. He was always attacking people, one day attacking a man who was lying under his vehicle who lifted his head so suddenly that he knocked himself out. I was working in my carpentry shop with the vehicle outside when suddenly I heard a rush and looked out and in came Peter Bell, the District Commissioner, who jumped onto the table with the turkey right behind him. I was told to get rid of the turkey, or words to that effect and as Christmas was very close, I said

-"All right, then it can be your Christmas present and you had better do something about it."

We did, but not until Christmas arrived. Peter Bell told me later that day that the Provincial Commissioner was coming to visit Mbulu, and that he would bring him to see me during the next two days. The reason for this meeting was that I had applied for a farm at Oldeani but the Veterinary Department had complained that I had not given them sufficient information when I had asked for permission to buy the farm. They wanted to point out that they thought I had a future in the Veterinary Department. Although I had no formal qualifications, I was told that a special sub-department, the Livestock Marketing Department, was to be formed within the jurisdiction of the Veterinary Department, and I was to lead it after a year or so. This would bring me up to the lowest veterinary officer's salary but that was as far as I would go and I made it clear that I was not interested in this. One or two kind people, like David White, Neil Reid himself (The Director of Veterinary Services), and Gordon Pevie, all tried to dissuade me from leaving the department but I decided that the only way to go about it was to give in my notice there and then. This gave me six months to look around for something before I left the Department.

Chapter Eleven
Becoming a Cattle Trader

Page-Jones had decided that I should have been allocated the farm at Oldeani and was prepared to back me. He also agreed that I was wasting my time remaining with the Veterinary Department, and although he would have liked me to stay on, it was a dead end for me, because without formal qualifications my chances of promotion would always be limited. He made no promises but told me that if I went up to Olmolog and had a look at the new farms up there, he would do all in his power to make sure that I got one. He also mentioned that he thought that would be a very good ending to the culling scheme, as Peter Bell had been awarded the O.B.E for it and, if I got a farm, that would just about level us off. Peter also backed me up and when Page-Jones came out and saw me making the body of my motor-car, this was used as one of the factors in my favour. He pointed out that I needed a job in which I was able to use my practical skills and experience.

We had a meeting with the Land Utilization Board, a very powerful unit, comprised of various government organisations and successful farmers, responsible for looking at areas suitable for farming and allocating farmers to each plot. I gathered that Page-Jones was on my side in opposition to two others, who were chosen by different members of the Board and he, in fact, had me brought back halfway through the meeting for more questions, which he put to me as Chairman of the Meeting. In the end, I believe I was awarded a farm mainly because of Page-Jones' support.

We were now just about through our second Rinderpest campaign in three years but fortunately I had very little to do with it as I had other work. John Pettifer, the Vet, was due for transfer and was about to go to Ngara Nairobi but on account of the Rinderpest campaign, the arrival of Pettifer's relief, Jimmy Garden was put back, as he had no experience with Rinderpest and he did not know the Mbulu people. It was felt that it would be better if he arrived when the campaign was over.

John had just come back from the Lake Tlawi area where he had been carrying out the last of the inoculations. He was in a bad mood because he had had a disagreeable argument with some of the cattlemen and his one thought was to leave the place and get back to West Kilimanjaro where he originally came from. Rosemary came up to my house that night at about half past seven and said,

-"Can you come over and talk to John? He's in such a bloody awful mood. I'm sure he's going to do something dreadful."

I went over and we had a few drinks and John's mood improved. Suddenly one of the local people came in and demanded compensation for his dog and his sheep which John's bull terrier Patch had killed. John was about to throw a chair at the fellow but I managed to quieten him down and pointed out that it was inevitable that if one's dog went nearly two miles away and killed another dog, for the owner to come and demand compensation. John turned around and said,

-"That bloody dog Patch, I've asked you to shoot him about ten times and you always say that you will, you will, and you never do anything about it. In any case," he said,"I cannot take him back to West Kilimanjaro as he will kill somebody's pet lap animals."

Eventually the fellow who had lost his dog and his sheep was paid Shs.15/-, which was about their value, and John, sitting down, turned to Rosemary and said,

-"Rosemary, please ask David, as he is more likely to listen to you than to me, to please shoot Patch."

-"I 'll shoot Patch if that is what you want, but don't turn round afterwards and complain. I must make it clear now that I personally will not take him on when you leave, as I dislike the dog and he is too much of a headache. I'm having no more to do with bull terriers unless I bring them up myself," I replied rather wearily.

- "All you have to do, David, is to take my .22 rifle, go outside and shoot the bloody thing. Can't you do that little thing for a friend?"

-"Where is the .22?", I sighed.

I was handed the rifle and I went outside on to the lawn and shot Patch. I went back inside, muttering

-"Thank God that's done."

It would seem that John did not believe me until we went outside and there was Patch at the end of the lawn where I had shot him. Seeing his dog actually lying there dead upset John terribly. He said,

-" I didn't mean you to shoot the poor thing, I was just joking."

Rosemary sighed.

-"John, you begged David on many occasions to shoot Patch and tonight you were quite abusive to him and he went and did what you asked him to do."

-"Oh, all you're keen on is David, anything that David says is right, anything I say is wrong.", before adding "Bugger David".

At this stage, I thought it was time for me to leave and go home, which I did. John had had quite a lot to drink.

Next morning, John came to the office and apologised. I showed him a telegram saying that Jimmy Garden and his wife Betty were arriving that day and that John should proceed to West Kilimanjaro as soon as possible so that Jimmy Garden could move into his house. John asked me where Jimmy was going to stay meanwhile and I said I didn't know but they could stay with me until they got settled. He said,

-"Well, it's going to take me a week before I can get everything packed and away."

-"That's all right," I replied, "With Pat in Arusha and Penny with my mother, I'm by myself and the house is fairly empty. If they want to, they can stay with me."

Later on that day, Jimmy and Betty Garden appeared. They were very tired after the journey and as my house was near the office, it was easy for me to see them arrive. I went and told them roughly the situation.

- "Do we have to go over to this fellow Pettifer?", Jimmy asked. "We hear that he's an awkward so-and-so."

- "He's not actually all that awkward," I assured them. "Only when he's been drinking. He's one of those people that you can put in his place easily. But you are welcome to stay in my house if you like."

They were quite pleased about this and decided to accept my offer. In those days of colonial department snobbery, it was not my place to invite somebody of a higher rank to stay with me unless it was suggested by my boss. I thought this was the sort of thing John Pettifer would take up but did not do so, as he was only too pleased. John left a week later and remained a great friend of mine and I was asked to be godfather to their second child. Later, Rosemary and John parted and I gather that, after Independence, John tried to go through the Tanzanian border in the boot of a car and got caught. Rosemary married someone with a title and I believe she is now living in Cape Town.

Jimmy Garden was a quiet man and a good vet, very pleasant and always willing to help and his wife, Betty, was outgoing, good-looking and lively. As John left so quickly after they arrived, the task of taking them round and showing them the district was left to me. They had not been out from the UK for very long, and so were very interested in everything that was happening around them, and I can remember one incident very clearly. Whilst we were at the Katesh market, there was a young Masai brander, responsible for cattle identification, who was obviously in a randy mood, as he had a huge erection most of the morning.

As Betty was watching the cattle coming into the ring, she suddenly noticed this and turned to me and said,

- "David, that man, the one in front there, sitting on that wall. Is what I can see what I think it is?"

-"Yes, Betty, but you should not be looking in that direction".

-"Do you mean to say that these little African girls can take that?", she asked in feigned shock.

-"Yes, they certainly can and they probably love it, too."

-"Oh, God. Oh, to be an African girl, just for one night," she sighed wistfully.

Jimmy's greatest weakness was that his knowledge of motor-cars was strictly limited to making it go forwards and backwards. He could hardly change a wheel when he came to Mbulu and I think that he was not much better when he left, but he did learn quite a little about his car, if only to realise that he should never buy another one of the same make - a 1949 Skoda. Jimmy often had to travel around with me because his car just could not take the gradients. Every time he came home, he tried it out but for some reason, that make of car just could not cope with our roads. It gave him a lot of experience blowing into the tank, changing points and all that sort of thing. The Gardens were only in Mbulu for a short time but they made their mark. Jimmy was particularly good at clinical work and so he was moved to Arusha where he was more suited. He must have been in Arusha for five or six years after which he returned to practise in England.

When I came back from my safaris, I found a letter from David White, who was then acting Director of Veterinary Services in the absence of Neil Reid, informing me that I was to go down to the Yaida to investigate the Tsetse position and to arrange for clearing to begin. He had also sent a copy to Hugh Newland, who was then the Provincial Veterinary Officer, in Arusha. At the same time I was to mark out an area and build a compound for a veterinary contingent, who would be going down to carry out an experimental project. A hundred and fifty head of cattle were to be brought in from outside from non-tsetse areas, to be inoculated against trypanosomiasis, before being taken into the area. This was to see how long they could survive with inoculation and care, once the area had been cleared of certain trees, such as acacia, thorn, and some of the bigger specimens of other varieties, that the tsetses nest in.

Geao, myself, my veterinary guard and three others went forth to the Yaida Valley with equipment for a full ten days' safari. This pleased me as I had been wanting to go to this area for some time and some of the other Mbulu Europeans had wanted to come down too and so I was able to invite a few of them down, over the weekends, once I was established. On arrival I found that in fact some clearing had already been done, rather half-heartedly, and abandoned some time back. A lot of ring-barking had been done and a fairly high proportion of this had been successful, which meant that about eighty per cent of the big acacia, fever trees, including tortillis, had died back and only required a push to bring them down. On the second evening my staff told me that the others who had been ordered down from the Mangola area on the shores of Lake Eyasi had arrived and they were very hungry for meat. There was a plain packed with game animals, right in front of the camp, and so I went out and shot a zebra. My veterinary guards complained that they did not like zebra meat, would I be so good as to shoot them an eland? I told them that I was not going to shoot animals at random all over the place, just to please individuals. If they wanted an eland, they could certainly have an eland but they had to make sure that the zebra would be eaten first. I was immediately told that the Tindiga, who were the local bushmen (Ndorobo tribe) were in the area and in no time at all they would eat the zebra, and one of my staff pointed them out, heading straight for the dead zebra.

This aroused my curiosity because I had been very interested in these people for some time and wanted to contact them, so I just let them carry on with it, hoping to see them later. I could not get near enough to the eland but I did get a wildebeest for my people before going back to the zebra to try and contact the Tindiga but they had disappeared.

Geao told me that he could contact them for me if I left him there and went off in the car until I was out of sight. It was not long before I heard a shot, which was the sign for me to come back and when I got there I was amazed to find that the zebra had been completely removed except for the skin and the excreta. Sitting next to Geao was an oldish man who was about to leave when I got there until Geao persuaded him to stay. He was a genuine Tindiga. I soon met quite a few of these people after the first man had been introduced to me and we all seemed to get on quite well. I gave him odd little things and after that it became a regular occurrence, when I went into that area, that one or two of them would come up and I would shoot for them. On this particular occasion, I shot quite a number of animals for them, including an elephant and a couple of buffalo, although, I did not shoot any eland for them, despite their requests, because they were scarce. In conversation, one of them told me about the spring and swamp at the top north-eastern end of the Yaida, where the water came from and so a fortnight later, I went up with my rod and did some fishing and caught some very large lungfish.

The place was teeming with barbus and on that first occasion I saw three large python all over fourteen foot long. Over the weekend some friends came down from Mbulu including the Scotts, Robert Collet and John Percy. Pat was not there as she was in Arusha at the time. The elephant I had shot for the Tindiga, mentioned earlier, was in fact John Percy's elephant, supposedly shot on his licence. The one thing that I could not understand was where all this meat had disappeared to. Whenever the Tindiga got stuck into meat, it all disappeared in no time. I asked them where they kept the meat. One of the old men said,

-"Ah, you come with me tomorrow and I will show you but you must not bring anyone else, just you and Geao."

The next day, I went with him and not very far away there was a large rocky outcrop, at least a thousand square yards, completely covered with meat at different stages of desiccation. The other thing I noticed was that a large number of people were deformed and disabled, with broken legs, broken arms and so on. When I enquired why, I was told that a lot of them had fallen out of trees, when trying to get their honey combs from the hives. I found out that there was a considerable amount of inbreeding - in fact the Tindiga group did not go in for formal marriage, they just took whatever woman they wanted and sometimes the woman would be a close relative. It seemed to me that incest was a custom and that, when a man felt like sex he would virtually go with whichever woman suited him at that moment and she was always willing unless she was very heavily pregnant or was menstruating.

I met a lot of Tindigas in the Yaida after this and got to know them quite well. Although they were very similar in their living habits and their customs to the proper Ndorobo, their language was different, but generally speaking they were like other bushmen and honey hunters. They were generous and cheerful people but it required patience to meet them in their normal groups. They could be standing in light bush, thirty yards away, and you would not see them because there would be absolutely no movement and when you turned they would either come into or go out of view and you would never see any movement whatever. Once, I had to approach an elephant very close to check a sore or injury on the inside of the rear leg, fairly high up, causing the animal to have a bad limp. One of these fellows asked what it was we were looking at and when I told him I saw him go to within about seven yards of the elephant and bend down and have a good look, the elephant never knew he was there. He came back and reported that it was just a bad sore, the elephant must have cut itself and there was a piece of wood stuck there but it was healing.

When we had completed the job of getting the site ready with all the cattle bomas and were well into building temporary houses for the staff, I returned to Mbulu. I succeeded in persuading two Watindiga to act as bodyguards for my staff until they got used to the area. These people would not accept cash for payment but wanted matches, salt and meat, shot for them when I came down.

When I got back to my house, there were two important letters waiting for me. One was from the Veterinary Department, suggesting that I might like to take on the job of Chief Cattle Buyer at the new

Tanganyika Packers factory in Arusha. This would entail buying and supplying the factory with their livestock requirements and seeing that the livestock got through to the slaughterhouses on time. This was perfectly suited to what I wanted, but for one thing that I was not prepared to accept, which was the fact that I was also to work part-time as their labour officer, managing the labour. Basil Stubbings, who had been a Provincial Commissioner, was going to be employed at the factory as overall Manager and I could have worked very well with him as I knew him well and liked him. I realised that I had only a few months more under the Veterinary Department's umbrella and after that I would be on my own. I had resigned and made my application for another farm, the resignation had been reluctantly accepted and it was just a matter of working out my time to the end of the year when I was due for some paid leave. I wrote to Tanganyika Packers and said that I was prepared to buy and sell cattle to anyone or any organisation that I wished, that I had a considerable amount of experience in this and I knew that once I got going, I could make a go of it. I soon had a reply agreeing to my suggestion and details were then to be worked out in Arusha and, in the meantime, a Mr Bill Timms would come out from Arusha and be the buyer for Tanganyika Packers, on my advice. He did not have much experience in this business but I did not have the necessary licences and I was still under the jurisdiction of Government so I would do the buying, but for him. He had been there only a short time when I got a cable from the Department releasing me to buy officially on contract, while I was on my terminal leave.

From time to time, I used to hold a special market at Masakaloda Clearings, at the foot of the Rift Valley escarpment, in the shadow of Mount Hanang. One day, just after the first showers of rain had fallen, I had set up my camp away from the swamp, on account of mosquitoes when Sakta, my cook, told me that we needed meat for supper. There was no game about and the market was not until the next day, when meat would be available but a great many sandgrouse could be seen flying to the swamp to the north of the main clearing where there was a little stream. I went over and saw there were little pools in the river which runs into the swamp where the sandgrouse were drinking, so I walked along the river and was able to shoot about 15 birds coming in to drink. When I went to pick them up, all except the three which I had shot with the last round had been taken by jackal. I saw that as I shot, the jackals in the bush would come out and take away the fallen birds, a problem I dealt with fairly quickly.

While returning to Mbulu, I had to go through Dabil. Unfortunately the road had been washed away and it was rough going. My near right-hand main leaf spring broke at the centre bolt but I managed to get as far as Dabilland where I parked my vehicle in the Dabil square. I collected as many odds and ends as I could to do a temporary repair, principally using a zebra skin which was cut into strips about one inch wide. As the rains had just started, the heat in the middle of the day was unbearable and my staff and I were all sweating like pigs. Having made up a block cut from a tree trunk to fit into the upper end of the spring and the chassis, I was binding this in place, first with ordinary half-inch sisal rope and then covering it over with the zebra hide strips which had been kept soaking in water, when suddenly a voice, a smooth Irish brogue, cut in,

-"Oh, Mr Read, and what would you be doing there?"

I told the owner of the voice that I was busy with my car, what did it seem like to him.

-"Oh, come and join us for a drink of some sort - it will make it easier for you to work."

It was early Saturday afternoon and so I refused before looking up to see it was Bishop Winters from the Mission next door. He tried to insist but I declined, postponing it until after I had finished the job because I knew very well that if I went into one of the shops where they were drinking, I would not be able to finish the repair that day. As soon as I had finished the job, I told him, I would be delighted to come and join them. At 4.30 pm, I did just that but as I had predicted, the drink kept coming with one drink leading to another, as the game of poker progressed. The Indians watched us but did not take any active part except by producing more and more Scotch, which went down very well and we carried on drinking until the early hours of the morning, when the Fathers had to go off to Mass. I am sure that by this time none of them were capable, but all the same they got off in time and seemed to be quite able to drive back to the Mission. They tried to make me promise to meet them later on the Sunday but I declined because I had to return home, promising that I would carry on the session next time I was at Dabil.

The Mission, including a small hospital well-run by the Sisters of Mary (medical sisters) who did all the nursing and medical work, was financed more or less entirely by the bishop, Monseigneur Winters. It belonged to a group of three missions, the main one at Dabil, another at Lake Tlawi and a new one being built down at Mbugwe. One evening one of the Fathers was coming back from Mbugwe on his way to the Ndareda Mission where there was a big party going on. As he passed very close to the road, he heard a faint little cry and one of his people in the vehicle also said they heard it and it must be a child. As they did not see any adults nearby, they decided to search and sure enough they found a new-born child, not more than an hour or two old. There was nobody there and the child was shivering with cold and so it was wrapped up, taken back to the Mission and taken over by the Sisters. Nobody claimed it, although the Mission tried to find its mother and it was christened Maria, rapidly becoming the pet of the sisters' quarters with her upbringing paid for by the mission and various people in the area. Maria was about the same age as my daughter Penny but a little bit smaller and so all Penny's clothes fitted her. She turned out to be a very pretty girl and was eventually old enough and well enough trained to help with the teaching. By this time, of course, her worth was assured and the local people started taking an interest in her leading to claims as to whose child she was, but nothing was ever proved. She was eventually taken to Ireland, where I understand she was trained as a nursing sister in the Church and came back to Dabil. I can remember one day going up there and she came running over to greet me and asked me where Pat and Penny were in perfect English with an Irish accent, quite at odds with her local dress. What happened to her when she returned to Mbulu I do not know as I was already out of the district and did not have contact with the Dabil Mission any longer but shortly after this, Bishop Winters was to be replaced by a local bishop because, I understand, that he refused to continue financing the Mission and returned to Ireland.

On my way back to Arusha, at a place called Kwakuchinja, we came across a large pack of baboons that were obviously playing some game that people claimed to be called "fire". What actually happened was that a few sticks of old bush were put in one particular spot and all the baboons sat around looking very much as if they were sitting around the fire like a bunch of old elders at a meeting. The youngsters were playing and suddenly one of the youngsters would be grabbed and shoved into the "fire". This would bring screams from the fire and the young one would dash off and run away, get caught by one of the adults and given a good smack. We sat and watched this for something like half an hour and no sooner had one young baboon been punished than another one went into the fire and so on. Some of my men, including Geao, seemed to think that this was a regular happening and he was quite convinced that the baboons knew exactly what they were teaching and having witnessed this myself, I was inclined to agree with him as they seemed very determined and intelligent. The baboon is not an animal that I like very much but I must be quite honest and admit to being intrigued by their antics. They are so like human beings, if they know they are being watched they will play up to the audience and are very good actors. One of my men decided to pull faces at one of the baboons and within seconds the baboon was doing exactly the same in return. Then the man turned around and showed his backside to the baboon and put his hands between his legs, and the baboon did the same back to him.

It was getting late and I decided that I had to get back to Arusha, particularly as the next day was a market day and I also had to collect cash from the bank. I had to operate a big cattle-buying organisation, which required anything up to Shs. 200,000/- in one round of markets and so it was arranged that I would have an overall credit facility of Shs. 50,000/- at Barclays Bank in Arusha. I went to see the Provincial Commissioner and pointed out that if I was at a place like Loliondo, miles away from everywhere, and there were a lot of cattle on the market during the dry season, I would need further finance. Would the Administration be prepared to lend me money to enable me to hold prices at the markets? The Provincial Commissioner agreed to consult his District Commissioners and District Officers and eventually it was agreed that while I was at these outlying stations and because the Government wanted as much money as possible to go into the cattle owners' pockets for tax purposes and famine relief requirements, they would help me out. I did not in fact have to use this facility until approximately a year later when there was a famine in Masailand and then I was able to draw a further Shs. 50,000/- out of native treasury funds, which had to be returned within a month.

It took me about a week to do three markets and at the end of this period, the cattle would all have to be herded together for their long trek back to Arusha. This would take ten days and an allowance of at least three days for quarantines *en route* would be made, so it was about three weeks before the cattle arrived at the other end. Once the animals were slaughtered I should have a cheque paid into my account but it did not always work this way, of course, and in effect, it took some time with long delays being the usual state of affairs.

At about this time I was also asked to go and see a friend of mine at Arusha Chini near Moshi at a big sugar factory. The manager and labour officer asked if I could buy cattle for them. They wanted a better quality than that provided for Tanganyika Packers and agreed to pay a higher rate. At Tanganyika Packers, quality did not matter so long as the animal was alive on arrival at the factory and Arusha Chini was prepared to pay up to a third more per head, but they expected much better quality animals and would be selective because they were to be slaughtered for the labour on the estate. They required approximately 150-200 head of cattle per month on a regular basis and they pointed out that if the price went up they would be prepared to pay a bit more. I signed a contract with them on the spot and then went to Tanganyika Packers to tell them exactly what had happened. They pointed out that it did not matter in the least as far as they were concerned, as the type of animal they needed was not of the standard required by Arusha Chini. Arusha Chini had promised that they would immediately put into my account Shs.30,000 and as soon as it was finished, it would be replaced, which helped considerably with my cash flow situation. In my first full month's cattle buying I made more profit than I had received in salary for two years in the Veterinary Department.

The month of December was even better than the previous one. I was now well launched into the cattle-buying business on my own account. There were a number of little matters that needed ironing out, such as the delay in Tanganyika Packers paying up when cattle were on the market in large numbers and I had one or two setbacks when I had to stop the market just because there was no money available. This gave the traders a free hand and prices toppled as the farmers were forced to sell at this time of year. Fortunately for me, the administration was very keen that the farmers should be paid a fair price and so they would stop the market at certain stages, giving me the opportunity to dash off to Arusha to sort out the financial side. Eventually, frustrated with Tanganyika Packers' slowness in paying up, I went to put my case to the Provincial Commissioner. I don't know what went on as a result but I do know that I was given another Shs.30,000 credit facility while Packers were sorting out their own accounts. I also received authorization from the Provincial Commissioner to draw as much as I could from the native treasuries in the different centres, particularly in Masailand. Between Waso and Ulala alone I had purchased over 1800 head of cattle and ninety-five per cent of these were Tanganyika

Packers' animals. As they were in poor condition due to the drought they would have to be trekked carefully to Arusha in order to get them there without losing too much weight. At this time of year it was impossible to take any herds larger than two hundred and fifty and even this number was only possible with the better conditioned animals so I carefully chose five hundred animals that I considered to be the best. These were put under one guard and some drovers, in two batches, approximately one hour behind each other. Instructions were given to travel only at night for the first fifty miles as there was a shortage of water and only small stock camps *en route*. The next five hundred were also divided into two groups and given the same instructions, to move a day later. A third group left a day later still and the last group was to stay for an extra two days before following slowly - by which time two lorries were to come up from Arusha, bringing water for the stragglers and ready to take back any animals incapable of doing the journey to the next stop, which was fifty miles away.

The plan worked extremely well, so well in fact that the whole batch got through with the exception of nine animals and every animal arrived either by lorry or on the hoof. Night travelling in Masailand did have its dangers, though, and the Masai warriors, who were cattle rustlers for want of a better phrase, were at this time very active as it was the right time of their Manyatta season. The few available water holes were also frequented by predators, which made a nuisance of themselves when we tried to water the cattle.

My other purchases from the Ngorongoro, Endulen and Mbulu districts were also very successful and I was now riding the crest of a wave and doing very well financially. To crown it all, when I returned to Arusha, Pat handed me a letter, which was to change my life completely. It was from the Land Utilization Board, informing me that I had been allocated a farm at Olmolog, on Mount Kilimanjaro. Olmolog farms are situated in the North-Western slopes of the mountain at an altitude of 5500 ft. It is a fertile area because of the high rainfall, that washes the volcanic soil of Kilimanjaro down into Lake Amboseli, and it had once been a wild olive forest burnt down by the former German farmer. Unit Three, as it was known, was not the best, by any stretch of the imagination, but it was certainly a very pleasant surprise. Thus, the Christmas of 1951 was spent in the bush, moving up cattle and it was the busiest Christmas I had spent in Tanzania. Despite this, I was able to get away from December 30th till January 4th, and so New Year was spent eating Peter Bell's turkey, which had chased him onto the carpenter's bench. On the morning of January 1st, I left with most of my possessions and a nucleus of seven staff, for the farm at Olmolog. When I arrived at about mid-day on January 2nd 1952, I did not sleep on my own farm because I didn't know the exact position of the boundary and I did not find out until later that I was actually fifty yards inside Derek Byrcasson's farm, next door. Brian Freyburg, who arrived next morning and went straight onto this farm, maintains that he was the first to arrive in Olmolog but that is not correct- of the eight farms allocated at the time, I was definitely the first arrival.

We immediately set about building bandas and I left a driver, Masudi, with my old Bedford for transporting things for the staff. I had to pick up another vehicle in Arusha and get off on safari again on January 4th to start the Mbulu round of markets. As they weren't very good at this time of year, I had trained one of my ex-market staff, the market-master's son, Ramadani Leseko to be a reliable and good buyer. I had also bought another second-hand vehicle, which I gave him, so that he was able to continue buying cattle with the Mbulu whilst I was free to return to the farm.

I now had one whole week on the farm and by the end of it I had moved a Fordson tractor in, together with other implements, and built a three-roomed shack from split sisal poles with a grass thatched roof. This shack remained for three years before I eventually handed it over, with considerable improvements, to an assistant. Later, during an argument with another assistant after a few drinks, it was burnt down. I also established temporary labour quarters and we had started making traces for the clearings. I then employed a young man as assistant but he was rather idle and didn't last long, as it seemed that as soon as my back was turned, he would decide that his camp bed was more attractive than work! However, his replacement, the district Commissioner's son, Chris Lewis, turned out to be a first class fellow. By the end of February I had two buyers, one in the Mbulu area and the other in Masailand, and with Chris now on the farm, I was able to get around easily, checking that everything was in order and running smoothly. Chris managed to get in a small five-acre crop of maize, which yielded quite a good crop that season and there is no doubt that his was the first crop on the eight farms.

In March I was asked to escort a party of twenty-two Transworld Airlines staff (TWA) who were on a fact-finding visit into Tanganyika, to see what potential the area offered for future tourism. I was amongst other things at that time, a professional Hunter and was guiding this safari for Russell Douglas Safaris at the request of the Provincial Commissioner, Mulholland, who wanted us to create a favourable impression of Tanganyika. At this time there were no lodges (nor were there in Kenya) and nor were there any National Parks, but the first game reserves had been gazetted by the British Administration, including the Serengeti. These safaris were always hunting safaris in those days and those who wanted to take pictures would join a group of hunters and simply shoot film rather than guns. The whole expedition was a lot harder because many of the animals were not used to vehicles or people and so would either charge or flee. Interestingly, though, this was not the case with the Masai, who are formed in clans, each with a sacred animal, which it undertakes to protect, especially from other clans. For instance, if a Masai wants to kill a lion for a ceremonial head-dress, they would need permission from the Lion Clan and would probably pay for the priviledge of doing so. I did once consider dressing the clients as Masai, to gain the confidence of the wildlife, but decided that if they had travelled this far, they would expect a little comfort. So the safari was a major operation with camps set up in advance for the 21 guests, and an army of gun bearers, trackers, camp staff, kitchen staff, drivers and guides, including Pat, who came along as the camp nurse.

On returning to Arusha, I was asked to go to the Amboni Pangani Ranch and acquire for them two thousand young steers, which were to be purchased in as many places as possible in the country because they wanted to do experimental ranching with them and needed to know which area was most suitable to buy them from. There was as always a problem with tsetse fly and East Coast fever, a tick-borne disease found on higher ground above 500feet. Some of these cattle were to come all the way from Ikoma on the shores of Lake Victoria. The worst problems would occur on the section from Kibaya through to Hendani and down to Mkwaja itself, just south of Pangani.

From Hendani, it would be necessary to survey and make a stock route from Mkwaja as there was no other way of getting the herds through other than through Tanga or Bagamoyo, which would require a boat trip that was completely out of the question. At Hendani, I picked up a couple of guides who claimed to know a way avoiding the local farms, deep rivers, swamps and ravines that cattle could not cross. I was also fortunate to have a map that was fairly reliable and which turned out to be quite useful for at least two thirds of the trip. Thus, early the next morning, my three staff, two guides and myself set off from Hendani. The Tsetse flies were in predatory mood that day and by midday we had reached a point from where we could no longer proceed by car and so carried on by foot. Two staff stayed with the vehicle and set up a small camp and the remainder of us carried on only for one of the guides to ask that he be paid off as he was near his home village and wanted to go home. We were all very thirsty and I was rapidly losing faith in the idea by about five o'clock when an old man suddenly appeared, greeting us and welcoming us to the area. We asked him where Mkwaja was and he told us we were just on the very edge of it but the actual ranch headquarters was still quite some distance - at least another two hours' walk. He then began to cut up *mdafu*, which are very young fresh coconuts, giving us the juice, which was very welcome and soothing but not content with this, he produced the largest pineapple I've ever seen in my life. It must have weighed nearly five kilograms and unfortunately I was too late to stop him from cutting it up. He was a nice old man and when I gave him five shillings for his trouble, he at first refused to accept it but I insisted despite the protests of my staff who felt I was grossly overpaying him. I later employed him to make the stock route and I set the work going for two night stockades and for some shelters for my drovers. Next day I returned to Hendani, where I met up with the visiting Veterinary Officer and District Officer. Instructions were given for the Government stockade, which had been unused for a long time, to be put back into service and the necessary drugs were supposedly ordered so that as the cattle came through they could be treated for 'fly'. The existing dip was rarely used and I would have to fill it if I wanted to use it. I made arrangements for this to be done but unfortunately a bad leak was found in the dip and I had to employ a local mason to carry out a temporary repair before I could use it in order to get my stock through. Luckily, the Government saw the work going on here and, feeling somewhat ashamed of themselves, decided to repair the dip. This they did and it was ready when my first lot of cattle came through although I still had to supply the dipping chemicals and it was fortunate that I had brought enough Dimidium Bromide with me for the 'fly' as the supply that was supposed to be at Hedani for me did not materialise.

Hendani had an old wind-up telephone, one of the few in the area, so I was able to speak to Pat in Arusha to warn her that I would not be returning that day as I was going to retrace the stock route all the way back to Kibaya first. She told me that I had a couple of hunting safaris booked for June and July in the Kibaya area and the Dodoma region. I had much to do at this time but I found that the more I had to do, the more efficient I became, because instead of putting things off I had to get cracking immediately. I was very tempted to turn these two safaris down. However, I did take them on and they were both very pleasant and successful.

At Hendani I picked up two veterinary guards who were returning to Kibaya and supposedly knew the stock route from Kibaya to Hendani. I say 'supposedly' because they knew where the stock route started but that was about the extent of their geographical knowledge and so it took us three days to reach Kibaya, moving at a steer's pace in my old Bedford lorry, but we did eventually get there. This was very important because we had to establish the water points along the route and get the Masai to open up some smaller ones, which had been abandoned. On reaching Ngassumet, I was able to see some of my cattle being bought for Tanganyika Packers and Arusha Chini and from there onwards as far as Endulen, the stock route was in reasonable condition and I knew the route well so no further checking was necessary.

I returned to Arusha and went on to the farm to check progress where Chris was doing a marvellous job with the machinery available. Few people appreciate that it is just about impossible to break new land with a Fordson Wheel Tractor and my land had previously been forested with olive and cedar, which had been burnt down by a previous German occupant before the 1914-1918 War. We tried a variety of things like doubling up back wheels, putting on chains and fitting pegged-tooth rims instead of rubber before I finally managed to get an old second-hand Clee track from Arusha Chini. This was a 90 hp machine, very heavy and very difficult to turn and it was one of the very first track machines to come onto the market. I also had on order an International D9 but there were very few coming through and so I put my name down for a John Deere 55 Combine but was told that it would not be available for quite some time so I bought myself a 12A, which is a small towed combine and not very efficient. Another difficulty was obtaining a planter and after finding out that there were three of these in Nairobi, I dashed up there and persuaded Gailey and Roberts to let me have one. It was sent to their Moshi branch, from where I collected it. Other equipment such as ploughs and harrows came onto the market every now and then and I was able to buy one of the big John Deere 606 ploughs together with some smaller ones, suitable for smaller tractors. I also had to buy another Fordson tractor and having installed all this equipment on the farm, I once again left for the cattle business and felt quite confident in leaving Chris in charge.

Next, for my cattle going to Mkwaja, I had to survey a route from Ikoma through to Ngasumet, as they were anxious to obtain animals from this region. It is on the edge of the Serengeti and absolutely teeming with game. Great care would have to be taken when moving animals along this route and they could only be moved during the wet season when water was plentiful, otherwise there would be no chance of getting any of the cattle through. The route was rough and rugged but not really too bad and the area was reasonably cool, allowing daytime movement. I had to hire twenty Masai warriors and I accompanied the livestock all the way along this particular section of the route through to Endulen.

I decided to move the cattle in two major groups, Masailand, Ikoma, Mwanza and all the lake animals as one lot and the second group from the Mbulu, Barabaig area and south Masailand. The first lot of animals I purchased at the end of the dry season and held them at Kwakuchinja for about three weeks, until the rain had some positive effect on their condition whereupon I moved them on. The whole journey took twenty-four days actual trekking and, despite heavy losses, they were nothing compared to what I'd expected, as some of these animals had to trek some six hundred miles. This first batch arrived at Mkwaja in better condition than they'd started because of the lush grass and the low speed at which we had moved. The second lot was moved six weeks later and I did not accompany them, except for the last stretch. They did not fare so well as many of them suffered from 'fly' between Kibaya and Hendani, where losses were heavy. So although there was little profit on this second group, the previous group had done so well that there was a good margin of profit overall. Two years later I was asked by the same ranch to repeat the operation with larger numbers but by then I had left the cattle business and had to decline.

Frequently when I decided to go on these trips, such as the safari from Tanga to Mkwanja, I would have no food with me. Sometimes I would be able to stay with friends from the Administration or Veterinary Department but often I had to camp down in the bush or in a Masai manyatta and eat the local food with the local people. The Masai, whom I knew very well and whose language I spoke, were very hospitable, as soon as they discovered my identity and realized I spoke their language, they would load me with gifts of food such as milk and sheep and sometimes I had great difficulty in refusing. The other difficulty was the payment for these things, as they would not accept my money but would pick on something such as a watch or a pair of shoes that I had and ask for that instead. I would explain that I was only too happy to pay them for their food but could not let them have, for example, my watch, as I needed it and it was the only one I had. Then the argument would start. "But you can always get another one." I would try to explain the difficulties in doing so but the Masai, particularly, are very awkward to say 'no' to and appear to be great beggars but this is not really the case. It is an old Masai custom that if you have something then you share it and when you've only got one of something they want, they feel they should have that 'share' and not you. Often I have pulled out a packet of cigarettes and smoked one and a Masai has turned to me and asked,

-"What about me?

So you give him one but then he says

-"But what about the rest? I want them all."

You reply that you need some to smoke yourself but the answer to this is

-"Oh, no! I'll smoke them for you. Give them to me".

And so the circle continues, but even when refused, the Masai accept it with a grace that few Europeans could summon in similar circumstances.

Once again, we have much to learn from those considered less "civilised" than ourselves.

Chapter Twelve
Saopunyo

The year was 1952 and I had now gone for quite a while without seeing my old friend Matanda, 18 years in fact. I was very keen to meet up with him again so when the opportunity arose to visit Loliondo on a cattle buying expedition, I took it up immediately. The market was at Wasso, about a mile and a half from our old farm, and it was to here that I went, sought out the spring in the forest and set up my camp, about 7 miles from Loliondo itself. The Mau Mau uprising against white settlers had spread across from Kenya closing down the market for some time and there was also a famine on, leaving the Masai people of that area in bad need of money and so this one was expected to be a big gathering. Tanganyika Packers, for whom I was buying cattle, requested me to purchase as many as possible, which required me to carry a considerable amount of money, more than I normally did. It was very difficult to get to Loliondo – over 200 miles of extremely bad roads and no communication in between and I was carrying enough money for the duration of the trip. I was putting up camp with my staff at Wasso when an elderly Masai arrived on the scene.

After some discussion he recognised me, and informed me that my old friend, Matanda, was no longer called Matanda but was now called Saopunyo, as a result of his having become a warrior. He would be at the market the following day and had already sent in a number of cattle for sale, which were, at the time, outside the market.

News gets around fast in Masailand, and whilst I was shaving next morning, a young elder came walking over towards me and announced that he was in fact, Saopunyo, and asked me where I had been for the last 18 years? Why had I not come back to visit him? Saopunyo, whom I will refer to as Matanda from now on, sat down on a spare chair, whilst I completed my ablutions. After finishing his cup of tea, which took about ten minutes, and a certain amount of small talk, he got up and announced that we would meet later on at the market as he had to go and keep an eye on his cattle that were for sale. After a heavy breakfast of curry, rice, eggs and bacon I proceeded to the market where I sat down and within a few seconds of getting myself settled, Matanda appeared and sat down next to me. We were not able to discuss very much as I had to concentrate on buying cattle, and he on selling his, which we did until 2 o'clock, when the afternoon break came. Within a minute or two the market was deserted and only Matanda and I were left.

Matanda started the conversation, asking why had I gone away and left him and never got in touch with him for all these years? I stated that it was impossible to make contact as I was a long way away and also that I had not been around during the war and had not come back until fairly recently. I told him that I had started working in the Veterinary Department in Dodoma and this was the first opportunity I had had of coming to visit him. Among other things he informed me that he had ordered a sheep to be killed a little way from the manyatta and that I was expected to go and stay with him at the manyatta that evening. He pointed out that he had three wives and all I had to do was choose which hut I wanted to go to. I said,

- "I am sorry Matanda, I would love to come and stay in the manyatta and take advantage of your hospitality but unfortunately I have a lot of money and my staff are very jittery because of all the Mau Mau about here."

-"Don't worry Debe" he replied, "that is no problem. I will send ten or even more Morans to protect your money and the camp, but you must come and stay at my manyatta."

At the time, very few Masai knew Swahili and the Masai had difficulty pronouncing David, so I was always called Debe.

-"They have guns," I said, "and spears are no good against guns."

-"The Kikuyu are frightened of the Masai and will not come any where near if I have my Morans out here."

-"Also, I am married," I continued, "and with our customs, if you are married, you do not go with other peoples' wives."

-" The people around here all say that the white men are your friends while you are useful to them but as soon as you are no longer useful they are not your friends. They think they are superior to us. I did not believe this because I knew you well but I am now beginning to think that there is a lot of truth in what they say. You are my friend Debe, and friends share everything – all my cattle are yours, and my wives, and my children, - to do with as you wish."

The market was about to start again and Matanda walked off without saying much, obviously not very happy with me. It had been a great feeling of belonging to turn up after eighteen years and stand there with Matanda sitting next to me, whilst I shaved. I did feel guilty about not being able to partake in the hospitality, which was an important Masai custom, and these feelings of guilt were to stay with me until a few days later when we finally seemed to understand each other again. However, back in camp a fat, healthy sheep arrived and whilst I did not want to slaughter it, I felt that I would have to do so because I would let my friend down badly if I did not. Later on he and a couple of his elder friends appeared on the scene, and we sat round the fire, ate meat from the sheep as it was roasting, and when he had enjoyed three bottles of beer laced with large brandies, Matanda opened up a bit and started to discuss other matters with me. His two companions also had their fair share of drinks but, apart from butting in occasionally, did not have very much to say.

-"I asked my father on many occasions if I could be prepared for circumcision. He told me that I was not ready, and, in any case, he needed me for his cattle herding as he did not have anybody else reliable at the time. Meanwhile, the period of the unbound Olpiron (which signified the circumcision season) would soon end, and I was getting very worried that I would miss my circumcision on this occasion. That would have meant another seven-year wait, before the next group was to be circumcised. Rumours were already going around that that particular circumcision period was going to finish fairly soon so I took the bull by the horns and went and saw my sponsor. I explained the situation to him, that if I waited, it would make me a very old fellow by the time the next unbound Olpiron came around. He did not make any comment at the time, but sent for me later and ordered me to appear before an elder sponsors' meeting at a time when the moon was in a certain place. I was by now about 15 or 16 years of age. At this meeting I was told to attend the next Nkapata. I was instructed to get myself an *Inoile*: that is a cedar base for a firestick (a softwood which is splintered and lit by friction with a firestick), beeswax for the arrowhead (to avoid damaging the birds) and a number of other requirements. This meant that my request had been accepted and my father would have no power to disagree. He could make things awkward for me, but he could not stop me having my circumcision. I was included in the next Nkapata without any special status.

-"The Nkapata consisted of taking off all my clothes and then painting my body with white ash, particularly my penis, to show that I was uncircumcised and therefore dirty. During the Nkapata we all begged to be circumcised: to be raised to the higher level of the clean people: Morans.

-"On the night of the Nkapata we went to the pond on your old farm, half way between Wasso and your house. We sang and danced in a clockwise direction whilst a mythical hyena moved in an anticlockwise direction on the outside of the dance ring. This went on until the early hours of the morning, whilst the elders were eating our roasted ox and waiting for daylight. At daybreak, we returned to our manyattas and dressed normally, continuing with our usual duties as before.

-"A few days later, I was out herding, having taken the cattle to water and was waiting for them to move away. I bent down to have a drink myself and suddenly, a gentle voice said to me:

-"Why are you lingering here, why don't you go with your cattle?"

I turned round and there was a young *siangiki* (woman) with whom I had often had sex, although she was circumcised and I was a *layoni* (uncircumcised). She continued:

-"I understand that you are about to become a moran, so if you would like to make love to me, it'll be fine."

We walked to the bush close by, and lay down. When we had finished, I turned to her and said:

-"Now is your opportunity to make me suffer for this."

She looked at me and said,

-"That I will never do. This maybe the last time we can be together until you become a morani. When that happens, we can meet, follow our traditions and make love, but I will never make you suffer for the pleasures you and I have had in the past, because I like you very much."

It was considered an insult for an uncircumcised *layoni* to make a pass at a *siangiki* and she could have made him suffer very badly for it later. This was generally done by waiting until the *layoni* had been circumcised and then going to his hut, removing her shirt and arousing him sufficiently for the fresh wound to reopen, and it happened more regularly than one would suspect.

-"After I had completely recovered from the circumcision and had had quite a bit of sex with other women, I met up with the same *siangiki*. I asked her why she did not make any trouble for me, why she did not make me suffer for having insulted her, when, as a *layoni*, I made love to her, a married woman and circumcised. She said:

-"For two reasons: One, I like you very much and I did not want to disrupt any future arrangements we might have - I want your children - and secondly, for the same reason as lots of other married women have sex with their *layoni* lovers of the past, purely and simply because the *layoni* don't have as much freedom to have sex as the *morani*, and therefore they are much more active and grateful for the sex they get. We women become a little tired of the *morani* just arriving and making love to us and leaving, before we have had our pleasure. We like to have a little bit of play before and after, which you *layoni* always give us because you don't have as much sex as the *morani*.'"

-"About two moons later my sponsor informed me that I was to prepare myself as I was shortly to be circumcised. After that particular day I noticed my mother was making plenty of beer and I asked her what it was for? She told me that it was for the changing-of-my-name ceremony. That meant that my circumcision was imminent as I knew that the changing of name was followed almost immediately by circumcision. In fact it was very much part of the same ceremony."

"Two days later an ox was slaughtered. This ox was chosen especially; pure black with no white markings on either the head or the tail. Both my father and my mother wore special sheepskins for the occasion."

"It was slaughtered outside my mother's gate and she was given the left hand side of the ribs. By this time I was also dressed in sheepskin. The meat from the right hand side was taken a short distance away and cooked for the elders. As this meat was seen and touched by women purposely there was no question of any moran having any part of the ox. The other women were given the rest of the left hand side of the beast and had to start eating first, ahead of the elders. My sponsor called me over to the elders, who gave me four notches of brisket, which I had to eat. As I did so, he named me after a wealthy elder, Saopunyo, and this was to be my name from now on.

"The ox hide was pegged out to dry directly in front of my mother's hut, where it remained for two days and was then cut up into thin strips. Next a fat sheep was slaughtered and this was called Olkiptupunyek. The right hand ribs and the liver were eaten by the women and the tail and brisket fat from this sheep was rendered down. Meanwhile, I was being shaved completely, from the top of my head to my toes, by my mother. The rendered down fat from the sheep was mixed with red ochre and spread all over my body and the next morning

I went into a compulsory trance, blanking myself off to everyone except my sponsor, and looked only into space. At some time in the day, I was taken out by two morani, given a blunt axe and made to cut an olive branch with it. The branch was then taken to my manyatta and hidden until next morning. After an ox had been bled, the following day, the olive branch was carried in to the manyatta by two warriors, in single file, in front of me. I was made to strip off my clothes and stand naked, meanwhile, the women collected water, which they poured in to an earthenware pot in which they placed a small axe, called Ndoluu, in preparation for the next day.

"The following morning, I was taken to the cold spring, near your house where we used to catch birds, and made to sit in it for quite a while. When I got up from the water, I ran to the manyatta where there was a cow hide laid out for me to sit on. I lifted it up and flung it about three or four yards away just to show my independence and authority. I then sat on it and indicated that they could get on and do what they liked with me. My sponsor came and sat behind me in the normal way, with his arms around my waist and his legs stretched out. An assistant of the circumcisor held my penis while the circumcisor cut off the end of the foreskin. He made a slit on top and pushed the head of the penis through the cut. I did not bleed at all whilst the operation took place. I was then carried into my mother's hut and there I bled slightly on the hide. Some of the audience threw fits and had to be held down. My sponsor, after handing me over to my mother, announced that I was a moran, a brave moran, and a moran to be considered in the future. I was then given blood from the special ox that was bled, mixed with sour milk and sheep's fat, to drink.

From that day on, until I became an elder, I could not eat meat or blood seen by a circumcised woman, but it was all right as long as the woman was a girl and uncircumcised. I was not to drink milk or eat anything alone and I had to do it in the company of other warriors if there was a woman about.

After a while in my mother's house, I came out of my trance and slowly began to feel a certain amount of pain but I would not at any time mention this. I had a fairly rough night but the pain was not as great as I expected it to be and I was grateful for what I had achieved. Next day I was visited by a couple of *mbarnoti* (recently circumcised warriors) from my own age group who had been circumcised a little bit earlier than me. After a while we went out on my first walk after circumcision. This took about half an hour. I went back and rested for a while, then went for another walk later on in the evening. I was dressed up in a very heavy, long, dark cloak which had been coated with fat and charcoal and I now became a *sokonyo*.

Matanda continued: The *sokonyo* are the warriors who have just been circumcised and are wandering around, dressed in black, hunting birds for their head dress until the official healing time is over. When the pain had gone, about three days after circumcision, I took my bird rack, bow and waxed arrow and joined other *sokonyo* in a group, looking for birds to put on my head-rack or frame. We carried no other weapons, even our meat had to be cut up for us as we were not allowed to carry a knife. I now began to feel very proud and full of myself, as it was only a matter of a few weeks or a couple of months at the most, before I became a proper moran. This was the ambition of my life, as was the case of every other young man. I did not worry about animals, in fact I did not consider at any time that there was any likelihood of any animals attacking us as we did not have any weapons. If they had done so, we could have run away but they wouldn't, for the simple reason we had the protection of our *Laibon* (witch-doctor) who had thrown a magical protective band round us. In the beginning, there were five of us in this *sokonyo* group, but then some new ones came in and others went off in a continuous movement. It was now a period when the young warriors were choosing whom they wanted to stay with, or they were called back by their sponsor for some reason or another, or they came from a different area, but our *sokonyo* group continued with the initial five until the end. There had been quite a few changes but we ended up with seven in our group.

I was quite lucky with my bird shooting. There was no particular cleverness on my part. After a while, I was adopted by our *sokonyo* and treated as their leader and this was the beginning of my short-lived leadership. When the time came for us to be shaved and raised into proper young *morani,* I was definitely accepted as the leader of this particular group of seven which went to the *olpul* (meat feast) together. At this ceremony, even the elder *morani* treated me as the leader of this little group. When we had abandoned our old clothes and put on new red ochre, and dressed smartly, we were addressed by one of the leading elders who told us how to behave as *morani*, which we were now, and directed me to see that this was done.

We were not to drink or eat anything alone in the presence of women and we were not, as I have already said, to eat meat in any form, that has been seen by a woman. We were also instructed how to behave towards our elders and how we were to behave in the presence of our juniors, how we should behave in the presence of women, and so on.

"My father then gave me a spear and a side arm and my mother presented me with a beautifully beaded belt for the side arm, and a beaded band for my elbow, which was given to me by my sister."

A goat was killed in a selected place a distance from the manyatta. The brisket was cut up by the elders into small pieces and then *morani* started eating it. When it was finished we immediately started eating the meat, cutting it with our own side arm and this was the sign that we would eat meat only in *morani* company and not meat that had been seen by a circumcised woman.

This is a ceremony, which is known as *olgine lolbine,* and we were now ready to go to the *moran olpul* where we would be staying for the period during which we ate all the cattle that were provided. Every man that took part had to produce one ox, which were specially chosen oxen kept for this particular purpose and were in very good condition and had to be slaughtered in a special way. The animals were held by the *morani,* upright. The head was pulled down and the *moran,* who owned the animal would then pierce it with his *simi,* (side arm), at the back of the neck down a hollow which went straight into the spine. The animal would immediately drop and that was the way these animals were killed. The blood was kept inside by using a tourniquet on the cut.

Having joined our new warrior group and sworn to follow the rules of this particular group, I was officially recognised as the leader. I do not know why I was chosen apart from the fact that my father was fairly influential and was a junior *laigwanan,* that is chief, and I had not at any time misbehaved, although I had not achieved anything in particular. However, the choice was unanimous. This group was the continuation of our *sokonyo* bird-hunting group and after I was made the leader, we immediately went off to the Mkutu, which is to choose the animals that would in fact be slaughtered. As there were seven of us, seven animals were chosen. All of us that were taking part were successful in persuading our fathers that they had to make an animal available for this particular occasion. It would take some time for our hair to grow and so some of us immediately got wigs and others just waited for their hair to grow sufficiently long for them to plait on wool and make their own head-dress for themselves. It was now our responsibility to make our shields for battle, our knob-kerries or truncheons, whichever we chose, made out of olive. Our sieves for our soup were also made out of shaved olive. Our head-dress to cover up our hair or wigs was made from the inside of the main stomach and this was spread over a frame until it dried and was carefully folded and when there was rain about, this went over our wigs for protection from the rain. We also made swizzle sticks for our soups, and this was a period of competition as each young *moran* tried to out-do the other by producing a better finished article than the other one. There was nothing wrong with the inferior one, but the better one was always looked upon as something somewhat superior. All our soups were made with either *kiloroti* or*kitoloswa,* which was a stimulant and made us throw epileptic fits when we got excited and it was up to the others to hold us down before we did any damage. During this period we all became extremely randy, and as we had a pretty free hand with the young uncircumcised girls, and were also acceptable within our own *olpiron* group's wives, whose ages ranged from 16 up to and including 50, we spent a considerable amount of our time "screwing" and picking up *Asanjas*. These are young, uncircumcised girls who request the moran to drink milk with them and vice versa followed by a ceremony whereby the girl's mother produces a calabash of fresh milk, gives it to the girl, takes a sip out of it, and then passes it on to the warrior and says: will you drink milk with me? Having done that, they go back to their huts and spend the night together. A girl may have a number of *Asanjas* and that goes for the warrior also and if he visits a manyatta and he has two or three *Asanjas* in that manyatta, he will then have to choose which one he wants to spend the night with. She may also have other *Asanjas* and if she has somebody whom she prefers, she may turn round and say; "No, tonight I am with somebody else, you must go to another hut or else share or go without me for the night."

None of us were able to make shields at this particular *olpul*, on account of the fact that there had been some hunting safaris in that area, and these had frightened away most of the buffalo into the forest, and the ones that remained in the plains and glades were all very shy and we could not get anywhere near them. I fortunately had a shield given to me until such time as I made my own. Whilst at this *olpul*, two other *morans* asked if they might come and join our group, this did in fact take place after our *olpul*. The choice of the place for our *olpul* was not very good as we were a long way from any activity and so we had a fairly pleasant but rather boring *olpul* and towards the end we decided that we would go to the *moran manyatta* as soon as possible. One of my aunts and two *nditos* went with me to the *moran manyatta*, the aunt to look after me and feed me, do the necessary work and the *nditos* were there purely and simply for my and others pleasures. We also took with us twenty head of cattle: two of these were for slaughter and the others were for milk. As my father was a fairly wealthy man,

I had no difficulty in this respect. The manyatta was situated between Morijo and Ndasegera in the Loita Hills. It was here that we did our training. From time to time we received instructions from the elder moran who were not of the same *olpiron* as ourselves - therefore we did not have any close association with them. Every evening the young *moran* would get their women to make a fire in the middle of the manyatta and they would sing and dance. The Masai had no musical instruments. All the Morans would put their knob-kerries, according to custom, in one heap in a single place, and just before the dancing or singing was over, the girls would dive for the pile of kerries, choosing the one belonging to the Moran they wanted to sleep with that night. Occasionally, there were odd fights started up between the girls, on account of one girl going for the same knob-kerrie night after night, not giving the other girls a chance.

Whilst here, an uncle of one of my group came and told him that there were two stray lions creating havoc in an area not very far from the manyatta. They had already raided cattle in three manyattas and also wounded a *layoni* out herding cattle in the day-time. He reckoned this was a good chance for this group to prove itself. My uncle told me in confidence, so without much ado we set out to where the lions were last seen. On our way there, we were told that the lions had come back to another manyatta during that particular night, and that one of the lions had been wounded by one of the occupants of the manyatta, an elder, and the lions were not very well-disposed towards human beings, so we should watch out. Shortly after this we were told that another group had gone after these lions but had returned home as they had got no trace of them, but since they had left, one of the *laiyoni* had come up and warned that the lions had taken cover in a bushy outcrop at a certain place not very far from one of the earlier manyattas that they had raided. There were some people keeping an eye on them and if the *morans* would like to go there, they could deal with them. We approached the *kopje* a little too closely and it was fortunate that one of the *morans*, right behind me, saw movement and immediately ran over to my right as the lion came, making straight for me, and he managed to put a spear into it. This held the lion up for a very short time, sufficient to give me an opportunity to turn, when I was able to put my spear into its heart and immediately three other morans pounced on it and the lion was dealt with fairly quickly. This turned out to be the wounded one, the other one went off and got away. The whole attack had been so sudden, we had not prepared ourselves sufficiently. However, the area had no more trouble from these particular lions and we had our first bit of excitement as a group, which turned out to be successful. In the following week we had quite a few young moran who tried to join our group because of our success. We did, in fact, allow six in, and no more as we did not want too big a group and I did not want to be responsible for too many people. I made it quite clear at this time that I was not prepared to be a big leader, as it had been requested that I take over two other groups. I refused point blank. This was not a good move on my part as the elders did not approve of it. I was shy of the responsibility of too many people. This was our first kill, as *moran* and it was desirable that each one of us should hold the lion by the tail while it was still alive. I was able to do this so I was very pleased with myself.

In the company of two other *morans*, I went visiting some of the manyattas. One of these was where an old girlfriend of mine lived at her husband's manyatta. In the company of two other *morans* from my group we were called out to deal with a mad rhino which had got into the manyatta and was killing cattle. The three of us were called upon to do something quickly. The night was fairly overcast and we could not see very well so had to be very cautious in our movement. When we spotted the rhino, the three of us made a very quick attack, spearing the rhino in the shoulder and before it had a chance to sort itself out, we were on our way to picking up other spears and weapons. The rhino stampeded off in the opposite direction and broke through the manyatta, collapsing on the other side and dying on the spot. No one saw this or what we did, except the three of us, as it was quite dark, so we got much more credit than we deserved. It was shortly after this that I picked up a dose of *olmerega* (syphilis). I tried to treat it with m*rututu* (copper sulphate) but it came back after a short while, each time. Some white men came into the area taking pictures and I was asked to help show them round. These white men found out what was wrong with me and took me to Narok where I was taken to the hospital and there I was given lots of injections with a *sindano* (needle) over a whole week, before I was allowed to go home again. These needles seemed to chase the *Olmerega* away, and it never came back again.

My father had been ill for quite a long time and he requested that I come home, as I was the eldest son and he needed help. My father had three wives living at the time. The first wife had two daughters, the second wife had a son and a daughter, but the son had only lived a few days before he died. Then came my mother who produced me and another son, and a daughter. The fourth wife was a Sonjo girl who produced two daughters and four sons. Just before my father took her on, the second wife got a sore in her leg, under the *segenge* (wire stocking) and this turned septic and by the time the witch doctor had finished mucking about with it, she died, which left him with three wives. My father had arranged for a wife for me when I was still very young. She was now pregnant, and about to produce and was still living in her father's manyatta. She could not live with me until such time as I became an elder and I was not yet even an elder warrior, about fifteen years away from elderhood. Meanwhile my father had found a second wife for me who was still a child but was the daughter of a great friend of my father's. My father's condition was now deteriorating fast so I abandoned the idea of going back to the *moran* manyatta and concentrated on taking over my father's responsibilities. I abandoned my warrior group and the leadership, which did not go down too well, but this could not be helped. I would have liked to have gone on another cattle raid, a proper big one, but unfortunately the opportunity did not arise, before my responsibilities became too great for me to do very much.

For a while, on returning home, I spent my time looking for medicines and treatment for my father. The *Laibons* were slowly losing their grip, and my father was getting worse and worse. One day I heard that there was a *Ngashomba* (white man) working in the Narok area, and in view of the success of my treatment for syphilis I thought that I would go and see him although I did not think that he could do very much, but my father was surely going to die very soon. I saw the *Ngashomba* and described my father's symptoms as best I could. He informed me that he could do nothing unless my father came to Narok but that he would be in the Olbosimoru area in about two weeks time when, if I could get my father there and he was still alive, he could look at him but he did not think there was much hope. He did, however, give me some *Oljani* (medicine) which I gave my father just before we took him away in one of Kerr Singh's lorries that was going in that direction and moved him to a manyatta of ours, very close to Olbosimoru. When the *Ngashomba* arrived, my father was still alive but was not at all well, but the *Oljani* of the *Ngashomba* seemed to work miracles, and he started improving considerably. The *Ngashomba* did not allow him to go home until he had finished his treatment, which took some time, and he had to go back to Narok to finish it. This could only be done by car, as he was incapable of walking even fifty yards. My sister went with him on Kerr Singh's lorry, and I followed on foot, a few days later. Whilst I was in Narok, my wife had her baby, and this was a little girl.

-"How can you say this, my friend?" I asked Matanda. "You were not even about when your baby was conceived. You were miles away – and you know it."

-"Of course it was my baby – did I not pay good cattle for my wife? And was she not waiting in her father's manyatta to come and join me? By the time she does come and join me in my manyatta, she may have four of five of MY children. I may not be the true father of those children, but what does that matter – they are my children – it was my wife that produced them," he answered.

-"Are you not annoyed with the people who are responsible for producing your babies?" I continued to question him.

-"No, I am not in the least worried, as long as I get babies, that's all I care about."

-"Would you not be annoyed at the person, if you knew who had fathered your child?"

-"Not at all," Matanda continued. "You told me that your wife has had a baby girl, like mine. Do you know if that child is your child?"

-"I think – I'm pretty certain it is." I assured him.

-"What about if your wife had a child by somebody else, would you mind?"

-"Very much so. In fact I would kick her out." A n eventuality that pleased Matanda immensely.

-"What if you have many wives and you are incapable of producing any children? Do you not want anybody else to help you out or do you want to turn your wives into thieves who take the medicine?"

-"By our customs, I would not in the first place, have many wives – I can only have one wife", I replied. "And I would not like anybody else to help me out, because if that child is born a boy and it inherits my property and so on, I would have taken my property out of my family and given it to another family, and my family could easily starve."

-"Are you telling me, Debe, that all white children are born to their fathers, their proper fathers?", asked Matanda disbelievingly.

-"No, there are cases where the wife goes off, but not openly.".

-"Well," he said, "that is just stealing. I do it openly and with approval." At this point Matanda said, "I am happy that I am not a white man."

He continued his story, "My father had returned home, very slowly, over lots of manyattas but his strength was getting better and better all the time. He was warned by the doctor that he must not drink any more because he had killed his liver but after a while, my father started drinking again. He took ill and two days later, he died. I was now responsible for the family."

Matanda then informed me that some missionaries had moved into the area, behind the (administrative centre) and to the north of the old boma, near the water springs.

"They are building big houses, and their *Laibon*, which they called Daktari (doctor in Kiswahili) were helping the people with medicine in the area, but most of the Masai would not believe in their medicine."

We had a long break when there was very little discussion. I turned to him and reminded him of the time when the aeroplane came and landed on our farm, years back. I told him that I had learnt to fly those planes during the war and that I was now about to get one and would come and visit him. When I did, I would take him up. He did not believe me, and informed me that I was to come to his manyatta the next night.

Reluctantly I had to tell him that I was going off and I would not be back for at least a month or two, but when I did come back, I would certainly come and see him. He left in a bit of a huff, but we had made a little ground and as he was going away, I said,

-"Now, Matanda, what would you like me to bring you the next time I come?"

Immediately he pricked up his ears and said,

-"I would like to have one of those bulls that the *Ngashombe* have, that produce so much milk. I have heard each one can produce a whole calabash of milk on its own. Also a tartan rug like you used to have."

-"We can discuss that, the next time I visit, as it is difficult to get a bull here and you would have to treat it very, very carefully, in order for it to stay alive, but I will bring the rug."

At this Matanda spat on the ground and left. I did not see him for some time and then I flew in - with the rug. I took him and his friends up in the 'plane, we renewed our friendship and things became very much more normal.

In retrospect, I suspect that I was indeed guilty, as Matanda claimed, of becoming something other than what I was when we were children. It was inevitable after all the years that had passed, and the differing experiences that we had undergone, that I would seem different to him and he to me. However, despite the different courses that our respective paths had taken and the different companions that we had collected on the way, this incident, in which we were able to rekindle our childhood friendship, was very important to me. Ultimately, it was only because of the experiences that separated us that I could realise this, the differences that restored our similarities, as it were, and so it was, that after everything we had done apart from each other, I returned to where I first started , and I finally recognised him for the first time.

Printed in the United States
105033LV00001B/130/A